The Indian Drum of the King-God and the Pakhāvaj of Nathdwara

The book studies the evolution of the ancient drum *mṛdaṅga* into the *pakhāvaj*, crossing more than 2,000 years of history. While focusing on the Nathdwara school of *pakhāvaj*, the author joins ethnographic, historical, religious and iconographic perspectives to argue a multifaceted interpretation of the role and function of the *pakhāvaj* in royal courts, temples and contemporary stages. Furthermore, he offers the first analysis of the visual and narrative contents of its repertoire.

Paolo Pacciolla is Tagore Fellow affiliated with the Indira Gandhi National Centre for the Arts of New Delhi, where he is conducting research on ritual drumming in Kerala. His main ethnographic focus is on music in India, and his research interests include Ethnomusicology, Organology, Iconography of Music, Indology and Religious Studies.

SOAS Studies in Music

SOAS Studies in Music is today one of the world's leading series in the discipline of ethnomusicology. Our core mission is to produce high-quality, ethnographically rich studies of music-making in the world's diverse musical cultures. We publish monographs and edited volumes that explore musical repertories and performance practice, critical issues in ethnomusicology, sound studies, historical and analytical approaches to music across the globe. We recognize the value of applied, interdisciplinary and collaborative research, and our authors draw on current approaches in musicology and anthropology, psychology, media and gender studies. We welcome monographs that investigate global contemporary, classical and popular musics, the effects of digital mediation and transnational flows.

Turkic Soundscapes
From Shamanic Voices to Hip-Hop
Edited by Razia Sultanova and Megan Rancier

The Indian Drum of the King-God and the Pakhāvaj of Nathdwara
Paolo Pacciolla

Asante Court Music and Verbal Arts in Ghana
The Porcupine and the Gold Stool
Kwasi Ampene

For more information about this series, please visit: www.routledge.com/music/series/SOASMS

The Indian Drum of the King-God and the Pakhāvaj of Nathdwara

Paolo Pacciolla

Routledge
Taylor & Francis Group
LONDON AND NEW YORK

First published 2020
by Routledge
2 Park Square, Milton Park, Abingdon, Oxon OX14 4RN

and by Routledge
52 Vanderbilt Avenue, New York, NY 10017

Routledge is an imprint of the Taylor & Francis Group, an informa business

British Library Cataloguing-in-Publication Data
A catalogue record for this book is available from the British Library

Library of Congress Cataloging-in-Publication Data
Names: Pacciolla, Paolo, author.
Title: The Indian drum of the King-God and the pakhāvaj of Nathdwara/
Paolo Pacciolla.
Description: [1.] | New York: Routledge, 2020. | Series: SOAS musicology
series | Includes bibliographical references and index.
Identifiers: LCCN 2019058856 | ISBN 9780367370237 (hardback) |
ISBN 9780367370244 (ebook)
Subjects: LCSH: Mridanga–History. | Music–Religious aspects–Hinduism. |
Music–India–Religious aspects. | Carnatic music–History and
criticism. | Music and mythology–India.
Classification: LCC ML1038.M74 P3 2020 | DDC 786.9/40954–dc23
LC record available at https://lccn.loc.gov/2019058856

ISBN: 978-0-367-37023-7 (hbk)
ISBN: 978-0-367-37024-4 (ebk)

Typeset in Times New Roman
by Swales & Willis, Exeter, Devon, UK

The audio and video examples can be accessed via the online Routledge Music Research Portal: www.routledgemusicresearch.co.uk. Please enter the activation word **RRMusic** and your email address when prompted. You will immediately be sent an automated email containing an access token and instructions, which will allow you to log in to the site.

To Piero and Rina

Contents

Figures

Music examples

Audio files

8.1 *Paṛāl, Cautāla*
9.1 *Gaṇeśa paran, Cautāla*
9.2 *Madhya lay ka prastār* composition, *Cautāla*
9.3 *Dhenanaka bāj* composition, *Cautāla*
9.4 *Dhenanaka bāj tigunī lay, Cautāla*
9.5 *Dhenanaka bāj caugunī lay, Cautāla*
9.6 *Paran udgatan pattu, Cautāla*
9.7 *Lay tāl torneka kata* composition and *tiśra jāti gati, Cautāla*
9.8 *Lay tāl torneka kata miśra jāti gati, Cautāla*
9.9 *Lay tāl torneka kata catuśra jāti gati, Cautāla*
9.10 *Thapyā ka bāj, Cautāla*
9.11 *Relā, Cautāla*
All tracks played by Dalchand Sharma and recorded by P. Pacciolla

Video files

Video 1	David Elkabir – Rudra Vina (2013) www.youtube.com/watch?v=QsQwo-K54VA (Accessed on 10 January 2017).
Video 2	Kenig Drum Brothers (2015) www.youtube.com/watch?v=KrUpH6XtklY (Accessed on 10 January 2017).

Acknowledgments

This study owes much to the inspiration of my *pakhāvaj* teacher Svāmī Ram Kishore Das who introduced me to the world of the ancient *mṛdaṅga*, but it would have been impossible without the collaboration with Pandit Dalchand Sharma, whose passionate and knowledgeable point of view on the history and language of the *dhrupad pakhāvaj* and its aesthetics has been extremely helpful and always stimulating.

I am grateful to all the *pakhāvaj* players I met, who have contributed to my research by providing information about the *pakhāvaj* and the peculiarities of their *gharānās*: (in alphabetical order) Akilesh Gundecha, Prakash Kumavat, Shrikant Mishra, Manik Munde, Ramashish Pathak and his sons Sangeet and Shubashish, Ramakant Pathak and his son Shashikant, Bhai Baldeep Singh, Ravishankar Upadhyay and his son Rishi and Bhagwat Upreti. I am particularly grateful to Kalyanray Mahārāja and his sons Hariray Gosvāmī and Wagdish Gosvāmī for their invitation to celebrate Holi with them in their family palace at Nathdwara. It was a unique experience, and extremely useful to understand specific aspects of their cult.

I owe to Martin Clayton and Laura Leante an enormous debt of gratitude for their insightful comments throughout the process of producing the dissertation of which this study is a revised version.

A warm thank you goes to Lyne Bansat-Boudon for the extremely interesting conversations we had on some aspects of this study and for her comments on Chapters 5 and 6.

My gratitude to Bulla and Neete Ray, more than friends, for their joyful support to my researches in Orissa.

I extend my heartfelt thanks to my brothers for their contribution in making me what I am. My infinite gratitude goes to my father Piero and my mother Rina.

My biggest thanks go to my wife, who has supported my idea of a study on the heritage of the *pakhāvaj* and has been sharing all my travels, efforts and work.

Notes on the transcriptions and transliteration

In this study, compositions and musical phrases are transcribed into Indian standard notation – based on the syllables used to indicate the strokes – transliterated in Latin alphabet letters. In order to provide a clearly structured space and an easier reading, I have adopted from Kippen's (2006) notation method the grid of boxes enclosing the *bols* and, to indicate the flow of dynamics, I have adopted a few symbols from the Western classical music notation system. The sections coloured in grey in each example indicate tihāīs. This indication is also provided at p. 133.

Throughout the text, diacritical marks for Indian words are used, according to the International Alphabet of Sanskrit Transliteration (IAST) system. Names of places (Nathdwara, Mathura, Sanci, Amaravati and so on) and languages (Sanskrit, Brajbhasha) are transliterated without diacritics in their conventional Romanized spelling. The final vowel (*rāga*, *tāla*, *bhāva*) is retained – unless in the case of traditional names of compositions (*lay tāl torneka kata*) – and English plurals are applied (*bhāvas*, *tālas*).

1 Introduction

Background

My first journey to India, in 1995, brought me to Bhubaneshvar, the capital of Orissa. I had been attracted to India by the repertoire for solo *tablā* and intended to learn it as well as *khyāl* singing. I was also deeply interested in *advaita* Vedānta philosophy which I had been studying for a few years and wished to understand better. Orissa seemed the right place to go since I could study *tablā* drumming and *khyāl* singing and visit one of the main monasteries founded by Shankaracharya, the great saint and philosopher of the 8th century C.E., at Puri. Furthermore, my wife intended to study Odissi dance with the famous dancer Sanjukta Panigrahi who lived in Bhubaneshvar.

Bhubaneshvar is an expanding city with a medieval old town and in 1995 was like a village, since Orissa was away from the main touristic routes. I soon started studying *khyāl* singing with Ragunath Panigrahi, husband of Sanjukta and himself a famous musician, but I was discouraged from studying *tablā*, since, I was told, the main local drum was the *mardala* and it had an ancient tradition while the *tablā* had been adopted only recently. The *mardala*, or the Odissi *pakhāvaj*, is the barrel drum accompanying the Odissi dance and, immediately captured by its sound, which was similar to that of the *tablā* but lower in register, I started studying with guru Banamali Maharana, an excellent musician, considered the main representative of the *mardala* tradition.

Banamali Maharana's house was in the middle of the old town, and to attend his lessons I had to pass near beautiful temples such as the Lingaraj, the Ananta Vasudeva, and the Vaital Deul. I thus had the chance to admire their architectural structures and the many figures of gods, celestial musicians (*gandharvas*) and dancers (*apsaras*), and human performers carved on their walls. Seeing these every day was so inspiring that I developed a strong interest in Indian art and architecture.

Busy with many things to do and to learn, I never went to Shankaracharya's monastery, but during one of my visits to the temples, I met a knowledgeable Mahārāja of the a, the monastic order founded by Svāmī

Vivekananda, with whom I had numerous conversations on *advaita* Vedānta and Indian culture.

When I arrived in Bhubaneshvar, Odissi dance was in full bloom and there were many opportunities to attend performances and listen to the *mardala*, which was, in fact, essential to the dance but also dependent on it, in the sense that it did not have a repertoire for solo recital and all the compositions were connected to dance. It was in its essence an accompanying instrument. While Odissi dance had been recognized as a classical dance form, Odissi music, notwithstanding the work done by musicians and scholars in order to obtain recognition from the government, had not yet been included in the list of national classical forms. Banamali Maharana was among those musicians and he was then working towards the creation of a solo *mardala* repertoire, considered an indispensable feature of a classical drumming tradition.

My introduction to the *mardala* and my subsequent discovery of its important historical role in the temple music of Orissa attested by the numerous representations on the walls of the temples, opened the way to the world of Indian barrel drums and led me in turn to the *dhrupad pakhāvaj*, which I discovered had an older tradition and, moreover, a rich repertoire for solo recital.

In 1996, when I returned to India with a scholarship from the Indian Council for Cultural Relations to study *khyāl* singing at New Delhi, I expected to start studying the *pakhāvaj* of the *dhrupad* tradition too, but the real training did not start until 2000. It was not an easy task to find a *pakhāvaj* guru in the capital. I took a few lessons from the famous *pakhāvaj* player Gopal Das and then continued to study with a young *tablā* and *pakhāvaj* player, who had a more effective didactical approach.

Every day, I used to go to the Sangeet Natak Akademi's library and audio/video archives for my research. There I met a *tablā* player of the Delhi *gharānā* who recommended that I go to the Kathak Kendra and to Svāmī Ram Kishore Das, a very high-ranking *pakhāvajī* – *pakhāvaj* player – and main disciple of the famous Pagal Das, and study with him.

I decided to follow the kind advice of the *tablā* player, and the next day I went to the Kathak Kendra, wishing to meet Svāmī Ram Kishore Das. He was in his classroom teaching his students and welcomed me and the porter who had guided me to his room. I explained that I had received some training in *mardala* but I was now interested in learning the *dhrupad pakhāvaj*. He replied that I should first listen to his music and he started playing for me in a very joyful and vibrant way. After quite a few minutes he ended his solo and invited me to play something for him. His style was powerful, rich and expressive, and I felt shy to play but I could not refuse and did so to the best of my ability. At the end of that musical meeting he told me that he was prepared to teach me, in his house, and under the traditional teaching system of *guruśiṣyaparamparā*, based on the direct relationship of the teacher (*guru*) with the disciple (*śiṣya*).

I accepted his invitation and went to his house at Shakarpur, a quarter of East Delhi where many musicians and dancers lived, since it is cheap and near to the centre. There, after offering me tea and sweets, he sat on his wooden seat, cross-legged in front of the *pakhāvaj* in meditative attitude, and played a sweet and clear stroke – the most resonant and important one, called ***dha*** – and taught me the first lesson: the sound of the *pakhāvaj* is equivalent to the monosyllable *Om*. This was to me an unexpected way to begin, but it was in line with the fact that he was a musician and ascetic (Svāmī). After a few lessons including music, as well as frequent references to mythology, literature and yoga, I decided to keep studying with Svāmī Ram Kishore Das because I wished to learn the language and repertoire of the *pakhāvaj* and study its association with meditative practices and religious rituals. From 2000 to 2003, I had extensive and intense discussions with him in the course of my daily meetings in his house or in theatres where he had to accompany musicians or *kathak* dancers. During those years I had the opportunity to meet and speak with several musicians and dancers but also to yogis and leaders of religious sects.

Svāmī Ram Kishore Das was a musician, but also an ascetic. He had long hair, used to wear an ochre robe and always drew a red *tilaka* on his forehead as a sign of devotion to Rāma and Hanumān. He had received training under ascetics and more than once told me that all the main representatives of his school (*gharānā*), the Avadhi *gharānā*, based at Ayodhya in Uttar Pradesh, were ascetics who had been playing the *pakhāvaj* as a path to enlightenment. He introduced me to the mythical, literary and 'religious' world of the *pakhāvaj* in a simple way, through his own way of life, through quotations from the epics, the courtly and devotional literature and from the oral tradition of the world of Svāmīs he came from, and with the aid of the many posters of gods, heroes and kings hanging on the walls of his house. In his vision, the *pakhāvaj* was identical with the ancient *mṛdaṅga*, the drum which resounded in Rāma's capital Ayodhya and was played both by kings such as Arjuna, and devotees such as Hanumān. He considered the *pakhāvaj* as a spiritual instrument, a drum having a soul, and its playing as a form of yoga leading to a state of supreme beatitude. Furthermore, according to him, it was a drum capable of telling stories – which he translated to me and a very few other privileged friends through words and gestures – and reciting prayers.

The basic idea of this study is rooted in the time spent with Ram Kishore Das but it evolved and became clearer when I was working on the book *La gioia e il potere. Musica e danza in India* (2008). Indeed, while writing about music in ancient and medieval courts, I read theatre and music treatises, many literary – epics, Purāṇas, dramas – and philosophical sources – Upaniṣads, yoga, Tantra, Śaiva, Vaiṣṇava texts – and looked at numerous representations of musical scenes carved on the walls of temples or painted in manuscripts and miniatures. The information provided by these sources helped me to realize that the *mṛdaṅga* – of which the *pakhāvaj* was a recent version – was considered the most important and auspicious drum in ancient India, at least from about the 3rd or 2nd century B.C.E. onward, and, at the same time, that it constituted an important element of a complex network of symbolical relationships. The view of the *pakhāvaj* that Ram Kishore Das embodied and transmitted to me with great passion and care was clearly connected to the world of ancient courts, and to ideas, canons and symbolical associations, expressed in ancient and medieval literature and represented in theatre and visual arts. To discover the presence of ancient ideas and symbols in a contemporary musical tradition was extremely interesting but at the same time problematic. Indeed, it raised several questions.

Was the world of the *pakhāvaj* presented by Ram Kishore Das exclusive knowledge of the Avadhi *gharānā*, whose main representatives were ascetics (*sādhus*), or was it part of the *pakhāvaj* heritage shared by all the *gharānās*? Considering that the system of the *gharānās* had developed during the 19th century, was it a centuries old oral tradition or had it been recently fashioned?

From the visual sources I had already collected and the corresponding description given by the *Nāṭyaśāstra*, it was clear that the *mṛdaṅga* had not always had the same organological features. Indeed, while from the 2nd century B.C.E. until the end of the 1st millennium C.E. it had been composed of a set of three drums, at the beginning of the 2nd millennium it had become a single barrel drum taking slightly different shapes according to the region. Furthermore, during the medieval period, other names were added to the ancient name *mṛdaṅga*, such as *mardala* or *pakhāvaj*, more recent or vernacular alternatives. In the light of organological changes, what was the constant crucial feature of the *mṛdaṅga*?

The technique of the *mṛdaṅga*, as it had been described in the *Nāṭyaśāstra*, was very similar to that of the contemporary *pakhāvaj*, but was its repertoire ancient too? And how ancient? What was the influence of Islam on its language and repertoire? And how could that influence be ascertained given the lack of textual sources in Sanskrit, Persian and other languages?

Many people, including musicians, used to pay respect to Ram Kishore Das, but it was only partially due to his musical abilities. Indeed he was a Svāmī, and Svāmīs are respected and feared. The status of the *pakhāvaj* player in Indian musical society is higher than that of the *tablā* player, since the drum is recognized as an ancient instrument and it is linked to the *dhrupad* style and devotional music, but it is nevertheless low since it is considered an accompanying instrument and it includes leather, an impure material. How can we explain the present-day low status of the drum and its previous high rank?

All these questions could be subsumed under a wider one: what is the relationship of the present-day *mṛdaṅga* – the *pakhāvaj* – with its past? This main question gives rise to the following sub-questions: why was the *mṛdaṅga* considered auspicious? Why was it associated with kings and kingship? Why was it linked to gods and so closely connected to the sphere of sacred music and meditative practices such as yoga? Is its contemporary repertoire connected with the ancient world presented by *pakhāvajīs*? Does the relationship of the drum with kings and gods influence its repertoire?

Fieldwork among *pakhāvajīs*

While addressing these questions it became immediately clear to me that my research had to follow two divergent routes: on the one hand I had to further investigate the present-day practice of the *pakhāvaj* and, on the other, I had to deepen my research on the history of the drum, its myths and symbolism.

In order to investigate the experience of the contemporary *pakhāvaj* player, I decided to meet representatives of the main schools (*gharānās*) of *pakhāvaj* – the Kudau Singh, the Nana Panse and the Nathdwara schools – and collect information on their heritage and their personal views on the drum, its antiquity and 'symbolical world'. Since, unfortunately, Svāmī Ram Kishore Das died in 2007, I could no longer rely on his knowledge and his help in introducing me to other *pakhāvajīs* of his own or other *gharānās*. However, during two fieldwork trips – from November 2011 to April 2012, and from November 2012 to April 2013 – I managed to interview and converse with Pandit Dalchand Sharma, Prakash Kumavat and Bhagwat Upreti of the Nathdwara *gharānā*, Ravishankar Upadhyay, Ramakant Pathak, Ramashish Pathak and sons, Shrikant Mishra, Akilesh Gundecha and Manik Munde, all of them belonging to different branches of the Kudau Singh *gharānā*, and with Baldeep Singh, leader of the Punjab *gharānā* which he himself had recently revived. I tried to meet important representatives of the Nana Panse *gharānā* but it was not possible. Nevertheless, I received some information about it from Ramakant Pathak, who told me that before entering the Kudau Singh *gharānā* he had received training in the Nana Panse *gharānā*, and from Kalyanray Mahārāja and his sons, Harirai Gosvāmī and Wagdish Gosvāmī, religious leaders of the Puṣṭimārg sect and good *pakhāvaj* players, who told me that they had received extensive training in Nana Panse *gharānā* at Indore. While, over several months, I had numerous conversations with Dalchand Sharma – excluding Bhagwat Upreti whom I met twice – I met all the other musicians only once. These one-off meetings, however, took the form of long conversations or semi-structured interviews.

All the *pakhāvajīs* identified the *pakhāvaj* with the ancient *mṛdaṅga* and hence considered it one of the most ancient musical instruments of Indian classical music, reported stories or legends connected to it, associated it and its repertoire with the gods Śiva, Viṣṇu and Gaṇeśa, and attributed to it the quality of auspiciousness. Almost all of them asserted that there were strong links between the instrument and the spheres of the 'religious' – associating it to gods and mentioning a particular kind of composition conceived as prayers, such as the *stuti parans* (compositions mixing the syllables referring to the strokes on the drum with the Sanskrit text of a prayer) – and with royal courts – associating the drum with the heavenly court of Indra, the king of gods. While some of them linked their school to court music exclusively (Ravishankar Upadhyay, Ramashish Pathak of the Kudau Singh *gharānā*), others told me that it had some relationship with temples, worship and yoga (Ram Kishore Das, Ramakant Pathak, Shrikant Mishra, Kalyanray Mahārāja and his sons). The position of the Nathdwara *gharānā* was unique since it had been, until the 20th century, a musical tradition connected to the worship of Kṛṣṇa in the temple of Nathdwara.

The new data collected were broadly consistent with the view of the *pakhāvaj* presented by Ram Kishore Das – a world of royal courts, where the drum was a symbol of power and sovereignty, and temples, where it was a spiritual drum representing God. Even though none of the musicians interviewed had proposed any explanation of its symbolism, since their views were based on the unquestionable truth that they had inherited from their musical tradition and from myths, it was clear that the *pakhāvaj* was not simply a musical instrument but a symbol of an ancient world which no longer existed on Indian soil but was still alive in the minds of the *pakhāvajīs*. A striking aspect shared by all of them was that the connections of the drum with gods and royal courts were not conceived as secondary but as very crucial aspects of the instrument. To know these features of the drum was considered a necessary accomplishment of the *pakhāvaj* player. Furthermore, since very few other instruments of classical music may boast such a high prestige and auspicious qualities, this specific knowledge had an impact on the drummers' lives. Indeed, the sound of the *pakhāvaj* was unanimously considered as auspicious and purifying. Hence, to play it was understood as a kind of privilege, notwithstanding the fact that drums are generally considered as low status, accompanying instruments in the classical music scene of contemporary India.

Thus, the main themes that came up in my interviews are the following: *pakhāvaj* and *mṛdaṅga* are alternative names of the same instrument; the *pakhāvaj* is an auspicious drum, symbol of kingship and representative of Śiva and Viṣṇu, the most important gods of the Hindu pantheon; it is an instrument used for worship and yoga and its sound is equated to the *Om*; it is linked with clouds, lightning and rain. In this study I will explore what lies behind these essential observations.

Ancient courts: the roots of a musical tradition

Evidence from fieldwork showed that the world that Ram Kishore Das had shown me was not exclusively his, or of his school, but was shared, in different degrees, by almost all the *pakhāvajīs*. Even the repertoires of each school were very similar, the differences consisting mostly in the playing style, forceful and vigorous in some cases, light and mellow in others. The *pakhāvaj* players did not simply relate their music to God – as many Indian classical musicians do, irrespective of the style and repertoire – but were acquainted with the mythology connected to the drum, its history and its relations with ancient literature (*kāvya*) and devotional verses in Sanskrit and other local languages. This was extremely interesting since those aspects had not been studied in depth, and delving into the links between mythology, religion, literature, symbolism and the *pakhāvaj* has, in fact, become one of this study's most original and significant contributions. In light of the lack of specific works on the history of the *pakhāvaj* and, moreover, on its mythology and symbolism, in order to deepen the research on these aspects and the context out of which it has evolved, I have turned my attention to some examples of scholarship related to the cultural and religious context of ancient and premodern Indian society. I have then focused on studies relating to the concepts of kingship and divine kingship and their symbols, the sacred–secular dichotomy in the field of performing arts, and the concept of auspiciousness and its role in ancient, premodern and contemporary India. These issues, which are crucial to an understanding of the symbolic world suggested by the *pakhāvaj* players, are interconnected since they were created and elaborated in ancient India and played an important role in royal courts (Ali 2006; Inden 1985; Marglin 1985b). Kingship was connected to auspiciousness and fertility as well as to music and dance, and the performing arts were related to kingship as harbingers of auspiciousness (Inden 1985; Marglin 1985a, 1985b; Pacciolla and Spagna 2008). Numerous literary and iconographic sources attest that, in ancient and premodern India, royal courts were conceived as earthly replicas of the court of Indra, the king of gods, and describe them as resounding with the voices of musical instruments played by celestial dancers (*apsaras*) and musicians (*gandharvas*) who were, in their turn, conceived as symbols of power. A court where the sound of musical instruments filled the air and moved the courtesans to dance was the expression of a powerful king, while a silent court meant a defeated king (*Rāmāyaṇa* 2, 67, 15; Iravati 2003; Pacciolla and Spagna 2008).

The origins of courtly culture in India date back to the court of the great Maurya empire and developed under the Śaka, Kuṣāṇa and Sātavāhana dynasties, appearing fully crystallized under the Guptas and other dynasties between the 4th and the 7th centuries C.E. (Ali 2006; Clothey 2006; Pollock 1996, 1998). During these centuries kingship had become a stable aspect of the North Indian landscape and the urban centers had become autonomous city-states. From this urban landscape emerged a new ethic suitable for urban life, an increased interest in the patronage of literature and arts, and new theisms with devotional character (Ali 2006; Clothey 2006; Thapar 1978). These cults, whose main gods were Śiva and Viṣṇu, evolved a new idea of the deity conceived as an all-embracing presence having a cosmic role (Samuel 2008) and a new ritual practice based on the worship of God in the form of an icon, treated as though it were a king (Ali 2006;

Buhnemann 1988; Clothey 2006). This religious phenomenon, which incorporated the idea of kingship – with all its symbols and paraphernalia – through the identification of God with the king, produced the King-God, a concept of deity which is still crucial for many sects (Clothey 2006; Gaston 1997; Marglin 1985a; Subramaniam 1998; Thielemann 1999). Parallel to this phenomenon was the spread of temple-building and the practice of worshipping God in the form of an icon conceived as His embodiment. The temple, which represented the residence of the King-God embodied in the icon located in the *sancta sanctorum*, corresponded to the palace of the king, and just as royal courts were filled with music and dance and crucial moments of the king's daily life were marked by the presence of auspicious music, the icon was worshipped through music and dance.

During this period of ancient Indian history an original courtly culture took form. The idea of the king and deity merged producing an intertwining of the spheres of the sacred and the secular, and performing arts started to be conceived as crucial ritual elements of both royal and divine courts. This period is crucial to an interpretation of the mythological and symbolical world of the *pakhāvaj* since it evolved out of this context and according to its cultural patterns. Indeed, it is clearly to this world and context that almost all the myths and ideas mentioned by *pakhāvajīs* refer, and, hence, it is through a thorough and critical study of the ancient courts and their world-view that the cultural heritage of the *pakhāvaj* has to be approached and studied.

Several scholars have written on the concept of kingship in ancient India (Clothey 2006; Coomaraswamy 1942; Davidson 2002; Gonda 1956a, 1956b, 1957a, 1957b; Heesterman 1985; Samuel 2008), on Sanskrit literature and aesthetics in courtly culture (Ali 2006; Pollock 1996, 1998, 2006), on temple culture and sacred music (Gaston 1997; Thielemann 1999, 2001, 2002), on the sacred and the secular in performing arts (Subramaniam 1980) and on auspiciousness in Indian culture and its relationship with performing arts (Dehejia 2009; Hart 1975, 1999; Kersenboom 1987; Marglin 1985a, 1985b; Sivaramamurti 1974, 1982).

During the first half of the 2nd millennium C.E. a new scenario became apparent on the Indian subcontinent. Continuous Muslim invasions and the formation of increasingly powerful Muslim reigns, internal rebellions against the rigid structure of the social organization and the emergence of new Indic cults, produced instability but, at the same time, introduced important new elements into the feudal order of early medieval India favouring the development of a multifaceted cultural context and, of course, new musical ideas. The turn of the second half of the 2nd millennium, with the establishment of the Mughal dynasty and its empire, inaugurated a new important political and cultural period which, while not producing any radical change in the feudal order or in the cultural world which had been developed until then, did add further new elements making it more complex and multifaceted. It was a particularly important period in the evolution of the *mṛdaṅga*; in fact, it was during Akbar's empire that the vernacular name *pakhāvaj* was utilized for the first time as an alternative to the ancient name *mṛdaṅga*, to indicate the most important court drum.

Recent interesting studies based not only on Sanskrit sources but also on texts in Persian and vernacular languages, such as those conducted in different fields by Brown (2003), Bush (2004), Butler Schofield (2010), De Bruijn and Bush (2010), Delvoye (1990, 1992, 1993), Orsini (2014), Orsini and Butler Schofield (2015), Sarmadee (2002, 2003) and Trivedi (2010) have significantly contributed to a deeper understanding of the Mughal world in its many aspects. While disclosing the complex interrelationships linking different cultural aspects, including music, and facets of the Mughal society, they show the growing importance of vernacular cultures and the strong impact that ancient Sanskrit courtly literature and Indian culture, arts and music, had on the Mughal world.

A critical assessment and careful analysis of all these studies have helped me to find answers to the questions about the antiquity of the tradition of the *mṛdaṅga*, its links with royalty – from early medieval to Mughal India – and the symbolic world connected to it by the contemporary *pakhāvaj* players.

However, while all these studies rely mainly on textual sources, I have included in the perspective of my study also visual sources, which provide valuable information not only on the instruments, their organological features and the ensembles in which they were included, but also on the contexts in which they were played. This wealth of material gives a visual form to and confirms the literary descriptions. Furthermore, the geographical collocation of these sources provides information on the spread and distribution of the instruments on the subcontinent.

Nathdwara, a contemporary reign of the King-God and his court

The two paths of my study, the investigation of the present-day practice of the *pakhāvaj* and the research on the history of the drum, its myths and symbolism, find a meeting point at Nathdwara.

Having met many *pakhāvaj* players, I decided to focus the research on the Nathdwara school (*gharānā*). Dalchand Sharma, one of the most important representatives of the tradition, had a deep understanding of the history and the language of the *pakhāvaj* and considered it a spiritual drum. He was an excellent and knowledgeable musician, a devotee – according to his own definition – of the *pakhāvaj*, but with a positive critical approach towards its tradition and oral tradition in general. Furthermore, he was ready to establish a relationship of collaboration with me – rather than that of *guru–śiṣya*, which all the other *pakhāvajīs* would have expected – and was happy to share his knowledge. Indeed, we soon started working on the repertoire of solo *pakhāvaj* of Nathdwara style and discussing the many issues connected to the drum, its history, symbolism and auspiciousness.

The history of the Nathdwara school of *pakhāvaj*, which is essentially the history of a family tradition, is documented in the *Mṛdaṅg Sāgar*, a book written by members of this family, which also includes a huge number of compositions and diagrams of the different rhythmic cycles (*tāla*). While I have seen the original handwritten copy held by Prakash Kumavat, the oldest living *pakhāvaj* player in the family, I have found only one Xerox copy of the printed version – published in 1911 under the name of Ghanshyam Das – in the library of the Sangeet Natak Akademi of New Delhi. The story starts at the beginning of the 18th century and goes on until the first decades of the 20th century, a period which is crucial not only for the *pakhāvaj* of Nathdwara but for the development of the *pakhāvaj* in general. According to the *Mṛdaṅg Sāgar*, the family's working association as *pakhāvajīs* in the Śrī Nāthjī temple started in 1802, but the story of their tradition as *pakhāvaj* players began in the early part of the 18th century at the court of Amber and Jaipur. The last professional *pakhāvaj* player in the family was Purushottam Das (1907–1991), who brought the art from the temple to music academies and wrote the *Mṛdaṅg Vādan* for his students, a book including a short history of his family and a large number of *pakhāvaj* compositions. Since its members found employment in both the centres of patronage, the history of this school shows the interrelations of royal courts and the temple of Nathdwara. Furthermore, it is also interesting since it retraces in synthesis the evolution of the ancient *mṛdaṅga* which was first played in royal courts, then was adopted into temples and from courts and temples reached the cities, where most of the *pakhāvajīs* presently live.

Another important reason to focus on the tradition of Nathdwara is that, for these particular musicians, music plays a crucial role in worship. Indeed, while the worldly courts of kings disappeared – and their palaces have often been converted into five-star hotels – temples, the courts of gods, still tend to remain in active service as places of worship and furnish interesting instances of the endurance of an ancient world and its symbols in contemporary India. The temple of Nāthjī is a noteworthy example. Notwithstanding the fact that it is located only about 40 kilometres away from Udaipur, one of the most visited places in Rajasthan by tourists from all over the world, to visit Nathdwara is an experience that gives a glimpse of what might have been a medieval town, and every time I have been there I was the only foreigner among Indian pilgrims. The town of Nathdwara is organized like a medieval kingdom where the temple/palace of the King-God with its ritual activities is the centre around which the life of the entire community turns. The music of the temple musicians (*kīrtankars*) – like the bards with their kings – awakens the King-God and accompanies all the other moments of his daily life, while people await, in and out of the temple/palace, the scheduled ritual time to see their beloved divine ruler. When the call of a priest announces the opening of the doors of the inner chamber where he resides, the hundreds of people start pushing to enter, and the general emotion of being in front of their King-God becomes palpable. The devotion and respect which are offered to the divine ruler of the town is granted also to the leaders (Mahārājas) of the sect. Indeed, in one of my visits to Nathdwara, as guest of Wagdish Gosvāmī, Harirai Gosvāmī and Kalyanray Mahārāja, I witnessed that they are worshipped like divine beings.

The continuity of medieval and contemporary traditions is a remarkable feature of the cult. In a visit into the temple I met Kapil, a young priest who guided me on a tour from the kitchen to the room of the outdoor instruments (*naqqārkhāna*), and to the roof, near to the flag on the top of the temple. He told me that he was a Brahmin and a cowherd, and that he belonged to the family of cowherds that lived at Mathura and moved with their cattle from there to Nathdwara, together with the icon of Nāthjī, during the second half of the 17th century. Indeed, the icon of Nāthjī was originally located at Mathura, but it was moved to Nathdwara where the Mahārana Rāja Singh of Mewar provided shelter (Ambalal 1987; Gaston 1997) after the edict issued by Aurangzeb (1669) ordering the demolition of Hindu temples and forbidding public worship.

Providing me with the collaboration of an excellent and knowledgeable musician such as Pandit Dalchand Sharma, the history of a family of *pakhāvaj* players developing between courts and the temple, and being the realm of a King-God in full life, Nathdwara turned out to be the best place to work on my research at the meeting point of present and past.

A multidimensional approach

The information collected from interviews and conversations includes a wide range of aspects; almost none of the *pakhāvajīs* spoke of their drum from a purely musical perspective, but they connected it to myths, religion, yoga and/or metaphors and symbols of ancient literature (*kāvya*). Myths and gods were not only quoted in relation to the creation of the *mṛdaṅga* but also in relation to compositions and, in turn, compositions were assimilated to ancient literary images and formulas based on water, rain, kings, courtesans or loving couples (*mithuna*). However, despite such copious mentions of aspects of the ancient past, religion and myths, the styles, techniques and lineages of the contemporary *pakhāvaj* are rooted in the 19th century, a golden period for the drum thanks to the presence of great musicians such as Kudau Singh and Nana Panse who founded the schools (*gharānā*) to which contemporary players still belong. What then is the relationship of the *pakhāvaj* to the world of the ancient *mṛdaṅga*? Is there really a continuous thread linking the contemporary drum to its ancestor or were it and its repertoire created during the last few centuries?

The fact that aspects of ancient and medieval India are so intertwined with the contemporary schools of *pakhāvaj* is not surprising if it is considered that rājas and Mahārājas had ruled in India until the last century according to patterns deriving from the ancient models of kingship and adopting similar symbols, among which music and dance were crucial, even when they became 'hollow crowns' subordinated to the British. Indeed, the arts were so important as symbols of royal courts that the Hindu reformers of the Renaissance movement of the 19th century concentrated part of their work on trying to recast them as purely spiritual arts sprouting from devotion to God (Bakhle 2005; Jones 2014; Subramaniam 2006a, 2006b). Even in the court of Baroda, which Bakhle considers emblematic of the new attitudes of kings and court administration being based on colonial models (Bakhle 2005: 34), the display of grandeur followed ancient symbols and modalities. The prince Sayajirao Gaekwad did not appreciate Indian 'classical' music and was very interested in and inclined towards Western culture. However, he was known as a patron of learning and of the arts, and his group of entertainers (*kalāwant kārkhānā*) served as a means to increase his royalty (Bakhle 2005: 32). If the court of Sayajirao Gaekwad of Baroda (1875–1939) was happily inclined to colonial policy, that of Rāja Chakradhar Singh of Raigarh (1905–1947), during almost the same period, followed the ancient model, since he was not only a patron of the arts but an expert and knowledgeable musician who composed four important books on *rāgas*, *pakhāvaj*, *tablā* and *kathak* (Ashirwadam 1990).

Questions intended to analyse the relationship of the Indian present to the ancient past, such as 'how does the present use the past?', are addressed by Romila Thapar in the essay 'Interpretations of Ancient Indian History' in his book (1978) and in several lectures. She argues that the views on Indian history which have dominated until the recent past, are those formulated by the antagonistic British and nationalistic historiographies, neither of which were interested in history per se, but which were intended to interpret the past in order to control the present. Those interpretations did not portray the complexity of the social reality but looked at it from a specific perspective. Indeed, British historiographers, claiming the absence of a historical sense in Indian culture, intended to construct a history in line with their colonial policy, while nationalists intended to glorify the ancient Indian past as a reaction to the British view and in order to build national self-respect and political unity whose foundation was seen in the Maurya empire (Thapar 1978: 12).

Interestingly, Thapar adds that the influence of Brahmanism and its ideological prejudices on both the historiographies was quite significant. On the one hand, the early nationalist writers came from Brahman families, who had easier access to the classical language but, at the same time, their cultural background tended to inhibit a critical and analytical study of the sources. On the other hand, British scholars based their works on Sanskrit texts which were mainly Brahmanical and relied on Brahmans themselves for their interpretations. Thus, the reliance on Pandits, an elite of ritual specialists, who considered those texts as the earliest and only ones worth knowing, caused them to ignore, until the end of 19th century, the many texts in the other languages and religions such as Buddhism, Jainism or Tantra. This restricted point of view on the Indian religious world influenced what they called Hinduism (Thapar 2010) which is, Thapar argues, a mosaic of sects and cults, in which the most important aspect is not the orthodoxy of the text but the practice of the sect, often coinciding with a caste (Thapar 2010). The omission of this aspect produced a split in scholarship between the experts on the texts, doing fine philological research, and the ethnographers, observing the non-textual religious practice which was considered to be at a lower level. For this reason, there was no dialogue between the different fields in order to understand whether there was any overlap or link between texts and practices (Thapar 2010).

The point that Thapar makes very clearly is that both historiographies not only manipulated Indian history but even Indian religion because they looked at it from the exclusive point of view of the Brahmins' texts. By contrast, she argues that a complex phenomenon such as Indian religion needs to be observed not only from the perspective of texts, in their many languages, but also from the perspective of practice, since while texts are static in their nature, actual ritual practices are in a continuous flux of change, and the most comprehensive image would necessarily emerge from the observation of the interrelations or overlapping of the two perspectives.

Similarly, Samuel points out in his *The Origins of Yoga and Tantra* (2008) that a religious tradition is not just a body of texts, but above all something that lives and is maintained through the lives of human beings:

> a text, unless we assume that certain texts are indeed divinely inspired and so beyond academic analysis or criticism, can only be the product of one or more human beings and has to make sense in terms of their lives and their understanding of their situation.

Samuel adds that:

> even a textual scholarship cannot be divorced from a reconstruction of the intellectual, emotional, social and political context of the people who produced those texts [...] which is the real object of study of scholars of Indian religion.
>
> (Samuel 2008: 21)

Thus, in order to try to reconstruct as much as possible about the life-world within which a particular religious development took place, including its social, cultural and political aspects, he adopts a kind of multidimensional approach where textual, epigraphic, iconographic and archaeological material are seen as mutually illuminating bodies of evidence (Samuel 2008: 22).

This kind of approach allows Samuel to widen his view through a large range of information and even to establish possible connections and similarities between ritual practices of the present with those of the ancient past. Thus, for instance, while explaining what he calls the Tantric pattern, he writes that

> the place that comes closest to representing it in modern times is probably the Kathmandu Valley. The valley today is nearly a thousand years distant from the period of which we are speaking [...] it has undergone two centuries of strongly pro-Hindu rule since the Gurkha conquest, but it is still suggestive in many ways of how a medieval Tantric polity might have operated.
>
> (Samuel 2008: 314)

And again, according to him, in modern times, ritual drummers within Tibetan societies in Ladakh and northern Nepal show clear parallels to those of the ancient Tamils described by Hart, and like them constitute a distinct low-status grouping (Samuel 2008: 237).

In line with Thapar and Samuel, I believe that, in order to be understood in the best possible way, religious phenomena and cultural products in general, such as music and musical instruments,[1] need to be observed from multiple perspectives, including the socio-cultural context within which they have been created and their function which, particularly in ancient societies, was very often connected to celebrations or religious rituals[2] (Ahuja 2001). A multidimensional approach is particularly needed for an instrument such as the *pakhāvaj*, which is a drum played by contemporary musicians belonging to various schools, connected to both kingship and religion through an interesting body of myths, with origins tracing back to at least the 2nd century B.C.E.

The *pakhāvaj* can be studied and narrated through ethnography, observing its present context and describing its contemporary practice, through its historical development in relation with the changing cultural, religious and social contexts, and through the myths attached to it which, as argued by Marglin, 'could illuminate particular aspects of the ethnography in a most helpful way' (Marglin 1985a: 17). Texts – ranging from literature to philosophy and from mythology to musical treatises – visual arts and present-day practice, constitute different sources and points of view to approach and study the drum and its heritage, but they need to be considered all together to create a complex and comprehensive picture. Of course, it would be possible to focus exclusively on one of these aspects such as, for instance, the analysis of the present-day language and repertoire, but this would leave out many others which are important in order to understand the roots of contemporary *pakhāvaj* playing and are considered by musicians themselves to be so intrinsic to the instrument as to constitute its 'identity'. Indeed, what makes the study of the *pakhāvaj* very interesting is the presence of numerous symbols and practices stratifying one upon the other over the centuries, and the fact that it incorporates and synthesizes tribal,[3] folk, court and religious music, providing a perfect instance of both the kind of overlapping of spheres that Thapar speaks about, and the local (*deśī*) – global (*mārga*) cultural exchange investigated by Pollock in his studies on Sanskrit and its relationship with vernacular languages from the 1st centuries of the 1st millennium C.E. onward (1998, 2006).

The multidimensional approach, combining the analysis of the textual and visual material, and the study of historical material with contemporary practices, has provided me with the data to understand the evolution of the *pakhāvaj* and its relationship with the ancient *mṛdaṅga*.

Thus, my aim is to study the *pakhāvaj* and its repertoire in contemporary India and to trace the origin of the ideas, symbols and metaphors associated with it and its repertoire. In other words, my aim is to see how the ideas connected to this instrument have been changing over the centuries according to different socio-religious contexts and to determine if and how they still inform contemporary playing. In order to achieve this aim, on the one hand I have conducted an ethnographic study focusing on the repertoire of the solo recital from the perspective of Dalchand Sharma, the main representative of the Nathdwara *gharānā*, while keeping as constant background the views and interpretations of other contemporary *gharānās*, while, on the other hand, I have conducted historical, socio-religious and iconographical research on the evolution of the drum and on the concepts and ideas associated with it over about two millennia. On the basis of the collected materials, I have argued that the *pakhāvaj* was a vernacular drum which was identified with the *mṛdaṅga* through a process of Sanskritization taking place in the Mughal era. In order to observe and analyse the creative processes connected to the cult of a King-God from the point of view of a contemporary temple/palace, I have studied the aesthetic ideas of the Nathdwara *gharānā* and their relationship with ritual worship established by the Vallabha sect. Finally, I have focused my analysis on the contemporary repertoire of the *pakhāvaj* of the Nathdwara *gharānā* and, on the basis of the information provided by *pakhāvajīs* belonging to various schools, I have argued the strong link of *pakhāvaj* drumming with images, and identified the presence of a few metaphors and symbols of ancient Sanskrit literature in some kinds of compositions.

For my methodology, I have adopted a multidimensional approach, including more than one perspective, and taking various fields of study as sources of information. Thus, in order to understand the organological evolution of the *pakhāvaj*, its heritage and the idea – shared by all the *pakhāvajīs* – that the drum is more than a musical instrument, while relying mostly on ethnographic data, I have utilized different kinds of sources, such as treatises (*śāstra*) on the performing arts, literary, philosophical and religious texts, visual sources and contemporary studies on the arts, history and the anthropology of India. Looking at the drum from the many angles, as implicitly or explicitly suggested by the contemporary musicians, or, in other words, combining the ethnographic data collected in fieldwork with historical, mythological, religious and iconographical information, I have analysed the heritage of the *pakhāvaj* and its relationship to contemporary practice and repertoire.

The study is composed of nine chapters followed by the Conclusion. In Chapter 1, the Introduction, I address the main questions and explain the research approach. In Chapter 2, I explain the point of view I have adopted to approach the concepts of sacred and secular, and to study the relationship between courts and temples and their contribution to the evolution of the ideas associated with the *mṛdaṅga-pakhāvaj*. In Chapter 3, I present the *pakhāvaj* and its players and their position in the contemporary musical scene. Then I report what *pakhāvajīs* of different schools told me about the heritage of the *pakhāvaj* and highlight the resulting main features, which are, its being considered an auspicious instrument, and its association with both kingship and godship, and with devotional and meditative practices. In Chapter 4, in order to understand the reasons of these associations, I turn to historical, socio-religious and iconographical research. First, I study the organology of the ancient *mṛdaṅga* as described by musical treatises and in comparison with iconographical sources. Then, I explore the concept of auspiciousness and its association with the drum through the analysis of its myth of origin narrated in the *Nāṭyaśāstra*, and other iconographical and textual sources. In Chapter 5, I proceed to study the reasons why the drum is linked with kings and gods through the analysis of the concept of the King-God in relation with the organological evolution of the ancient royal drum *mṛdaṅga*. In Chapter 6, I follow the organological development of the *mṛdaṅga* during the 2nd millennium until its identification with the vernacular drum *pakhāvaj* in the Mughal period, and argue that the *pakhāvaj* was a vernacular drum identified with the *mṛdaṅga* and legitimated as the social elite's most representative drum under the Mughals. In Chapter 7, I focus on Nathdwara and Pandit Dalchand Sharma, the main representative of the Nathdwara school and the main informant of the study. I first trace the story of the Vallabha sect and then analyse the role of music in the cult which centres on the King-God Nāthjī, who is, at the same time, the supreme god and the king of the universe residing in his temple/palace at Nathdwara. Next, I study the history of the main family of *pakhāvaj* players associated with the temple and its playing style strongly connected with ritual worship and imbued with the precise aesthetic approach of the sect. In Chapter 8, I analyse the contemporary repertoire, and – combining the information regarding contemporary musicians with the data resulting from the previous three chapters – I argue that aspects of the ancient symbols and metaphors of ancient and medieval India may still be traced in compositions included in the contemporary repertoire. In Chapter 9, I analyse the sequence of compositions stringed together in a solo *pakhāvaj* recital and its symbolical relationship with a garland of flowers, and then focus on the solo recital by Dalchand Sharma. In the Conclusion, I summarize the main steps of the study and point out the importance of further research on the relationship of drumming and images in India.

Notes

1 One of the aims of my *La gioia e il potere* (2008) was to argue the crucial role that music and dance had in ancient India, particularly for the ruling caste of *kṣatriyas*, and hence that the materials connected to performing arts might be used as important sources of information complementary to the texts transmitted by the Brahmans.

2 Notwithstanding this strong relationship, unlike texts, music and musical instruments have rarely been considered as sources of information in the study of ideas and religions.

3 I use the term tribal to refer to those communities which have their own beliefs and live or have lived in geographical isolation, away from the urban centres and outside the mainstream of Hindu society. I use the term folk to refer to those communities having their own beliefs and living away from urban centres, but having cultural and economic interaction with the socially dominant groups.

2 A drum between courts and temples

The *pakhāvaj* occupies a unique position in the classical music scene of contemporary India. Identified with the ancient *mṛdaṅga* and associated with gods and kings, it is the most respected of the Indian drums by musicians and, according to textual sources, the most authoritative. It is an auspicious drum and there is more than one origin myth to explain its creation. Its 'body' has gone through many changes over time and its repertoire includes compositions which musicians connect to literature in Sanskrit or vernacular languages and to prayer. Each one of these aspects needs a specific analysis in order to understand its contribution to the present-day image of the *pakhāvaj* as it is projected by musicians who consider it not only an ancient and important musical instrument but a symbol of an ancient world. For this reason, as I have argued in the Introduction, I have adopted a multidimensional approach which allows me to observe the drum from different points of view in order to address my research question. In this chapter I will point out the perspective I have adopted to approach the concepts of sacred and secular, and to study the relationship between courts and temples and their contribution to the evolution of the ideas associated with the *mṛdaṅga-pakhāvaj*.

Music, religions, the sacred and the secular in India

The many facets and multiple symbolic associations of the *pakhāvaj* raise several questions about their origin, meaning and, moreover, their interconnection. To approach such questions I initially sought to investigate what the most recent scholarship on classical music could tell us about the cluster of ideas and symbols associated with the *pakhāvaj*. However, instead of providing answers regarding the *pakhāvaj*'s relationship with ancient India, gods and kings, such an approach merely raised new questions. Since I have not found satisfying answers to any of the questions in any single existing field of scholarship, I have collected information from different fields and, considering the importance attributed to religion by musicians and both Indian and Western academics, I first tried to understand why the *pakhāvaj* was so deeply associated with gods and kings, as emphasized by all the musicians I met. This led me to investigate some aspects of the relationship of music to religion, and the realms of the sacred and the secular in India.

Issues relating to historical aspects or connected to the theory of music in ancient and medieval India have been widely investigated by Indian scholars,[1] although some of these studies, which are extremely valuable in many aspects, are mainly based on Sanskrit Hindu sources and adhere to the prevailing Indian view, according to which Indian musical tradition descends from the Vedas, and hence has an exclusively spiritual aim and Sanskrit as its main theoretical language. Indeed, this is also what is maintained by contemporary musicians and dancers who, generally, lay emphasis on the spirituality of Indian arts. The contribution of Western scholars to the same fields has also been significant,[2] although some of them clearly show their adhesion to the Sanskrit-centric view. Neuman, for instance, looks at Indian music as essentially Hindu and devotional in character, an avocation and not a profession, a means to attain liberation maintained and practised by Brahmans (Neuman 1985). Rowell, in a similar way, looks at ancient Indian music from the perspective of religion and metaphysics, and attributes to it a religious origin, hence identifying a process of musical generation from the sacred ritual *mārga* music to the local *deśī* music (Rowell 1998). A similar approach is also taken by Thielemann who, in order to demonstrate the religious character of the courtly *dhrupad*, writes that most of the *dhrupad* musicians were Hindu Brahmans who converted to Islam for political reasons, and this did not prevent them from keeping their traditions and repertoire alive (Thielemann 1997).

Although Sanskrit Hindu sources are undoubtedly crucial for understanding the evolution of Indian music, they are not the only ones. As shown by the scholarly widespread preference for Hindu music, early Buddhist music remains quite neglected,[3] although it seems to have played a significant role – attested by the numerous quotations of music and musical instruments in Buddhist texts and carvings of music scenes depicted on Buddhist monuments – until the 8th century C.E., when Buddhism disappeared from India. A few texts such as, for instance, Aśvagoṣa's *Buddhacarita* provide very interesting descriptions of the ancient *mṛdaṅga* set, and some of its most ancient representations are those carved in numerous bas-reliefs on the railings and the gateways of the stupas at Sanci, Amaravati and Bharhut.

Several studies published over the last ten years have clarified the process at work with the Hindu Sanskritic approach to Indian music and its evolution. They have revised recent Indian history highlighting the relationship of music, and performing arts in general, with nationalist movements, while considering the emphasis on the spiritual approach to music as a part of the nationalist project of Hindu reinterpretation of India's past. The research of Bakhle (2005), Subramaniam (2006a, 2006b) and Kippen (2006) shows from the perspective of music – Thapar's writings (Thapar 1978, 2010) do it from a wider historical perspective – that the spiritual aura attributed to Indian performing arts is the deliberate creation of a specific group of people and a political invention useful to the needs of a particular historical moment. Even the studies of scholars such as Coomaraswamy (1929, 1991, 2001), Kramrish (1976) and Danielou (1943, 1949), which laid down the basis for a better and deeper understanding of the role and value of arts in Indian society and culture, are being updated. Recent scholarly works on Indian arts have argued that, notwithstanding their important contribution, they have to be reconsidered in the light of their excessive reliance on Sanskrit texts and Brahmin sources, hence for having a Brahmanical neo-Vedantic perspective. This is maintained, for instance, by *The Sacred and the Secular in India's Performing Arts* (1980), a book edited by Subramaniam in which several writers examine critically the theory that identifies art with religion and suggests different interactions between the sacred and the secular in various traditions of Indian performing arts. In a similar way, Davies (1989) clearly affirms that the privilege attributed by art historians to the *advaita* Vedānta position on image worship is a fundamental flaw and contrasts it with the Śaiva *siddhānta* view.

The view proposed by both Western Orientalists and Indian nationalists, exalting the Hindu roots of Indian music and projecting the image of Muslim musicians as ignorant and responsible for the decline of Indian music, has been revised. Indeed, the studies on Indian music centred on Persian texts conducted by Delvoye (1990, 1992, 1993), Sarmadee (2002, 2003), Trivedi (2010), Brown (2003), Butler Schofield (2010) and De Bruijn and Bush (2014) produce a picture of the Mughal period much more nuanced than before, and demonstrate that the contribution of Muslim musicians to the evolution of Indian music was considerable. They show the many other parallel histories of music happening during the late medieval and the early modern periods in India and highlight that other streams of thought entered South Asia with Islamic invaders and intertwined with local culture producing an extremely interesting cultural variety.

A significant idea emerging from these studies is that the notion of Indian music as purely religious and spiritual is actually quite a recent phenomenon. The identity of spirituality and music commonly claimed by contemporary musicians is a product of recent Indian history and it cannot be considered as a major character of Indian music throughout its history. In other words, it may be said that the historic-religious and socio-cultural context resulting from the fall of the Mughal empire, the spread of the *bhakta* cults, the rise of British rule and its values and the development of Indian nationalism, produced a new idea of spirituality which was rooted in Brahmanism and Vaiṣṇavism, and presented as purely Hindu. This new Hindu/Indian spirituality, which was essentially devotional and was divulged as the 'eternal truth' of India (Subramaniam V. 1998, Subramaniam L. 2006a), promoted the idea that Indian arts were in their essence religious, with music being the most spiritual and devotional among them (Bakhle 2005; Coomaraswamy 1991; Subramaniam 2006a).

The new readings of recent Indian music history and the understanding that our received idea of the Indian world is only about one century old, stimulate new questions. If music is not spiritual in itself what makes it religious and/or sacred? Is music considered religious or sacred in the same way by the different sects that have used it in their rituals? What was the idea of the sacred and the secular in early modern, medieval and ancient India? Were the sacred and the secular conceived as separate realms? What was the function of music in each of them? Was it different? What are the differences?

Questions such as these are readily stimulated from the study of an ancient instrument such as the *pakhāvaj* or *mṛdaṅga*, which has been strongly associated with both courts and temples. Indeed, the relationship of the *mṛdaṅga* with Śiva, Viṣṇu and Gaṇeśa is a fact that all the *pakhāvaj* players I spoke to took for granted and is also expressed in literature and mythology. However, at the same time, both musicians and literature emphasize the importance of music in royal courts and the auspiciousness of the *mṛdaṅga* and its association with kings. Courts and temples, the two main contexts of performing arts and arts in general, are strongly intertwined and their relationship has been an important aspect of ancient, medieval and modern Indian history. The *pakhāvaj*, as successor of the ancient *mṛdaṅga*, symbolizes both the temple and the court, and helps reveal the relationship between the two; indeed, this is one of the instrument's most interesting aspects and a major reason for studying it. As a representative of both these institutions it incorporates their most significant aspects and generates several questions: did the drum play the same function in all the cults to which it was associated even when they held contrasting views, as in the cases of Śaivas and Vaiṣṇavas? Was it conceived in the same manner by all of them? Why was it associated also to kings and royal courts? Were courts and temples, secular and sacred, distinct realms and categories?

The questions stimulated by the new revisionist history and those deriving from the analysis of the heritage of the *pakhāvaj* coincide, and this is true because the recent Hindu nationalist re-elaboration of music as purely spiritual calls for an analysis of the historic-religious context that is the same as that in which the *pakhāvaj* was nurtured.

While nationalist, neo-Vedantic or Vaiṣṇava ideologies assume that Brahmin and temple culture are more ancient and valuable than courtly culture (Bakhle 2005; Beck 2011; Kippen 2006; Peerera 1994; Subramaniam 2006a, 2006b; Thielemann 1997), and some Western scholars until the first decade of the 21st century agree with them (Bakhle 2005; Beck 2011; Farrell 1999; Rowell 1998; Subramaniam 2006a, 2006b; Thielemann 1997), the new data demand a renewed and more profound study and raise the new questions indicated above. While nationalist histories emphasize the association of the *pakhāvaj* with temples and Brahman families to claim its purity and sacredness, and do not mention that it was at the same time played to accompany dances which were identified with the courtesans (*ṭawā'if*) (Francom 2012; Gaston 1997; Kippen 2006; Walker 2004), Western scholars use the association with Hindu temples to explain its high status (Dick 1984d: 697; Gaston 1997: 108; Sanyal and Widdess 2004: 41). These discussions stimulate one to consider whether there are, in fact, other features in addition to the instrument's association with Vaiṣṇava temple worship that have contributed towards its high status.

Due to the adoption of music and theatre for religious purposes by the numerous medieval *bhakta* movements and their fortune since at least the 16th century until recent times, the literature on devotional music and theatre in India is quite extensive. The strong relationship of Kṛṣṇa worship with performing arts, the crucial role played by the *Gīta Govinda* of Jayadeva in this field, and the widespread presence of regional theatres based on his cult such as the Rās Līlā and the Rām Līlā in Uttar Pradesh, Rajasthan and Madhya Pradesh, the Ankhiya Bhaona in Assam, the Prahlad Nātak in Orissa, the Bhāgavata Mela Nātaka in Tamil Nadu and the Kṛiṣṇāṭṭam of Kerala, have stimulated the production of essays on each of these forms and a few monographs on traditional theatres. Most of these studies are useful to the understanding of each of these theatrical forms, but all of them pivot around the religious and devotional utilization of music and theatre.

All these studies provide useful and interesting specific information, but their approach is marked by the assumption of the devotional religiosity of music and theatre, or the intrinsic association of Indian music and devotion, as if they could not be separated, and often do not consider the many facets and complexities of the Indian religious landscape.

There is no doubt that music has been the main religious means for the majority of the cults flourishing in medieval India, including Vaiṣṇava, Śaiva, Nāths, Sikhs and, Sufis (Jones 2009; Qureshi 1986; Sathyanarayana 1988; Singh 2012; Thielemann 2001). All of these sects adopted music in their worship, but a close look at the way they interpret music from a philosophical or theological perspective and use it in rituals, and the rules they follow while playing, show significant differences. It is also important to distinguish the idea of music and its ritual function in each one of these sects, since there may be different interpretations even among those belonging to the same major cult (Beck 2011; Tanaka 2008; Thielemann 2001). Differences may be seen even in the musical instruments they play for worship; indeed, Vaiṣṇava sects, for instance, have adopted barrel drums – *pakhāvaj*, *khol*, *puṅg*, *mṛdaṅgam*, *maddaḷam* – belonging to the family of the *mṛdaṅga* and have associated them to Viṣṇu or Kṛṣṇa, but the specific organological features, their sound, the rhythmic systems and the details of their symbolical association are different.

While contextualization is necessary to an understanding of the birth and evolution of the cults which emerged during the 2nd millennium, it is also essential when addressing the music of the 1st millennium, and it has to be taken into account that the concepts of sacred power and religiosity were then different from the later period. During the 2nd millennium, gods dominated human life and legitimated kingship, with Islam spreading over the subcontinent and devotional cults increasing in number and variety. The situation appeared quite different in the 1st millennium, when kings had the same status as gods, Buddhism was still being practised in India, Brahmanism was generating new forms and new cults and deities emerged from the lower strata of the society (see Chapter 5, pp. 76–77).

The concept of kingship in India, with the figure of the king being conceived of as representative of sacred divine power and an embodiment or representative of gods, has been extensively investigated by Coomaraswamy (1942), Gonda (1956a, 1956b, 1957a, 1957b), Heesterman (1985) and Pollock (1984) – academics who posit this idea as being a fundamental conception at the heart of ancient Indian culture, promoting a merging of ideas of sacred and secular and profoundly informing the ways in which performing arts are understood. Nationalist, neo-Vedantic and Vaiṣṇava perspectives would establish a strong distinction between the two realms, contrasting the religious as sacred and spiritual with the courtly as lascivious and entertaining. However, an analysis of these concepts from another point of view shows a different situation in which there is not a distinction between the sacred and the secular but rather a coincidence in the double figure of the King-God, a figure which Clothey (2006), Samuel (2008) and Davidson (2002) associate with the emergence, at the beginning of the 1st millennium, of new models of kingship and the gods Śiva and Viṣṇu conceived as universal overlords. While king and god merged into a single figure who appeared like a king performing dances of victory accompanied by a music ensemble and was represented as such in visual arts (Huntington 1994; Kaimal 1999; Kalidos 1999; Sitanarasimhan 2004; Sivaramamurti 1974), two separate buildings, the palace and the temple, started representing his sacred power architecturally. Indeed, the presence of two main centres of power and sacredness, the royal palace and the temple, in which king and gods reside and are celebrated with music and dance is a notable feature of medieval India (Hart 1975, 1999; Subramaniam 1980).

The importance of music in courts is testified in a number of ancient Sanskrit literary sources (Hart 1975; Lienhard 1984; Warder 1988) and, interestingly, it is not only sectarian theologians that confer a special status to music, but also early Sanskrit musical treatises (*saṅgīta śāstra*), texts produced by and for kings, which similarly attribute to it a metaphysical value. Both Sanskrit literature and music treatises emphasize the importance of the *mṛdaṅga* – alternatively called *muraja*, *mardala* and, later on, *pakhāvaj* – and its relation with kings, as do contemporary musicians.

In the worlds ruled by divine kings who had their own courts, music and dance were conceived as auspicious and promoting fertility (Dehejia 2009; Kersenboom 1987; Marglin 1985a, 1985b; Pacciolla and Spagna 2008). Indeed, in ancient India, the ideas of power and auspiciousness were connected, since sexual power and the power of conquering land and people were thought of as bringing fertility and guaranteeing the prosperity of a kingdom (Davidson 2002; Hart 1975; Marglin 1985a, 1985b; Samuel 2008). Women were conceived as harbingers of sacred power, and as such they were necessary in ritual auspicious activities directed to the empowerment of the king or the god and, at the same time, were considered dangerous and needing to be controlled (Hart 1975; Kersenboom 1987; Marglin 1985a, 1985b). Interestingly, literary and iconographic sources tell that in royal courts, and later in temples, music and dance were mostly performed by women, clearly because of their auspicious power.

The interrelation of royal palace and temple, conceived as the palace of the God-King, and the ritual importance of the temple courtesans (*devadāsīs*), clearly emerges from Marglin (1985a) whose contribution is also significant to an understanding of the concept of auspiciousness conceived as female power (*śakti*) and permeating Indian culture to a remarkable extent. Indeed, notwithstanding its widespread mention in literature and the arts, the centrality of the concept of auspiciousness in Indian thought and society has been properly highlighted and treated as a major research issue in anthropological and religious studies only in recent years.

Studies devoted to the auspiciousness of music in South Asia are still scanty. The most thorough contribution is provided by Tingey (1994) who, following the theoretical route traced by Marglin (1985a, 1985b), focuses her research on auspiciousness in Nepalese music. This study provides a valuable analysis of the Damāi musicians, their instruments, their repertoire and the fascinating relationship between low-caste status and auspiciousness. Terada (2008) and Booth (2008) study the concept of auspiciousness and the transformation of its meaning in the context of South Indian and North Indian wedding rituals respectively. Auspiciousness is a major aspect of my research too, but I have adopted a different perspective because, while the Damāis as well as wedding musicians and their instruments belong to low castes and play outdoor music, the *mṛdaṅga* is intimately associated with sovereignty and godship and is, therefore, an instrument of the highest rank. Although contemporary players are listed as accompanists, the *pakhāvaj* was played by kings, such as Chakradar Singh and Chatrapati Singh, until the last century, and is still played by several religious leaders. Furthermore, it is noteworthy that while Damāis and other low-caste musicians are themselves considered auspicious – as well as the instrument they play – *pakhāvajīs* do not consider themselves, and neither are they considered by others, auspicious, although the drum they play is still respected as a harbinger of auspiciousness.

The fact that the *mṛdaṅga-pakhāvaj* has been played by kings and high-rank religious figures and, moreover, its being played directly in front of the deity, are important features that clearly distinguish it from other instruments having connections with royal courts and temples. Indeed, a few other drums such as *naqqāra* and *tavil*, and reeds such as *shahnāī* or *nāgasvaram* also have strong links with sovereignty and godship, but their function is different. All these instruments, which are played by specific communities with the right to do so, produce loud auspicious sounds and for this reason are mostly played in the outdoor areas of the temples to accompany the processions of the deities. Thus, while the *mṛdaṅga-pakhāvaj* is played to give energy to the deity and the king in the inner chamber of the temple or the palace,[4] the others are played in open areas to convey a sonic representation of royal and divine power and splendour to people.

Historical and religious studies show that the realms of the sacred and the secular were not separate. Rather they constituted a whole within which both the figure of the king and the god were invested with sacred power. Although these two aspects have not always been balanced and have taken different forms throughout history, this conception remained a prevalent force within South Asian thought from the beginning of the 1st century C.E. until the early modern period, and it is still present in the rituals of cults which evolved during those periods as demonstrated by ethnographic studies.

A crucial aspect which has to be highlighted is that the concept of aesthetics evolved in ancient India, in a period in which kings were equated to gods and gods were conceived as kings. One of the most sophisticated and non-religious interpretations of the role of aesthetics in medieval India has been proposed by Pollock, whose argument is based on Sanskrit and Sanskrit literature. He argues that the power of Sanskrit 'derived, not from sacral associations, but from aesthetic capacities, its ability to make reality more real – more complex and more beautiful – as evinced by its literary idiom and style' (1998: 13), and that Sanskrit gave voice to imperial politics not as an actual, material force but as an aesthetic practice, and it was this poetry of politics that gave presence to the globalized cultural formation which he calls the Sanskrit cosmopolis (1998: 15). Reducing the religious power attributed to Sanskrit while highlighting its aesthetic capacities, Pollock almost identifies aesthetics with politics, and considers it the main instrument of political expression in the creation of the Sanskrit cosmopolis. Another very interesting approach to aesthetics has been provided by Ali who analyses the court as a somewhat segregated and isolated society, arguing that performing arts and courtly literature assisted the education of the elites shaping their emotions, manners and relations (2006: 23). He considers courtly aesthetics, the elites' obsession with beauty and refinement, 'as means through which they acted upon themselves as well as negotiated their relations with others in the wider world of the court' (Ali 2006: 182).

While Pollock (1998) centres his arguments exclusively on the transformative power of Sanskrit and Sanskrit literature (*kāvya*), with its associated disciplines of grammar, rhetoric and metrics, I argue that the other arts shared the same aesthetic interpretation of reality and projected the same view. They constituted an integral world based on a holistic understanding of the arts in which each one of them had its own language but in which they all communicated the same ideas and were based on the same metaphorical images and symbolical associations. Furthermore, while even Ali (2006), who bases most of his arguments on the *Nāṭyaśāstra*, does not highlight the function of music, I argue that music was an important element of the aesthetic world – as was clearly stated by Bharata who defined music as the 'resting place of the drama' (*Nāṭyaśāstra* 32, 493) – and while he (Ali) concentrates on aesthetics' supposed ability to produce virtuous and ethical behaviour among the people of the court, I argue that aesthetics were mostly conceived as a powerful source of auspiciousness. The aesthetic production of beauty was also identified with ritual. In other words, the arts were practised because they produced beauty and beauty produced auspiciousness and fertility (Ali 2006; Dehejia 2009; Donaldson 1975; Sivaramamurti 1982), which in turn guaranteed the life force of the king and the entire kingdom. Among the arts, music and dance, together with Sanskrit, were part of the training of the kings and as such were appreciated by them. Thus, an aesthetic theory developed in the courts within which music and dance were considered powerful because of their capacity to produce beauty, auspiciousness and fertility, and it was in courts that a refined grammar and a detailed technique were developed to control these powers, and they were described and codified in authoritative treatises (*śāstras*) that attribute a metaphysical status to performing arts and equate their effects to Vedic sacrifice (*Nāṭyaśāstra* 36, 23–28; Lidova 1996; Vatsyayan 1983). Music, dance and theatre became sacred because they increased the life power of the king, of his kingdom and people. They were not devotionally performed to supplicate gods to send their blessings and grace, but were executed because their performance itself produced welfare, it was a ritual expected to produce specific effects.

The understanding of performing arts as ritually powerful has been a constant feature of Indian thought and religions. This aspect has linked the arts with religions for at least two millennia. However, the relationship of sacred to secular and the concept of religion evolved and the function of music changed accordingly. Thus, while during the 1st millennium C.E. music was conceived as a ritual and magical act intending to celebrate and empower the king by producing auspiciousness, with the spread of *bhakti* cults during the 2nd millennium C.E., it was mostly transformed into an act of service done in order to receive the grace of the Lord. The powerful, magical and beautiful action of performing arts was transformed into a prayer.

In this study I will analyse the development of the concept of auspiciousness and its relationship with the performing arts, and the correlated concept of King-God, from the perspective of both courts and temples. The results of this analysis will allow me to understand the cultural and social contexts which have nurtured the development of the *mṛdaṅga* and the *pakhāvaj*.

Paramparās and *gharānās* according to contemporary *pakhāvaj* players

As soon as I started working on the history of the *pakhāvaj*, I realized that I had to consider several aspects deriving from its connection to both royal courts and temples as well as the scarcity of studies on it and on drums in general. Indeed, although drums as a category are quite a rich and interesting field to explore due to their connection with the most important ritual moments of Indian life, and are very useful to the understanding of several aspects of Indian culture, research on Indian drums other than the *tablā*, and the southern barrel drum *mṛdaṅgam*[5] to a lesser degree, has been rather scanty. The *pakhāvaj*, notwithstanding the fact that it is the most popular drum of North Indian classical music, is a noteworthy instance of this kind of disinterest. Aban Mistry's *Pakhawaj and Tabla: History, Schools and Traditions* (1999) is the only study on the history and the different contemporary schools of *pakhāvaj*.

The *pakhāvaj* is strongly associated with *dhrupad*, the late medieval court musical form to which several important studies (Peerera 1994; Sanyal and Widdess 2004; Srivastava 1980; Thielemann 1997) have been dedicated, but all of them look at the *pakhāvaj* as a purely accompanying instrument and devote a very small space to it. By contrast, valuable information on the history of the *pakhāvaj*, its role in temple rituals and on the families of musicians associated with temples, is provided – in addition to Mistry's (1999) account on Vaiṣṇava schools – by studies on the musical tradition of the Puṣṭimārg sect, such as those of Gaston (1997) and Ho (2006).

While all these studies mention that the *pakhāvaj* was played both in temple and courts, none of them treat the relationship between the two contexts and the effects of such relationships upon the music played, and addressing this gap is one of the main aims of my research. Indeed, as already explained, closely examining the relationship between courts and temples is essential to develop a sophisticated understanding of the *mṛdaṅga*'s evolution, and I have chosen to focus on the Nathdwara tradition because it provides an interesting example for studying such a relationship from the perspective of a contemporary *gharānā* developed from a temple tradition.

The transmission of musical knowledge according to the system of *gharānās* has been studied in a wide perspective by Neuman (1990), and among lineages of *tablā* drummers by Stewart (1974), Shepherd (1976), Gottlieb (1977) and Kippen (2005). While Stewart's and Gottlieb's pioneering studies adopt a comparative approach and are mostly centred on the repertoire, providing detailed notations of the solos of the main representatives of each school, Shepherd and Kippen – who adopt a socio-cultural approach – study a single school, the Benares and the Lukhnow *gharānā* respectively. In line with Shepherd (1976: 2), Kippen argues that the term *gharānā* does not represent exclusively professional family lineages of soloists, as maintained by Neuman (1990) – or even more exclusively *khyāl* singers as maintained by Deshpande (Shepherd 1976: 3) – but is also commonly used by *tablā* players to define their own lineage and style (Kippen 2005: 63–66).

The system of *gharānā* was adopted also by *pakhāvaj* players during the 19th century. However, the importance of *gharānās* is valued by contemporary *pakhāvajīs* in their own ways, and it is often considered in relation with the term *paramparā*. While the term *gharānā* – whose literal meaning is 'family or household' but in musical contexts is commonly used to indicate a school of playing – has often been used almost synonymously with the word *paramparā* (Mistry 1999; Neuman 1990; Shepherd 1976) – whose literal meaning is uninterrupted series, succession and tradition – the data which I have collected from my research provides different information. Neither Shrikant Mishra – mentioning it as the opinion of his guru Amarnath Mishra too – nor Akilesh Gundecha,[6] attributed any meaning to *gharānā*; Harirai Gosvāmī and Wagdish Gosvāmī[7] considered *gharānā* as a minor system lasting a small period in comparison with the history of the *pakhāvaj*; Ravishankar Upadhyay[8] and Ramashish Pathak[9] considered it less meaningful and much more recent than *paramparā*; while, according to Dalchand Sharma, the concepts of *paramparā* and *gharānā* are connected since a *paramparā* becomes a *gharānā* when one of his members moves from playing as a service to God (*sevā*) to playing as a professional artist, and hence receiving remuneration in cash. Dalchand Sharma expressed his view while telling me the history of his '*paramparā*/*gharānā*'. Indeed, he said that the tradition started as a family lineage, *paramparā*, and became a school, *gharānā*, when Purushottam Das moved to New Delhi and started teaching numerous students at public institutions.[10]

This interpretation, which is also implicit in Gaston's (1997) telling of the history of Purushottam Das's life, although contrasting with the literal meaning of the two words, is quite rational and may be explained by the fact that the *pakhāvaj* was played in courts as well as in temples. Indeed, it suggests that before the introduction of the word *gharānā*, the family lineages of *pakhāvaj* players were defined, or defined themselves, using the term *paramparā* and that there were two different streams of schools: the family traditions (*paramparā*) of musicians playing in temples and the family traditions (*paramparā*) of musicians playing in courts. During the 19th century, the members of the latter group, started to be called, or to define themselves, as *gharānā*. The life of the members of the two groups followed different patterns and their jobs required different skills. The *paramparās* of musicians employed by a temple were specialized in the repertoire of the sect to which they belonged and were usually paid in kind, with food offerings. They could marry only members of the same caste group (Gaston 1997), their post was hereditary and their work was based on the timings of the rituals of the temple. The musicians playing at Nathdwara, at Puri in Orissa, or in other even smaller temples, are an instance of this kind of performer. The *gharānās* included musicians who played in royal courts and were paid in cash. They had a wide repertoire which had to be suited to the various contexts and situations that they might be requested to play in, and was also necessary when they had to defend their post in musical battles. Although mostly based on familial transmission, the *gharānās* might absorb external individuals through marriage.

Within this context, the family tradition of Nathdwara has a particular place, but what makes the Nathdwara *gharānā* a unique and interesting case for study is not only the fact that the family of Purushottam Das was strongly connected with both court and temple traditions, but also the way in which it evolved. Indeed, the two different streams of lineages of *pakhāvaj* players were not completely separated but often intertwined. The histories of the founders of the main *gharānās* insist that they were Brahmans by birth, on their personal devotion to gods or goddesses and stress that they studied under musician saints (see Chapter 3, p. 40). At the same time, Gaston, for instance, reports that the musicians of the temple of Nathdwara had excellent relationships with professional visiting musicians and shared their knowledge with each other (Gaston 1997: 152–154). Thus they communicated, since they were not in competition, but retained separate traditions connected to different contexts. It is in this respect that the family tradition of Purushottam Das was particular. This *paramparā* was started at the court of Amber at the beginning of the 17th century, and then moved to Nathdwara in 1802, where it was included among the other families of temple musicians. When during the 1940s Purushottam Das, the last member of the family, moved to New Delhi to teach at the Bharatiya Kala Kendra and later on at the Kathak Kendra and started sharing the family heritage with his students, he transformed his *paramparā* into a *gharānā*. Thus the Nathdwara *gharānā* is quite recent as a *gharānā* but has a longer life as a *paramparā*. In this sense, this interpretation coincides with that of Ravishakar Upadhyay who told me that while a *gharānā* is short and recent, a *paramparā* implies the transmission of knowledge over several generations.[11]

We have seen that the Indian religious landscape is multifaceted and has to be analysed in its historical and social context and in association with a specific community. In the same way, different musical traditions in India are represented by and associated with specific groups or castes and religious beliefs, and as such they need to be studied from an appropriate perspective. A significant difference between *gharānās* of *tablā* and *sārangi* and *gharānās* of *pakhāvaj* relates to their religious affiliation. Indeed, while the *gharānās* of *tablā* and *sārangi* have been almost exclusively associated with Muslim lineages of professional court musicians (Gottlieb 1977; Kippen 2005; Qureshi 1997; Shepherd 1976; Stewart 1974), the *gharānās* of *pakhāvaj* include mostly Hindu musicians (Gaston 1997; Mistry 1999), although, as we will see in Chapter 3, the landscape of Hindu beliefs embraced by the *pakhāvaj* players is quite nuanced. The strong association of the *pakhāvaj* with Hindu temples explains its status and the reason why, as noted by

Gaston, 'although the *pakhavaj* is played for dance, the instrumentalists who play it have never suffered the same opprobrium as *tabla* and *sarangi* players' (Gaston 1997: 116).

Due to these particular aspects of the *pakhāvaj* traditions and the significant presence of symbols and ideas belonging to both courtly and temple culture, I have analysed the information I gathered from contemporary *pakhāvaj* players both in the present-day context and, with the help of textual and iconographical sources, from historical and religious perspectives.

Notes

1 Among them, Ghosh (1950, 1961), Prajnanananda (1963, 1973), and Sharma P.L (1992), Shringy (1978), Raghavan (1955, 1956), Ramanathan (1999, 2003, 2008), Sathyanarayana (1988), Vijay Lakshmi (1996, 2004, 2011) and Gupt (1986, 2006).
2 Katz (1987), Nijenhuis and Delvoye (1974, 1977, 2010), Widdess (1995) and Rowell (1998).
3 There are only a few articles on music in early Buddhism and most of the studies focus on Tibetan music. One of the most extended studies on Buddhist music is Ellingson's doctoral thesis, *The Mandala of Sound* (1979), which includes the chapter 'Music in Indian Buddhism'.
4 Even the *vīnā* has a high status and strong associations with kinship, but while the *mṛdaṅga* represents power and sovereignty it stands for elegance and refinement.
5 Monographs on the *mṛdaṅgam*, its history and technique have been published by Sankaram (1994), Rama Murthy and Rao (2004) and Gopal (2004); Brown wrote his doctoral thesis (1965) on it. Several videos on the technique and the repertoire of the *mṛdaṅgam* have been published, such as the *Mṛdaṅga Cintāmaṇiḥ* by Sivaraman (2008).
6 Conversation held on 24 February 2012.
7 Conversation held on 12 March 2012.
8 Interview held on 14 November 2012.
9 Interview held on 17 January 2012.
10 Conversation held on 17 November 2011.
11 Interview held on 14 January 2012.

3 The *pakhāvaj* in contemporary India

This chapter introduces the *pakhāvaj*, its organology and the main playing schools. On the basis of the data collected in the field, it traces the situation of the instrument and its players in the contemporary musical scene, and summarizes their views on the *pakhāvaj* and its heritage.

The *pakhāvaj*

The *pakhāvaj* is a two-faced drum, with a body shaped from a single piece of wood in the form of two truncated cones of different sizes connected at their bases (Figure 3.1). It is most commonly crafted from *shisam* wood (Dalbergia Sissoo) but *vijaisar* wood is considered the best.[1]

The drumheads (*purī*) have different diameters and consist of three overlapped goatskins[2] stitched around a circular support (*gajrī*) – made of a strap of buffalo-skin coiled up in four circles – a little wider than the extremity that has to be covered. From the first skin layer, the outer one (Figure 3.1. n.1) and from the last, the inner one (Figure 3.1 n.3), a circular surface is cut so that there remains only about 3 cm and 2 cm, respectively, around the edge. The section of the outer skin is called *cāṇṭi* or *kinār*. As I was told by *pakhāvaj* makers, the measure of the *cāṇṭi* of the smaller membrane – called *mādīn*, or female, for its high pitch – may vary according to the needs of the style of the different schools since its width influences the sound of the drum, and the strokes on the rim in particular. Confirming the information, Dalchand Sharma (Figure 3.2a) explained that the Nathdwara school adopts a larger *cāṇṭi* in order to obtain a bright sound, suiting its extensive use of the stroke (*bol*) *na*, produced by striking this section of the skin with the forefinger. On the central skin of both the membranes, a tuning paste is applied in the middle. On the face with the smaller diameter (*mādīn*) – ranging from 16.5 to 19 cm – the application, called *siyāhi*, is permanent. It is composed of glue, iron oxide, charcoal and other components which vary according to different makers, and is applied in layers that are each fixed and polished with a stone. By contrast, the tuning paste (*āṭā*) applied to the larger membrane – ranging from 21 to 25 cm and called *nar*, or male, for its bass pitch – is temporary. Made out of a mix of flour and

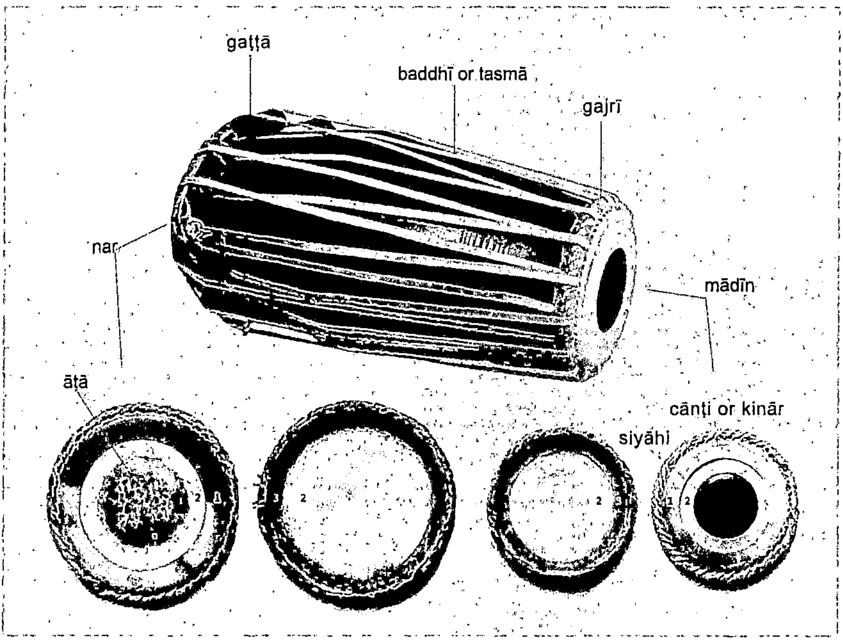

Figure 3.1 The *pakhāvaj*. The numbers 1, 2 and 3 indicate the different layers of skin in the drumheads. Photos and image composition by P. Pacciolla.

water, it has to be applied before playing and then removed soon after. The weight of the flour-paste and the humidity released by it dramatically modify the sound of this skin. Indeed, the high pitch of the dry and 'empty' skin, after the flour-paste is applied to it, is replaced by a low-pitched resonating sound which is the most distinctive feature of the *pakhāvaj*. The two membranes are kept in tension by a strap of buffalo-skin (*baddhī* or *tasmā*) going through 16 holes in the circular support of each of them and from eight wood cylinders (*gaṭṭā*) which, inserted under the connecting strap, allow the player to tune the instrument. The precise intonation is determined by striking the support of the skins with a special hammer.

The length of the body ranges from 55 to 75 cm and its thickness is of about 1 cm. The overall size of the drum defines its tuning; smaller and high-pitched *pakhāvajs* are chosen to accompany *dhrupad vīnā* recitals.

Each of the areas of the two skins produces precise and clearly distinguishable open and closed sounds. However, only the open strokes resulting by striking the *cānṭi* and the *siyāhi* of the smaller membrane and the open stroke of the bigger membrane produce finely tuneable sounds. Almost unanimously, all the *pakhāvajīs* that I met told me that the two drumheads are usually tuned at the distance of an octave, and that while playing with

a. b.

Figure 3.2 a. Dalchand Sharma (2012); b. Svāmī Ram Kishore Das (2003). Photos by P. Pacciolla.

other instruments both the faces are tuned to the tonic of the *rāga*. Only Dalchand Sharma provided a different and more detailed explanation based on his experience and research. According to him, although tuning the bigger skin to the lower *sa* is a good choice, the lower major third (*śuddha gandhāra*) is an appropriate alternative, particularly for those drums whose skins do not produce a good lower *sa*. Furthermore, he is of the opinion that, in order to produce the best consonance, it may be tuned to the main note of the *rāga* which is being played.

Nowadays, the *pakhāvaj*, positioned on a support of cloth in front of the musician or directly on his legs, is played by the performer sitting on the floor, both in the context of art music such as *dhrupad* and in temple music (*havelī saṅgīt*) too. This seems to be a recent habit, since iconographical sources from the 17th century onward mostly show musicians playing in a standing position with the instruments suspended by a strap across the shoulder.

Pakhāvaj is a vernacular word. Almost all the musicians explained it as constituted by the words *paksh*, or *pakhwā*, which mean side and arm, and *bāj*, which means to play, since the *pakhāvaj* is played through sideways movements of the hands and arms. Dalchand Sharma and Ravishankar Upadhyay also attributed to the word *paksh* the meaning of wing, and associated the movement of the hands and arms to the beating of a bird's wings.[3] Some scholars claim that it could derive from the Sanskrit words *pakṣā*, sides, and *vādya* or *atodya*, instrument; the two words would have been modified into a simpler spoken form becoming *pakh* and *bāj*, hence *pakhwāj* (Mistry 1999: 38), which is how *pakhāvaj* is presently pronounced in Gujarat, Maharastra and Bengal (Mistry 1999: 38). Another suggested derivation involves the presence of the vernacular *āwaj* of the term *atodya*, hence *pakhāvaj* (Deva 2000: 78; Mistry 1999: 38). All the musicians I met identified the *pakhāvaj* with the ancient *mṛdaṅga* spoken about in music treatises and Sanskrit literature. Ravishankar Upadhyay said that it was also called *pakshavādya*, and Ram Kishore Das and Sangeet Pathak added three more names, the ancient and medieval *suraj*, *muraj* and *mardal*, providing in this way a line of continuity of the instrument from the ancient past, represented by the *mṛdaṅga*, to the present time.

The *pakhāvaj* and the *pakhāvaj* players in the classical music scene of contemporary India

Presently, there are three main[4] schools (*gharānā*) of professional musicians playing the *pakhāvaj* in classical music. Two of them are traced back to their founders, the 19th-century musicians Kudau Singh and Nana Panse, and the third one is connected to the temple tradition of Nathdwara. The Kudau Singh and Nana Panse are the largest *gharānās* and include several sub-schools. The Avadhi *gharānā*, for instance, was established at Ayodhya by Svāmī Ram Kumar Das (Mistry 1999), who was a student of Kudau Singh. Both the Benares school, whose most renowned representatives were Amarnath Mishra and his disciple Shrikant Mishra, and the Darbhanga *gharānā* of Bihar, whose main *pakhāvaj* representative was Ramashish Pathak,[5] were founded in a similar way. According to Mistry's genealogical tree of the Kudau Singh *gharānā* (1999), another such instance is the Pandit Vasudev Upadhyaya *gharānā*/*paramparā* of Gaya in Bihar, whereas, according to Ravishankar Upadhyay,[6] its contemporary leading representative, the family tradition was started about 400 years ago in Rajasthan, and Pandit Vasudev Upadhyaya was a contemporary of Kudau Singh, and a musician of the same level.

Along with the main ones, there are other *gharānās*, such as the Punjab *gharānā* – which has been recently revived by Bhai Baldeep Singh – the Bengal *gharānā* and a few other schools associated with specific towns or courts, such as the Gwalior *gharānā* (Mistry 1999), the Raigarh *gharānā* (Ashirwadam 1990; Mistry 1999) and the Jaipur *gharānā* (Mistry 1999).

While two books, the *Mṛdaṅg Sāgar* (Das 1911) and the *Mṛdaṅg Vādan* (Das 1982), report the history of the family of *pakhāvaj* players connected to the temple of Nathdwara, there are no clear written sources providing a reliable account of the historical evolution of the other schools. However, both *pakhāvajīs* and musicologists trace all of them back to the same source identified as the 18th-century musician [Lala] Bhavani Din or Bhavani Das (Mistry 1999; Raja 2012). He was the guru of Kudau Sinh Mahārāja and of Babu Jodh Sinh, a well-known musician and the teacher of Nana Panse. He is also considered the founder of the Punjab school and, according to some elderly Vaiṣṇava teachers, was also tied to the Braj temple tradition (Mistry 1999: 64). There is no precise information about Bhavani Din and it is quite difficult to trace his ancestry. However, as reported by Mistry, some scholars, musicologists and musicians (Mistry 1999: 44) ascribe the very foundation of the contemporary *pakhāvaj* playing to Bhagwan Das, a musician at the court of Akbar (1553–1605). They argue that his legacy was continued by his grand disciple Krupalrai, and then diffused throughout the nation thanks to the work of two of Krupalrai's students: Ghasiram Pakhāvajī and Bhavani Din or Bhavani Das.

The *pakhāvaj* schools are nowadays spread all over North India in many branches, in Maharastra, Bengal and even in Andhra Pradesh (Mistry 1999) and, since New Delhi is the capital and a major centre for North Indian classical music, many leading musicians reside there. Most of the *pakhāvajīs* I interviewed or conversed with live in New Delhi, including Dalchand Sharma, who is a member of staff at Delhi University, Ravishankar Upadhyay, who holds the chair of *pakhāvaj* at the Kathak Kendra – the same position once held by Ram Kishore Das – Ramashish Pathak, Bhai Baldeep Singh and Bhagwat Upreti. Some of the most important auditoriums and academies of performing arts in the metropolis are located in the area of Mandi House. This is a central area, full of huge trees and evergreen plants encircling white colonial-style buildings, which represents the pulsating musical centre of New Delhi. Not far away, but on the opposite side of the Yamuna River, are the more recent and still expanding, fascinating and noisy Lakshmi Nagar, Sakkarpur and Malviya Nagar areas, where many musicians reside and where several musical instrument makers have their shops.

Delhi is an international and globalized city in which many venues, including the embassies, host numerous cultural events of diverse varieties. Music is an important component of the acoustic landscape, but it is really very rare to have the chance to listen to classical Indian music in places other than auditoriums.

Dhrupad concerts are not frequent and are mostly presented in selected and specific festivals, and solo *pakhāvaj* recitals are very rare. During the period of my fieldwork – always conducted between November and March, which is the densest festival period of the year – I have come to know of only three solo *pakhāvaj* recitals, mostly organized between February and March, around the festival of Holi. Indeed, it is a very sharp contrast that may be felt while conducting research on the *dhrupad pakhāvaj* in a city like New Delhi, and such a contrast becomes even sharper when the 'aura' surrounding the *dhrupad* musicians is considered. Although it is a well-established fact that *dhrupad* is considered the oldest and purest style of North Indian classical music and as such it is revered and esteemed, it is not by attending a single concert that the high status and religious character attributed to it may be grasped, but by attending a whole *dhrupad* festival, where most of the *dhrupad* musicians gather. These festivals, which are presented in different cities according to the same format and almost always include the same performers in the programme, appear like *dhrupad* sanctuaries and religious meetings following precise rules and hierarchies. The Benares Dhrupad Mela – the most renowned one – is quite emblematic of such an atmosphere. I attended the 2012 event invited by Dalchand Sharma – with whom I had already started collaborating – who encouraged me to go there to have the chance to listen to many *pakhāvaj* players, to understand better the differences among the schools and the particularity of each one of them, and thus comprehend better his own work. His advice was very good. At Benares I attended the concerts of numerous *pakhāvajīs* and had informal conversations with Ramakant Pathak from Lucknow and his son, Shrikant Mishra, Akilesh Gundecha and Manik Munde, all of whom belong to the Benares branch of the Kudau Singh *gharānā* but reside at Varanasi, Bhopal and Pune respectively. Over the five-day festival, I had the opportunity to observe the dynamics among the members of the *dhrupad* society and the many groups inside it. I came to know the opinions of musicians on the festival, such as that of Shrikant Mishra and Akilesh Gundecha, who lamented that too much space was given to the non-professional musicians and that some kind of remuneration was needed for professionals. At the same time, I met Prabhu Datt, nephew of Amarnath Mishra, the founder of the festival, himself a *pakhāvaj* player and member of the organizing staff, who, from his perspective, explained the organizers' point of view. I also had the opportunity to note the significant presence – relatively to the audience as a whole – of Westerners in the audience, mostly busy recording concerts, and their contribution to the fortune and propagation of *dhrupad* music.[7]

A very interesting analysis of the vision and ideas at the base of the *dhrupad* festivals has been provided by Widdess in the article 'Festivals of Dhrupad in Northern India: New Contexts for an Ancient Art' (1994a). He argues that the revival festivals, which were inaugurated in the 1970s and multiplied during the 1980s, are based on a specific ideology according to which *dhrupad* is a sacred music played for the delight of God, a kind of private contemplation played, without expectation of any monetary gain, for a restricted circle of connoisseurs. Widdess shows that these aspects are emphasized by the fact that these festivals are always held at sacred places such as Varanasi or Vrindavan, and at a sacred time, such as the season of the major religious festivals. They are open to all *dhrupad* singers or players without any restrictions, and the musicians receive only travel expenses and a small honorarium (Widdess 1994a: 96). Besides this, the presence of lamp-flames on earthen jars painted with the word *dhrupad* and the auspicious sign of the swastika, denoting the association of the musical form to worship and its auspiciousness, and the symbol of the elephant, an animal associated with kingship and royal power, in the logo of the festival, enforce the Brahmanical view according to which music is a kind of worship and a religious discipline (Widdess 1994a: 102).

The ideology described by Widdess is still at work in *dhrupad* festivals, and evident in the religious approach of musicians to *dhrupad*, and in the spirituality and the yogic qualities attributed to it by musicians. These qualities seem to be accepted even by the numerous members of the audiences listening to the concerts in yogic positions and/or with their eyes closed. Nowadays, in fact, *dhrupad* is almost synonymous with *nāda* yoga, meditation and spirituality. An instance of such identification is provided by a video on *nāda* yoga recently uploaded on YouTube – with the explicit intention of explaining what this yoga really is – in which the interviewed Gundecha brothers affirm the identity of *dhrupad* and *nāda* yoga.[8]

The *pakhāvaj*, being the drum associated with *dhrupad*, has been invested with a similar religious and meditative aura. However, while *dhrupad*, on the basis of such associations and ideas, is 'officially' considered as the most ancient and authoritative style of music of India, the *pakhāvaj* is esteemed for its association with gods such as Brahmā, Gaṇeśa and Śiva (Raja 2012) more than for its aesthetic qualities, and the *pakhāvajīs* are not respected as much as singers and *vīnā* players. This unbalanced position is quite evident to anyone going regularly to *dhrupad* concerts and is often manifest in the relationship of the soloist with the subordinate accompanist.

Although it was easy to understand that the reason for this subordinate position was connected to their role of accompanist I could feel that for them there was a kind of discomfort, and this was particularly true for Dalchand Sharma – who had proudly told me about his numerous fights with the most renowned singers and *vīnā* players for the recognition of the status of the *pakhāvaj* player – and for his own position on the stage. Indeed, according to him, the relationship between the singer or the *vīnā* player and the *pakhāvajī* should be equal, and their performance should be a *jugalbandī*, a meeting of soloists. An attitude similar to that of Dalchand Sharma was attributed by Chaubey (1958) to Ayodhya Prasad, one of the main *pakhāvaj* players of the 19th century, about whom he wrote that

> when it comes to fighting the good fight, he keeps his gun-powder dry and plunges into the battle of the *tāl* like a hero of old. He has a system and a plan and these he follows to the best of his ability. He avoids improvisation for the sake of it. Even when he sits applying a quarter pound of dough to his *pakhāvaj*, he quietly waits for the assault like a well-trained strategist. Once the initial skirmish leads to the heat and fury of warfare, he is never in a mood to lose the battle. Like a soldier, with a thousand bruises and half a dozen wounds, he never surrenders but keeps on fighting.
>
> (Chaubey 1958: 56)

Another detail that helps reveal the present position of the *pakhāvaj* and the *pakhāvaj* players is that, while the number of recordings of vocal *dhrupad* and *vīnā* has increased dramatically over the last 20 years, the recordings of solo *pakhāvaj* are still quite rare.[9] The first publication of a recording devoted to a solo recital to my knowledge is *Pakhawaj solo* (1982) by Chatrapati Singh, which was followed by solo recordings by Shrikant Mishra (1996), Arjun Shejwal (1998), Bhavani Shankar (1998) and Ashutosh Upadhyay (1999). The number of recordings increased slightly during the first 15 years of the 21st century[10] but have now fallen again.

The *pakhāvaj* is quite present on the internet, and more precisely on YouTube. Indeed, thanks to the files uploaded by musicians themselves and by many *dhrupad* and *pakhāvaj* lovers, both Indian and Western,[11] it is possible to watch numerous solo recitals of some of the most renowned players. Many of these videos were recorded at the Benares Dhrupad Mela from 2011 onwards. Performers have a good relationship with the internet and use it to spread information about themselves and their music, as well as a means to showcase their performing skills, but they have not yet started using the internet as a platform for teaching.

Thanks to the revival of *dhrupad*, the *pakhāvaj* is recently living a moment of relative fame in India and abroad. Indeed, the experience of the concerts in Western countries, and the meeting of new audiences with different expectations, is modifying the musicians' approach to the drum. Parallel to this, the increasing number of Western students and practitioners of Indian music is producing effects on the evolution of the musical forms, the instruments and the teaching techniques. Thus, even in the stronghold of the past represented by the *dhrupad* some of the musicians are aware of the fact that they have to adjust their repertoire and their approach to the taste of the audience – who may perceive the old repertoire as boring – but remain close to the *dhrupad* style. The most representative of this approach in *pakhāvaj* is that of Dalchand Sharma. His attitude towards the tradition is one of deep respect, but he has been able to give to the solo repertoire a new flavour by providing it with creative interpretation and a very sensitive use of dynamics. He does not compose new pieces, but reinterprets old compositions highlighting their beauty and meaning through an amazing capability of producing different sounds on the drum. Ravishankar Upadhyay also proceeds in a similar way, and, aware of the appreciation received by the *pakhāvaj* outside India and convinced of the necessity to play new compositions and music which the audience may understand, he has preferred to work on a new repertoire, in line with his school and the *dhrupad pakhāvaj* tradition. An original contribution to the language of the instrument and its popularity has been given by Bhavani Shankar, a well-known musician on the Mumbai cinema scene. However, since his style relies more on the *tablā* tradition than on the *dhrupad pakhāvaj*, he is not considered as a *dhrupad pakhāvaj* player by the *pakhāvajīs* of the *dhrupad* society.

Another recent phenomenon worthy of note is the entrance on the scene of women players. At least for the last two centuries, the playing of the *pakhāvaj* has been a man's prerogative, as with most instruments. In fact the charts with the list of the members of the different schools of *pakhāvaj* provided by Mistry (1999) include exclusively men. The only women players of the past that she can mention are an accomplished elderly female *pakhāvajī* met by the famous singer Kesarbai Kelkar at the court of Hyderabad, and identified by her as the daughter of Nana Panse, and, among the players of the last generation, Geetabhen, daughter of an industrialist in Ahmedabad and disciple of Pandit Govindrao Burhanpurkar (Mistry 1999: 339). However, it is interesting to note that the picture provided by iconographical sources for the period from the 17th to the mid-19th century, is quite different. Indeed, women playing the *pakhāvaj* for noble ladies in their apartments, for royal figures or to celebrate Holi, are depicted in numerous miniatures of Northern India and the Deccan, and probably appear more often than men.

Over the last decade, women have started studying the *pakhāvaj*, although they are still very few. Ramakant Pathak has women students, and Ram Kishore Das had at least one female student whom I met, but the cultural and social barriers are still numerous and strong, making it quite difficult for a woman to choose to become a professional *pakhāvaj* player. The most famous among contemporary professionals is Chitrangana Agle Reswale. According to her own account,[12] although she belongs to a family of *pakhāvaj* players, she was taught the *pakhāvaj* secretly by her brother, until her father realized her talent and started teaching her. Another emerging *pakhāvaj* player is Mahima Upadhyay. Daughter of Ravishankar Upadhyay, with whom she often plays in concerts, she is the first female *pakhāvajī* of her family tradition (*paramparā*).[13]

An article in the *Hindustan Times*[14] on Anupama Roy, a *pakhāvaj* player disciple of Ramakant Pathak, helps reveal the aura surrounding the instrument and how it relates to women:

> The younger of the sister-duo, Arunima Roy is a dancer. And, when she takes to the stage, her elder sister, Anupama sits down amongst the accompanying musicians [...] She is one of the very few women exponents of the pakhawaj in India. The pakhawaj is mainly an instrument played by men. Even among the men, few dare to take up the pakhawaj! [...] She tells [...] 'Pakhawaj is a divine instrument and is very much adored by Lord Shiva as it is played by his followers (ganas) when he performs various forms of tandav dance. It is not played in accompaniment with any "ordinary" instrument like the tabla.'

The article, depicting the *pakhāvaj* as a divine instrument, shows that the cluster of ideas and symbols stratified over the centuries on it are not shaken by the new interpretations or innovations of the repertoire, and the male-dominated world of the *pakhāvaj* is not challenged by the recent attempts to create a space for women.

The *pakhāvaj* heritage according to its players

The present-day position of the *pakhāvaj* and the *pakhāvaj* players in contemporary India sharply contrasts with the image emerging from the information gained from the history and legends connected to the drum and the lives of the founders of the most important schools of the last two centuries. Both Kudau Singh Mahārāja and Nana Panse are described not only as extraordinary musicians highly respected in musical society and the courts, but also as fervent devotees having special spiritual or yogic powers deriving from their musical practice.

According to the information provided by his family members, Kudau Singh Mahārāja was born in 1815 in a Brahmin family of Banda in Uttar Pradesh (Misra 1981; Mistry 1999). Having suddenly lost his parents at the age of 9, after a period of wandering he eventually settled at the ashram of Shridas, who was one of the foremost *pakhāvaj* players of the time (Misra 1981: 36; Mistry 1999: 73). Once he had completed his training, he performed in some of the most important courts gaining fame and rewards. It is said that he was a fervent devotee of Kali – the goddess whom he used to worship through continuous *pakhāvaj* playing – and received from her extraordinary musical and 'spiritual' powers (Mistry 1999: 74; Ranade 1997: 107). These powers were such that, according to legend, he once flung the *pakhāvaj* into the air chanting the name of Kali and the drum then played the main stroke (*thāp*) by itself (Mistry 1999: 72). The most interesting among the numerous legends surrounding him has it that, in Samthar, he gained control over a crazy elephant by playing a *pakhāvaj* composition, receiving from the king a present of an elephant and a reward of 1,000 Rs. According to the version of this story reported by Mistry, 'after subduing the pachyderm, Kudau Singh Mahārāja's crown had burst open and he attained instant salvation' (Mistry 1999: 73), while Naimpalli writes that he 'went into an ecstasy' while playing the *gaj paran* and people witnessed the miracle that the elephant stopped in front of him and started dancing (Naimpalli 2005: 116).

While it is said that Kudau Singh Mahārāja had an imposing personality, Nana Panse was an unassuming person, but equally filled with spiritual qualities. According to oral sources (Misra 1990; Mistry 1999), he was born in a family of Brahmin *kīrtankars* in the village of Bavadhan in Maharastra, and from a young age used to accompany devotional music in the temple. He studied under a well-known *pakhāvaj* player of the court of Pune, and later joined a group of *kīrtankars* travelling with them to all the important pilgrimage centres of India. At Kashi, he met Babu Jodh Sinh, who was an outstanding *pakhāvajī* and fervent devotee of Sarasvatī, and became his disciple. After 12 years of teaching, Babu Jodh Sinh himself sent Nana Panse to study under Yogiraj Madhav Svāmī, who was a saint and excellent *pakhāvaj* player. Once Nana Panse had completed his studies, the saint blessed his disciple and, having left to him his sacred books and *pakhāvaj*, voluntarily ended his life by entering the rapid waters of the Gange (Misra 1990: 46; Mistry 1999: 88). Nana Panse spent most of his life as court musician at Indore, enjoying fame and esteem, and training a large number of students.

Both the stories of the two *gharānā* founders are based on oral tradition and describe them as court musicians of the highest rank and saintly human beings. We can infer from these stories that music was highly appreciated by kings, that qualified musicians had opportunities to travel, present their abilities and be adequately remunerated, that music accompanied the ritual activities of temples and was played by a special group of musicians, and that music was also considered as a spiritual path, followed by a restricted number of musicians who devoted their entire life to the sonic art in order to attain liberation. Kudau Singh and Nana Panse synthesized the world of the courts, where they lived and played, and the world of religion, represented by temples and the practice of music conceived as a path to liberation. The *pakhāvaj* shared their ambiguous position and was an important instrument of court music as well as a means for worship; it was played for the enjoyment of the kings and to pray to the gods, and was thought to be capable of profoundly benefitting listeners and even producing magical effects. In both the stories the *pakhāvaj* is an instrument of power helpful on the spiritual path. Another interesting aspect of the stories is that both Kudau Singh and Nana Panse were Brahmins and fervent devotees; the association of the *pakhāvaj* with the worship of a deity is so strong and deep that the styles of the two schools are said to have germinated from it. Indeed, the vigorous and powerful *bols* of the Kudau Singh style are commonly explained by musicians as deriving from his playing for the fierce goddess Kali, while Nana Panse's soft style is justified by his devotional attitude and humble temperament (Mistry 1999: 92). On the basis of these well-known associations, Ram Kishore Das linked the Kudau Singh *gharānā* to *vīra rasa* and the Nana Panse *gharānā* to *śṛngāra rasa* respectively. The strong link of the drum with worship and gods is confirmed also by the already mentioned association of the *pakhāvaj* with Kṛṣṇa in the tradition of Nathdwara.

Within Indian culture, symbols deemed to be particularly significant are commonly linked to gods and included in myths, thereby emphasizing the high extent of their importance. In a similar way, Indian music has often been interwoven with mythology, and a few especially significant musical instruments have been provided with creation myths and legends. The *pakhāvaj* is one such instrument. It is the most ancient drum of the so-called *mārga* (ancient) tradition and numerous myths about its creation have stratified over more than two millennia up to the present day. Taking into account this feature and being particularly interested in understanding the cultural reasons behind the sacred aura attributed to the *pakhāvaj* and its contrast with the current position of the *pakhāvajīs* within Indian music scenes, I asked many representatives, from a variety of schools, during my fieldwork whether they had inherited an origin myth for the instrument or any other legends linking the drum to gods, and whether their school – or they themselves – considered the *pakhāvaj* an auspicious instrument, a *śubha-mangaḷa vādya*.

The most detailed picture of the relations of the *pakhāvaj* with myth, literature and art was transmitted to me by Svāmī Ram Kishore Das (Figure 3.2b), the main disciple of Pagal Das, who was one of the most famous *pakhāvajīs* of the 20th century and who wrote several books on the repertoire and history of *tablā* and *pakhāvaj*. When I met him he was teaching *pakhāvaj* at the Kathak Kendra of New Delhi but, as he told me, he was born in a village in Bihar around 1942/43. Son of a *sārangi* player, he started studying *tablā* but his father did not approve of it so, at about the age of 13 or 14, he left home. After some time, he met a Svāmī and became his disciple, and with him went to Ayodhya where he lived for two decades. In the sacred city, a renowned centre for the *pakhāvaj*, he studied for five years under Ram Mohini Sharan and then ten years under the tutelage of Svāmī Bhagwan Das. Being very poor, he used to serve his guru doing kitchen chores and preparing flowers for his rituals, and had to wait a long time before getting his first *pakhāvaj*. After learning from Svāmī Bhagwan Das, Guru Ram Kishore Das learnt from Svāmī Pagal Das. During those years he used to accompany the ascetics (*sādhus*) singing devotional songs in the temples. He was so completely devoted to the study of the *pakhāvaj* that his hair became all matted, growing in such a way that he had to pile it under his head like a pillow to sleep. Then, one day, Svāmī Pagal Das sent him to Bombay to participate in the Sur Singar Samiti's festival, and there he was awarded the *Tāl Mani*, and later the *Tāl Vilas* too, which are two of the highest prizes that an Indian drummer can attain. He taught for some years at the Kathak Kendra of Jaipur and then was taken on at the same institution in New Delhi. He was a top-grade All India Radio artist and, as accompanist of both *kathak* dancers and *dhrupad* musicians, travelled to many foreign countries including within Europe.

Ram Kishore Das told me that he was once a member of the Bairagi Viṣṇu Samaj but, at a certain point of his life, he had to leave it to go back home to accomplish his duties as householder because in his youth his parents had married him to a girl. He had two children but as soon as they grew up and married he reverted to the life of a *sādhu*. During the time I studied with him he lived alone at Shakarpur, excluding a short period during which his grandnephew spent some time in his house.

He often used to recall his years among the *sādhus* and more than once told me that all the main representatives of his school, the Ayodhya branch of the Kudau Singh called Avadhi school, were faqirs who had been playing the *pakhāvaj* as a path to enlightenment. The assiduous practice of playing the *pakhāvaj* as devotional service to a beloved deity had bestowed them with particular powers or *siddhis*.[15] According to Ram Kishore Das, Kudau

Singh attained Devī *siddhis*, Ram Mohini Sharan attained Hanumān *siddhis*, Bhagwan Das attained Sītā Rāma *siddhis*, Pagal Das attained Śiva and Hanumān *siddhis* and he himself attained Hanumān *siddhis* after 12 years of *tapas* yoga practice playing the *pakhāvaj* in Hanumān's temples.[16] Indeed, Ram Kishore Das considered the *pakhāvaj* as a spiritual (*ādhyātimikī*) instrument, coming from the *damaru* of Lord Śiva. He used to play in front of an icon as a form of prayer and sometimes equated the *pakhāvaj* to prayer beads (*mālā*).

Once I met in his house a man who was eager to tell me that Ram Kishore Das had cured him from a mental illness. He told me that some years before, while listening to someone playing the *tablā*, something had badly upset his mind and nobody had been able to drive him back to his proper mental health status until he met, by chance, the Svāmī. His cure was a musical one; indeed, according to this man, Ram Kishore Das had been able to free him from his illness through his unique way of playing the *pakhāvaj* and the singing of some devotional songs (*bhajan*) from Ayodhya. The disordered rhythm produced by a *tablā* player had produced a mental disorder in the man, while the sound of the *pakhāvaj* properly and lovingly played by a saintly musician had cured him. The man, who later told me he was a yogi, did not contrast the sound of the *tablā* to that of the *pakhāvaj* as respectively bad and good, but emphasized the spiritual power of the sound of the *pakhāvaj*. His story shows quite clearly the power attributed to rhythm and the sound of specific instruments and highlights that they can be both positive and negative; they can harm and cure.

I asked Ram Kishore Das whether there was any symbolism attached to the three areas of the skins. His answer was that they corresponded to the three worlds of the universe and the three main gods of the Hindu pantheon (*trimūrti*): the outer circle to Brahmā and the earth (*prithvī*), the middle one to Viṣṇu and the worlds below the earth (*pātāla*) and the black spot to Śiva and the sky (*ākāśa*). I asked him what the meaning was of the 16 holes on the leather hoop (*gajrī*) encircling the three gods, and he replied that they were all the other gods hymning – but only when wheat was applied – '*jay! jay!*' ('victory! victory!') to them. He said that the meaning was the same for the other skin (*bāyāṅ*) too, and that the *āṭā*, the flour applied on it, was the soul of the *pakhāvaj*. In a previous meeting he had already established another symbolical connection between the strokes ***tā dhi thun na***, the main *bols* of the *pakhāvaj*, with the four faces of Brahmā, saying that for that reason they were referred to as *Brahmā chaumukha prastuti karanā* (those who make the praise of the four faces of Brahmā). In the same way, according to Abhinavagupta (10th/11th century), the four *akṣaras* *ca*, *cat*, *pa* and *ṭa* of the ancient *caccatpuṭa* and *cacapuṭa tālas* were the exhalations of the four faces of Śiva and their repetition was a bearer of prosperity and the words *caccatpuṭa* and *cacapuṭa* had been created for that reason (Chaudary 1997: 41).

I found the image of all the gods hymning to the *trimūrti* so beautiful that it remained in my mind, and so I asked the other *pakhāvajīs* I met about it, but none of them had anything to say about this specific symbolism. However, according to Ramashish Pathak, head of the *Darbhanga* branch of the Kudau Singh school, the relationship of the *pakhāvaj* with the three gods is hidden in its name. Recognizing the identity of the *pakhāvaj* and the *mṛdaṅga* and quoting a Sanskrit *śloka* of his school[17] about the ancient name (*ādi nām*) of the *mṛdaṅga*, he explained to me that the word *mṛdaṅga* is composed of three parts, *mṛ-da-aṅg*, of which *mṛ* stands for Viṣṇu, *da* for Brahmā and *aṅga* for Māhesh. To make the concept clearer to me, his son Shubashish[18] said that the association of the three gods with the name of the instrument implied that they actually live in the *pakhāvaj*. While the interpretation of Ram Kishore Das was coherent with the tripartite universe of Hindu mythology and cosmology, the explanation of Ramashish Pathak was creative, but they were equally meaningful and provided me with the same information: the *mṛdaṅga*, or *pakhāvaj*, is a sacred drum since Brahmā, Viṣṇu and Śiva reside in it.

The explanation given by Ramashish Pathak and his son echoed the *Saṅgīta Makaranda* (7th/11th century) and a similar attribution stated in the more recent treatise *Saṅgīta Dāmodara* (15th/16th century) in a translation I found in '*Sri Krishna Katamrita Bindu*', a journal of the Gauḍīya Vaiṣṇava community, which affirms that 'Lord Brahmā is always situated in the *mṛdaṅga*'s middle part. The demigods who reside in Brahmā's planet are also situated there. Because all the demigods reside within it, the *mṛdaṅga* is all-auspicious (*sarva mangaḷa*)'.[19]

Sangeet Pathak, the son of Ramashish, was quite emphatic saying that the *sama*, or proper conjunction, of the sounds of the two membranes (*mādīn* and *nar*) of the *pakhāvaj* produces the *Om*,[20] and Ramakant Pathak, from Lucknow, affirmed that the sound of *pakhāvaj* is the *pratimā* or *mūrti* of the *Om*.[21] However, the clearest assertion of the auspiciousness of the sound of the *pakhāvaj* was given to me by Ravishankar Upadhyay, the major representative of the Vasudev Upadhyaya *paramparā* of Gaya in Bihar. While speaking about the origin of the drum, he told me that the drum created by Śiva out of the body of the demon Tripura produced the *Om* when struck and, according to his tradition, it is therefore believed that the powerful sound of the *pakhāvaj* purifies the environment.[22]

Kalyanray Mahārāja, religious leader of the Puṣṭimārg *sampradāya*, who I met at Nathdwara together with his two sons Harirai and Wagdish Gosvāmī, all of them expert *pakhāvaj* players, told me that the *pakhāvaj* is the instrument of Viṣṇu (Viṣṇu *vādya*) and its sound is *nādarūpa svayamhari*, the sonic form of the self of Hari or Viṣṇu. The *Śiva Prādoṣa Stotra*, which narrates the *Sāndhya Tāṇḍava*, or the twilight dance of Śiva, describes a scene where the god dances for the goddess, accompanied by the music of a divine ensemble including Sarasvatī on the *vīnā*, Indra on the flute, Brahmā holding the cymbals and Viṣṇu playing the *mṛdaṅga*. All the gods and all the beings dwelling in the three worlds assemble there to witness the celestial dance and hear the celestial music of the divine choir (Coomaraswamy 1991: 84).

The depth of the sound of the *pakhāvaj* was very important for Ram Kishore Das; indeed, he loved to play the *mahapakhāvaj*, a *pakhāvaj* of almost one meter in length and with wide skins (of about 28 cm for the smaller membrane and 30 cm for the larger), which he had designed and constructed for himself. He was the first player I heard comparing the sound of the *pakhāvaj* and the instrument itself to a cloud or a bolt of lightning and to recognize its relationship to rain. He established this comparison the day he taught me how to apply the wheat on the lower-pitched skin and after listening to the deep sound produced by one of his *pakhāvajs*. I had already read the myth in the *Nāṭyaśāstra* and other ancient treatises and literary sources comparing the *mṛdaṅga* to clouds and lightning and linking it to rain and water in general, but he gave me the first proof that the ancient connection was still alive. He taught me the *Bādal bijulī paran*, the *paran* of the cloud and the thunderbolt, one of the various rain *parans*.

Ramakant Pathak of Lucknow, exponent of the Kudau Singh school and disciple of Ayodhya Prasad,[23] who I met during the Benares Dhrupad Mela of 2012, established the same kind of relationship between the *pakhāvaj* and clouds,[24] saying that the *mṛdaṅga* is the instrument of Indra, and Indra and the cloud are the same thing; Indra himself plays the *mṛdaṅga* and the *apsaras* of his court play it too.

Another important typology of compositions linked to images, literature, gods and producing auspiciousness is that of the *stuti parans* (see Chapter 8, pp. 136–139 and Chapter 9 pp. 157–158. They are particularly meaningful because they conjugate, in the form of a prayer (*stuti*) or invocation, the *bols* of the drum with Sanskrit or Brajbhasha words describing the god to whom they are dedicated. These *parans*, generally first recited and then played, carry at once sounds and images; they are sonic icons. The words evoke a chosen deity creating his/her appearance and attributes, while the *bols* enliven his/her movements and *rasa*. *Dhrupad pakhāvaj*, the Avadhi school in particular, is rich with such compositions eulogizing a chosen deity.

According to Ram Kishore Das, the *mṛdaṅga* was strictly connected to the kings, and more than once he said that by playing the *pakhāvaj* in the 'right' way a person becomes like a king. He used to mention the many references to the drum in the *Rāmāyaṇa* and the *Mahābhārata*. Indeed, the expertise of Arjuna and Hanumān as *mṛdaṅga* players was a recurring subject of my lessons with him, who was a devotee of Hanumān. His house was full of posters of deities, as they are represented in popular iconography, and there were many images of Hanumān's deeds featuring his love and devotion for Rāma and Sītā, among which there was a beautiful and very rare image of Hanumān *pakhāvajī* which I have never seen anywhere else.

Ramakant Pathak, after having emphasized the already mentioned relationship of the *mṛdaṅga* with Indra, added that Arjuna played the drum too and that Hanumān was a good *mṛdaṅga* player in the Rāma court (*darbār*). Arjuna was the son of Indra and at the court of his father learned, together with the martial arts, vocal music (*gīta*), instrumental music (*vādya*) and dance (*nṛtya*) from the eminent *gandharva* Citrasenā (*Mahābhārata*, 3, 44), and Hanumān is known to have been a music and dance expert.

Excluding Kalyanray Mahārāja and his sons Harirai Gosvāmī and Wagdish Gosvāmī,[25] who are religious leaders of the Puṣṭimārg and hence have a deep knowledge of myths and philosophy of the sect, the representatives of the Nathdwara *gharānā* were not particularly attracted by the mythology connected to the *pakhāvaj*. However, while speaking about its auspiciousness they became enthusiastic.

During the many meetings and conversations I had with Dalchand Sharma, I shared many of my thoughts and arguments on various aspects of the *pakhāvaj* and once I told him that I was researching the topic of auspiciousness because I considered it to be one of the most defining characteristic features of the drum. Furthermore, I explained that it had been the first thing that Kalyanray Mahārāja and his sons had told me. Dalchand Sharma replied with the typical expression of approval used during concerts, '*kya baat hai*, this is a very nice point!' He said that in present times the *shahnāī* is considered a *mangaḷa vādya*, but in ancient India the *mṛdaṅga* – and together with it the *paṇava* and *dardura* – was the most auspicious instrument and it is written in every *śāstra*. To explain clearly the concept of the *mangal vādya*, he said that it is played on auspicious occasions like festivals, being the first sound executed, marking the start of the event. According to him, *mangaḷa* also denotes spirituality and it is because of this meaning that the instrument is played by many of the gods in the Hindu pantheon; specifically, it is a *śuddha vādya*, a pure instrument. He considers this aspect to be crucial and, in his lectures, always emphasizes that the *pakhāvaj* is a *mangaḷa vādya*.

Prakash Kumavat, the grandson of Purushottam Das, considered the instrument a *mangaḷa vādya*, a drum to be played on 'good occasions', for being a devotional instrument. He explained that it had been made by Gaṇeśa,[26] the god defeating all the obstacles, and hence is auspicious. He created the drum for the *tāṇḍava* dance of his father who used to play the *damaru*. Being a god with a huge body, Gaṇeśa created a very big instrument for himself – an instrument with sound resembling clouds, lightning and rain. It had to sound like Brahmā-*nāda*, to reproduce the sound of Brahmā, and hence it was auspicious. It was already used in Kṛṣṇa's time, and it was played during his *rās līlās*.

According to Bhagwat Upreti, one of the foremost disciples of Purushottam Das, the *pakhāvaj* 'is a good sign!' It is a *mangaḷa vādya* because it is related to temples like that of Nathdwara where, even today, *dhrupad* is played with the accompaniment of the *pakhāvaj*. He told me that Purushottam Das never spoke about this aspect, but added that the *kīrtankars* of Nathdwara worship the drum; they put a red cover on it and offer their salutation to it before starting to play. He concluded by saying that the *pakhāvaj* is played in the temples of Mathura, Vrindavan and even in the temple of Puri, in Orissa.

A subject that almost always arose during my conversations and interviews with the drummers was the relationship of *pakhāvaj* playing to yoga. Each one had his own view about it. According to Ram Kishore Das, who explained it to me at the first lesson in his house, the playing of the *pakhāvaj* with the mind focused on the energetic plexus located at the level of the forehead (*ājñā cakra*) was 'the best of the yogas', *nāda* yoga; its practice transforms a person into a king and leads to a state of *paramānanda*. However, to become fruitful it requires continuous exercise, devotion and faithfulness in the practice itself. Bhimsen, a *pakhāvaj* player whom I met at Ram Kishore Das's house, proposed a similar view. He was employed at the Kathak Kendra as *pakhāvaj* assistant and had been a student of Purushottam Das. I asked him whether he knew about any relationship of the *tāla* lotuses, or *tāla cakras*, in the book of Purushottam Das and the *cakras* in the body, and he replied that they were only musical means to explain the different *lays* of the *tāla*. However, he told me that, according to his own research, the sound of the *pakhāvaj* was connected to the plexus located at the navel (*maṇipūra cakra*) and it had to be the main focus of concentration of the *pakhāvajī* while playing. In order to produce benefits for himself and the earth, the musician should concentrate on the *ājñā cakra*, and then move down through the other centres in the body.

Although from a different perspective, even Dalchand Sharma considered 'classical' music, the music 'based on rules and regulations', as a meditative art based on discipline (*maryādā*), a form of yoga in which the practice of playing sitting on the floor without shoes is meant to create a direct contact of the spine with the earth. According to him, a proper training (*riyāẓ*) and a wholehearted and devout participation may lead the musician to a state of *samādhi* (meditative 'trance' state), and increase the participation and appreciation of the listeners. He associated his trance states to the playing of rhythmic patterns (*chand*), and told me that, although he experienced them even in concerts with others, they happened more often in his solo recital and during his practice.[27] According to Dalchand Sharma, this is an experience which does not happen to every musician for it requires a deep devotional attitude (*bhakti*) towards music and God, since 'the source of music is God'.[28] Indeed, he thought that the practice of meditation does not lead to experiencing *samādhi* unless it is accompanied by *bhakti*. For these reasons he considered music as an art with a spiritual aim which should not be commercial or aim at entertainment.

Ramakant Pathak considered the playing of the *pakhāvaj* as a form of worship of the *nāda Brahman* – God (*Brahman*) in the form of sound (*nāda*) – and associated both the playing of the drum and the verbal recitation (*paṛhant*) of the compositions with a meditative practice (*dhyāna*); he specified that he recited compositions every day, from four to five o'clock in the morning, and that doing this was once a compulsory part of his practice. Ravishankar Upadhyay intended the relation of the *pakhāvaj* with yoga in terms of physical exercises to be useful for the improvement of bodily strength and flexibility, both essential qualities for the *pakhāvaj* player, and defined *nāda* yoga as concentration and peacefulness of mind.

The information provided by the *pakhāvajīs* shows the multiple links of the drum with religion, mythology and kingship. However, these links appear partial and simplistic, and this impression is enhanced by the fact that none of the musicians explained in a rational way either the myths they mentioned or the religious and symbolical associations they established. Indeed, almost all the answers were based on aspects and elements considered by all the musicians as indisputably true for their being mentioned in myths or religious texts.

All these aspects are linked with Hindu nationalist ideology. The spiritualization of music and the reappropriation of ancient Hindu history have been some of the most significant goals of nationalist movements (Bakhle 2005; Thapar 2010). The antiquity and high status generally attributed to the *mṛdaṅga*, as well as its strong association with Vaiṣṇava temples, made it quite natural for nationalists to adopt it as a symbol of their view of the spirituality and ancient heritage of Hindu music (Kippen 2006). In other words, the association of the drum with religious ideas was not newly established by nationalists for political reasons but had quite a long tradition. Indeed, nationalists did not produce any significant theoretical explanation for the symbolical meaning of the drum. Various books on *mṛdaṅga* and *tablā* were published from the beginning of the 20th century onwards (Kippen 2007), but they were focused on the technique and concerned with notations. The *Mṛdaṅg aur Tablā Vādanpaddhati* by Patwardan, for instance, puts emphasis on the importance of the study of the *mṛdaṅga* and *tablā* for the knowledge of the rhythm (*tāla*) in music (Kippen 2006), but just highlights that the *mṛdaṅga* is an ancient instrument – contrasting it with the modern *tablā* – without adding anything else (Kippen 2006: 190). Patwardhan was a close associate of the nationalist Vishnu Digambar Paluskar and the vice-principal of his first public music institution, thus the manual includes many compositions which are familiar to 21st-century players but are not representative of any specific *gharānās* (Kippen 2006: 4).

Notable exceptions to this kind of approach are the books on dance and drumming by Rāja Chakradhar Singh (Ashirwadam 1990). His *Muraj Paran Puśpākar*, for instance, lists 430 compositions for *pakhāvaj* and *tablā* including the ones he collected from the many musicians of various schools visiting his court and his own pieces. Many of these pieces are devoted to elephants, rain, clouds, peacocks and other elements strongly connected with the *mṛdaṅga-pakhāvaj*; furthermore, the text includes watercolour paintings which depict the meaning of some *parans* (Ashirwadam 1990: 124) showing that Chakradhar Singh was acquainted with the heritage of the drum, and with its value and function in the ancient world (see Chapter 8, pp. 145–146).

None of the *pakhāvajīs* I met mentioned any political meaning connected with the spirituality and high status attributed to the drum, and their emphasis was on religious aspects associated with music and the *pakhāvaj* in particular. In other words, for them it was crucial to highlight the high religious pedigree of the *pakhāvaj* and its deep association with kings and gods in order to demonstrate the value of its heritage and the uniqueness of their musicianship. As already pointed out, the *pakhāvaj*, notwithstanding its significant symbolical value, is presently considered as an accompanying instrument and as such its importance is valued much less than *dhrupad* singing.

During the first decades of the *dhrupad* revival represented by the Dhrupad Melas, musicologists engaged themselves in the philosophical interpretation of the spiritual content of *dhrupad* music on the basis of ancient Sanskrit treatises of music (Sanyal 1986; Sanyal and Widdess 2004; Srivastava 1980); they studied the structure of *dhrupad* and its relation with ancient forms, analysed the different schools of *dhrupad* singing with their own particular features and studied the texts, but did not treat the *pakhāvaj* either for its own heritage or for its contribution to *dhrupad* in general.[29] Indeed, while Dhrupad Melas have been instrumental in spreading, both in India and abroad, the *dhrupad* ideology centred on vocal music and *rāgas*, and in raising the status of *dhrupad* singers, they have only partially contributed to a proper understanding of the heritage of the *pakhāvaj*. Dhrupad Melas have been beneficial only regarding general knowledge of the *pakhāvaj* and in spreading part of its repertoire, in particular the *stuti parans* that *pakhāvajīs* very often include in their concerts because of their religious content. Even the comments and explanations that *pakhāvaj* players provide to audiences during their solos at the Melas do not adequately contribute to an understanding of the rich and complex heritage of the *pakhāvaj*. The result of the approach of the *dhrupad* revival is that *dhrupad* singers are often keen to provide Sanskrit textual references to argue the antiquity and spirituality of their music while most of the *pakhāvaj* players provide very interesting information free of any interpretation.

The Hindu nationalist approach and the *dhrupad* revival have certainly strengthened the Hindu religious aura of the *pakhāvaj*, but the strong and deep association of the drum with Vaiṣṇava sects and in particular with the Puṣṭimārg has significantly marked its evolution through the engagement of Hindu musicians. These elements, together with the gradual disappearance of the Punjab school – which included mostly Muslim musicians – during the first decades of the 20th century may explain the fact that presently there are very few Muslim *pakhāvajīs*, and the contribution of Muslim musicians to the evolution of the drum – although certain – is not quite evident and clearly arguable. By contrast, the field of instrument making is at present dominated by Muslim artisans. In New Delhi almost all of the *tablā* and *pakhāvaj* makers are Muslim and this may be explained by the fact that working with leather is considered as polluting by high-caste Hindus.

A careful analysis of the various items of information provided by the *pakhāvajīs* allows us to explain contrasting aspects, while the presence of several interesting and coherent themes helps us to understand their context.

The first things that have to be considered to shed light on this material are that the Indic religious world is complex and multifaceted, that it includes even contrasting religions or cults – such as, for instance, Brahmanism and Tantrism, or Śaivism and Vaiṣṇavism – and that, over the course of time, they have blended to produce syncretized forms in which similar rituals have been interpreted in differing ways. The analysis of the three main contemporary *gharānās* of *pakhāvaj* from a religious perspective shows that they are based on different religious approaches and provides an instance of such complexity. As has been seen, Kudau Singh was a Brahmin but, at the same time, a devotee of the goddess and her power (*śakti*), which is an important aspect of Tantra cults. In contrast, Nana Panse was an orthodox Brahmin, while the Nathdwara *gharānā* is representative of the Puṣṭimārg, a specific Vaiṣṇava sect. Different approaches are also clearly reflected in the association of the drum with deities such as Śiva or Viṣṇu, who represent contrasting religious perspectives. Even the interpretation of the word yoga at the level of the single musician has shown a similarly nuanced variety of approaches which, again, may be explained by conceiving them as resulting from different religious views and personal experiences.

Because complexity and diversification are constant aspects of Indic thought, it is necessary to analyse historical and socio-religious contexts in great detail to comprehend any specific cultural element. Focusing on the *pakhāvaj*, it is important to verify whether the religious associations reported by the musicians are rooted in the past, as they often claim, or have been recently established.

Finally, it has to be considered that the heritage of the *pakhāvaj* includes several religious symbols deriving from its association with Vaiṣṇava sects and temples.

Thus, the information provided by *pakhāvajīs* may become clearer if studied in relation to specific historical, social and religious contexts. Furthermore, importantly, it does not only show contrasting perspectives, but also constant themes which are very helpful in revealing the symbols and metaphors associated with the *pakhāvaj* and the functions attributed to it. The themes emerging from this preliminary investigation are:

1. The *pakhāvaj* is an auspicious instrument.
2. Its sound is conceived as a representation of the *Om*.
3. It is a spiritual instrument used for worship and yogic practices.
4. It is linked with kingship.
5. It is linked with clouds, lightning and rain.
6. It creates images and tells stories through association. As I will explain in Chapter 8, these images and stories become apparent only by knowing the rich network of religious and literary symbols and ideas associated with the body and the sound of the *pakhāvaj*.

While the association of the sound of the *pakhāvaj* with the monosyllable *Om* and its utilization in ritual worship highlight its relationship with religion, the auspiciousness attributed to the *pakhāvaj*, along with its links with kingship, clouds, lightning and rain, and its capability to tell stories, are aspects and themes mostly connected to courtly culture.

Notes

1 This is the opinion of musicians and *pakhāvaj* makers based in New Delhi, such as Qasim Khan Niyazi and Mohammad Sharif; interviews held on March 2013.

2 While other regional versions of the *mṛdaṅga* such as the southern *mṛdaṅgam*, the Orissan *mardala*, the Manipuri *puṅg* and the Assamese *khol* adopt goatskins for the internal and the intermediate layers and cow-skins for the external layer of the bigger membrane, the skins of the *pakhāvaj* include only goatskins, although each one of them is selected from a specific part of the skin of a goat's back.

3 According to the John Platts' dictionary *pakhwā*, s.m., means side, flank (=*paksh*); arm; gable end of a house, while *paksh*, s.m., means wing; feather; fin; flank; side; party; class; faction (Platts 1884: 265).

4 I have distinguished *gharānās* as main and minor on the basis of their dimension and their presence in different parts of India. The Kudau Singh and Nana Panse *gharānās* include branches established in various centres that count numerous members; the Nathdwara *gharāna* is not as large as them, but is rapidly increasing its membership. The Punjab *gharānā* expired last century, the Bengal *gharānā*, the Gwalior *gharānā*, the Raigarh *gharānā* and the Jaipur *gharānā* count a relative small number of members.

5 He is mentioned as a prominent *pakhāvaj* player of the Darbhanga *gharānā* on the website of the school, darbhangagharana.com/darbhanga_gharana.html (Accessed 6 November 2016). In the interview held on 17 January 2012, he told me that he had been trained in Darbhanga by his grandfather Vishnudeo Pathak of the Kudau Singh *gharānā*.

6 Interview held on 14 January 2012.

7 Ashish Sankrityayan highlights this contribution in his article 'The fundamental Concepts of *Dhrupad*' in which he writes that 'it would not be an exaggeration to say that the interest of people in the West has made *dhrupad* singing, financially a more viable profession for its few remaining practitioners' klangzeitort.de/uploads/documentation2/AshishSankrityayan.pdf (Accessed 21 July 2016).

8 Video available at: www.youtube.com/watch?v=ghdCs9bD4_o (Accessed on 21 July 2016).

9 There is a 4.56-minute track of solo *pakhāvaj* by Chatrapati Singh in Alain Danielou's 1960s *A Music Anthology of the Orient, India III, Dhrupad* (Unesco Collection), and an eight-minute solo recording by Pagal Das in the 1974 LP *Rudra Veena Recital* (HMW), by Zia Mohinuddin Dagar. Audio recordings of solo *pakhāvaj* are not numerous even in the archives of the Sangeet Natak Akademi of New Delhi, where the oldest and unique until the 1970s is a wire recording copy of a solo by Ayodhya Prasad.

10 Since the beginning of the 21st century, solo recording have been released by Bhavani Shankar (2001 and 2002), Mohan Sharma (2002), Ravishankar Upadhyay (2006 and 2007), Hari Bagade (2010) and Dalchand Sharma (2012). The Insync label released, in 2014, *Rhythm Divine*, a recording of solo *pakhāvaj* including Bhavani Shankar, Mridang Kirtan, Keshav Jagdale, Gian Singh Namdhariand Chitrangana Agle Reshwal.

11 Instances of these channels are, '*pakhawajlover*', run by Sukad, the son of Manik Munde, '*Rishi Upadhyay*', run by Rishi, the son of Ravishankar Upadhyay, '*pakhawajplayer*', run by a disciple of Bhavani Shankar and '*elkabir123*', '*KenigDrumBrothers*', '*Darren Sangita*', etc., run by Western players or lovers of Indian music.
12 Available at: www.artindia.net/chitrangana/index.html (Accessed 29 April 2016).
13 See meetkalakar.com/Artist/1678-Mahima-Upadhyay (Accessed 29 April 2016).
14 Vinayak Sinha, *Hindustan Times*, 12 October 2016.
15 From the point of view of the devotee addressing his/her prayer to a deity, the *mṛdaṅga* is a perfect mediator: it carries to the god the devotee's prayers and love, and brings back *siddhi* and *ananda* as gift of the beloved.
16 Another aspect of his life among *sādhus* he often used to quote while speaking about myths or symbolism of the *pakhāvaj* was that they had a secret language that he used to refer to as *sādhu bāṣā*.
17 He often quoted this *śloka* at the beginning of his solo recitals.
18 Interview held on 17 January 2012.
19 *Bindu*, Issue No. 83, 20 July 2004, email mini-magazine from Gopal Jiu Publications, p. 3.
20 Interview held on 17 January 2012.
21 Informal conversation held on 21 February 2012.
22 Interview held on 14 January 2012.
23 Ramakant Pathak told me that he started receiving training under the Nana Panse school but then he won a scholarship to study with the Ayodhya Prasad, one of the most eminent representatives of the Kudau Singh school.
24 About this aspect see also Prakash Kumavat below.
25 However, they do not consider themselves as representatives of the Nathdwara *gharānā*; they live in Indore – excluding the festival periods which they spend in their palace at Nathdwara – and thus they mostly studied under gurus of the Nana Panse *gharānā*.
26 While Prakash Kumavat attributes the creation of the *mṛdaṅga* to Gaṇeśa, the most widespread version of the same myth, reported in Chapter 5, p. 84, ascribes it to Brahmā. This kind of discrepancy is quite recurrent in Indian myths and is generally due to different religious interpretations. In this case, since nobody else of the Nathdwara school has mentioned the myth in the same way, the discrepancy may be explained by the fact that Prakash Kumavat's version belongs exclusively to his family.
27 Conversation held on 8 January 2012.
28 Conversation held on 8 January 2012.
29 Gaston's (1989) article on Purushottam Das is the most detailed writing devoted to the *pakhāvaj* published in *Dhrupad Annual*, the journal devoted to the revival of the Dhrupad Melas.

4 Auspicious drumming

Auspiciousness is an important quality attributed to the *mṛdaṅga* in musical treatises, in the literature and in all the contemporary *gharānās*. Many of the musicians I spoke to declared that the *pakhāvaj* is a *mangaḷa vādya*. But while its quality was taken for granted, the reasons for its auspiciousness were never fully explained. The most common answer was that its auspiciousness derives from its being played by the gods, but this was a truth that seemed not to require further explanation.

The issue of auspiciousness of music and musical instruments in South Asia has scarcely been analysed. The auspiciousness–inauspiciousness dichotomy in India and its relationship with a more widely and deeply studied dichotomy such as purity–impurity has been examined from sociological and anthropological perspectives (Carman and Marglin 1985; Kersenboom 1987; Marglin 1985a). In music, studies have focused in particular on wedding music (Booth 2008; Terada 2005), which represents the most auspicious of the moments of the life of Hindus.

In this chapter I will trace the symbolism connected to the *mṛdaṅga-pakhāvaj* and its cultural context in order to propose a coherent explanation for its auspiciousness. The study has been based on the information I gathered from fieldwork interviews, the literature on the auspiciousness of music and musical instruments in South Asia, socio-anthropological sources on the concept of auspiciousness and philosophical and iconographical sources. The analysis of material from different disciplines has produced two new, different but interlaced original interpretations of the functions of the *mṛdaṅga*: the *mṛdaṅga* as representative and harbinger of fertility and auspiciousness and the *mṛdaṅga* as representative and harbinger of liberation.

Auspiciousness

Auspiciousness in Indian thought is connected with the idea of life, its essence and flow. It relates to that energy which constitutes the life force of everything, hence to fertility, prosperity, health and happiness. It relates to human life and its connections with the life of the whole universe. By contrast, inauspiciousness denotes those moments when the flux of life is weakened or interrupted, first of all death. Life itself is auspicious and auspiciousness is the normal status of things (Marglin 1985b; Tingey 1994). However, in order not to give space to inauspiciousness, it needs to be constantly reiterated, reaffirmed and strengthened (Narayanan 1985: 58). This is particularly necessary at specific moments of time and passages of the human life such as births and deaths, puberty or weddings, when life force is concentrated. Specific rituals, involving time, objects and actions particularly charged with life force and hence more auspicious, accomplish this task. Indeed, the efficacy of the life cycle rituals lies on the calculation of auspicious dates, auspicious places, directions, elements, persons and objects.

Mangaḷa and *śubha* seem to be the most recurrent Sanskrit words used to denote auspiciousness and they both imply welfare, prosperity, good fortune and happiness. These words are used as a prefix to designate various events such as a festival (*śubha utsava*) or a season (*śubha ritu*); objects such as a vessel (*mangaḷa kalaśa*), the wedding thread (*mangaḷa sūtra*) or a musical instrument (*mangaḷa tūrya*); rituals (*mangaḷa pūjā*); and women (*mangaḷa narī*). Their opposites *amangaḷa* and *aśubha* denote inauspiciousness (Dehejia 2009; Marglin 1985a, 1985b; Madan 1985; Narayanan 1985).

Everything in the world is charged with auspiciousness, but not in the same way; there are moments of time, seasons, human beings, animals and objects, bearing the highest degree of auspiciousness. As the representation of procreation and life, the fertile woman is considered the embodiment of auspiciousness and as such she is presented in treatises, literature and arts. Indeed, even the image of woman is auspicious because she symbolizes fertility and is beautiful; beauty itself is auspicious and synonymous with fertility. Representing femininity in its purest and supreme form, Śrī-Lakṣmī is the most auspicious goddess. She is connected with water as the primeval generative force of life; beauty, fertility and prosperity are her attributes; a lotus flower and a pot (*kalaśa*) full of water are her symbolic representations (Gonda 1969; Singh 1983; Sivaramamurti 1982).

The king (*rāja*), like fertile women, embodies auspiciousness. He himself is supposed to be a fertilizing agent, bringing well-being to his domain through the daily execution of rituals designated as auspicious (Gonda 1956a, 1956b, 1957a, 1957b; Inden 1985; Marglin 1985b). He is considered a rain-maker, and being the representation of Indra, the king of gods, is endowed with the power to cause the rain. As water symbolizes the primeval generative force, rain represents the fertilizing power of water ensuring the growth of crops and the prosperity of a country.

According to a widespread medieval Indian view, the couple and the sexual union of male and female, guarantee the regular flow of life, 'the stable state of auspiciousness' (Marglin 1985b: 81). The *mithuna* (couple), is one of the most frequent iconographical motifs carved on the walls of temples as a representation of auspiciousness (Dehejia 2009; Donaldson 1975).

In such a framework, sound, both as musical and lexical, plays an important role; it is conceived as a form of the life force itself and therefore is charged with the highest degree of auspiciousness. It can be inferred by the role of the monosyllable Om: it is the first sound to be uttered in any rituals or prayers and in a number of other undertakings because its sound is considered a means of conferring auspiciousness and blessings. The same function is attributed to the sound of a conch which is, indeed, together with bells, the most important ritual instrument of temples. Coming out of the ocean, the conch represents the sonic form of waters and is charged with their generative force, and therefore its sound is auspicious. Among the musical instruments, the voice of the *mṛdaṅga* is the most propitious: it sounds like thunders and is auspicious like a cloud full of rain.

Music and dance are particularly needed at the time of childbirth, during weddings and during sacrifices for the prosperity of the kings and their kingdoms in order to keep away destructive forces and any kind of negative influence; they are auspicious and creative, protective and nutritious. Since prosperity is the main purpose of the king, many rituals have to be performed and hence music and dance are a regular and steady requirement of a court. A specific feature of auspiciousness is that when two or more auspicious things join their auspicious qualities increase by addition; thus, music and dance, which are themselves full of life force, become even more powerful when performed by women. It is for this reason that the heavenly, and hence the earthly royal courts, are full to the brim with music and dance performed, almost always, by women. Another specific feature of auspiciousness is that even an image, a graphic or carved representation of an auspicious thing conveys and projects prosperity; in other words, the representations of auspicious things are endowed with the same auspicious power as the original ones and project it into the space (Dehejia 2009; Donaldson 1975). It is for this reason that the walls of the temples are covered with carvings of heavenly or earthly courtesans dancing and playing music, of erotic scenes and other auspicious images like the vase of abundance, lotuses, trees, elephants and other animals (Dehejia 2009; Donaldson 1975). For their auspicious power, images of *kalaśa* and musical instruments such as the *shahnāī*, the *naqqāra* and barrel drums are still painted at the entrance of huts and houses and they provide decorations even for trucks.

Auspiciousness and its roots

The concept of auspiciousness – as opposed to inauspiciousness – is very old in India and associated with a primarily agricultural society and with the cult of goddesses and local deities referred to by the generic terms *yakṣas*, *nāgas* or *devas*. Figurines of goddesses of fertility and auspiciousness and of loving couples or dance and music scenes showing a religious attitude towards sexuality conceived as a symbolical representation of fertility, have been abundantly found in terra-cottas of the post-Maurya period in numerous sites such as Taxila, Mathura, Kaushambi, Ayodhya, Chandraketugarh, Mahasthangarh, Tamluk and Midnapore (Ahuja 2001; Samuel 2008). The worship of deities of nature, trees and fertility was equally widespread in India during the 1st millennium B.C.E. (Ahuja 2001; Coomaraswamy 2001; Samuel 2008). When Buddhism and Jainism became major religious cults they were incorporated becoming minor deities, although they kept their strong relationship with fertility (Samuel 2008). Numerous *yakṣas* were carved on the railings of early Buddhist stupas such as those of Bharhut (2nd century B.C.E.) and Sanci (1st century B.C.E.), along with *yakṣinis*, represented as women and trees, lotuses and lotus creepers intertwined in various ways (Coomaraswamy 2001), *nāgas* and *nāginis*, *mithunas* and the goddess with the elephants, or Gaja-Lakṣmī. Gaja-Lakṣmī, identified with Lakṣmī and depicted as a woman sitting or standing on a lotus in a lotus pond, was the goddess of fertility and wealth, and the representation of sovereignty. Indeed, the king, who was at the very core of ancient Indian society and had to guarantee welfare for his kingdom, hence rain and good crops, was deeply associated with the most auspicious goddess (Coomaraswamy 1929; Gonda 1956a, 1956b, 1957a, 1957b; Marglin 1985a). Śrī-Lakṣmī was incorporated by the king through the coronation ceremony (*rājasūya*) but, since his was an exalted position, he had to be sanctified every day (Rodhes Bailly 2000). As shown by iconographic and textual evidence, this ritual function was performed by the courtesans who filled the courts with their presence and by performing the auspicious arts of music and dance for the king (Dehejia 2009; Kersenboom 1987; Marglin 1985a).

Auspiciousness is rooted in an agricultural world ruled by kings, in which courtesans, sex, music, dance and drama were means to protect the ruler and guarantee his sovereignty. Indeed, in ancient, medieval and, even, in premodern India, all of them were essential for the welfare of a kingdom (Dehejia 2009; Kersenboom 1987; Marglin 1985a, 1985b). It was a world coming out of a universal god and ordered in a hierarchy of domains commanded by an appropriate lord; it was greater than the human world but continuous with it. All earthly events were conceived as actions coming from a higher level realm and the various worlds were in a situation of continuous interaction governed by strict rules which the lords of each one of them had to follow in order to maintain a balanced relationship and avoid negative results (Inden 1985). In such a world, a science of reading auspicious and inauspicious signs, as well as a set of auspicious rituals capable of keeping the balance among the many kingdoms of the universe or restoring the broken equilibrium, was a strong necessity.

The auspicious arts in literature and other textual sources

The importance of the performing arts in the ancient courts is emphasized by the epics. According to the *Mahābhārata*, Indra, the king of the gods, whose city resounded with celestial music, had a court full of beautiful courtesans (*apsaras*), experts in the arts of love (*kāma*) and musicians (*gandharvas*), producing outstanding performances of dance and music (*Mahābhārata* 3, 43). The *Rāmāyaṇa* describes Ayodhya, Rāma's city, as 'sounding with the drumbeats of great drums, and with musical rhythm instruments like *mṛdaṅga*, cymbals, and with string instruments like *vīnā*' (*Rāmāyaṇa* 1, 5, 18). Even the kingdom of Rāvaṇa, the Rākṣasa enemy of Rāma, was brimmed with singing and dancing courtesans (*Rāmāyaṇa* 5, 10, 31–45).

The importance of the performing arts in the ancient courts is reported also in other textual sources such as the *Arthaśāstra* of Kautilya, a treatise on statecraft written under the Maurya empire, around the 2nd century B.C.E. This text devotes a whole section, the *Gaṇikā Prakaraṇa*, to the courtesans (*gaṇikās*), described as young and beautiful, adept in dancing, singing and acting and in other kinds of arts (Iravati 2003; Varadapande 1978; Vatsyayan 1968).

The real and symbolic relevance of the role played by the dancing courtesan was such that Iśvarakṛṣṇa, in his *Sāṃkhyakārikā*, one of the most important texts of the Sāṃkhya system (*darśana*) of Indian philosophy composed around the 2nd century B.C.E., compares the relationship between Prakṛti, the first cause of the manifest material universe, and Puruśa, the pure consciousness, to a dancer (*nartakī*) and her audience (*Sāṃkhyakārikā*, 59).

Music and dance were particularly needed on occasions such as princely childbirths, weddings and festivals (*Rāmāyaṇa* 1, 18, 17–18; Kulshreshtha 1989–1990: 216). If the capital filled with women, music and dance was the clearest representation of the power and wealth of a king, the silent court, the one where music and dance were missing, showed the lack of life and strength of a kingdom (*Mahābhārata* 7, 85; *Rāmāyaṇa* 2, 67, 15).

The epics abound with descriptions of the ancient courts and court scenes are carved on the stupas and in caves of the last centuries of the 1st millennium B.C.E. Another very useful source of information is the *Nāṭyaśāstra*, the most ancient treatise on drama (*nāṭya*), including music, dance and allied arts, ascribed to the sage Bharata and dated between the 2nd century B.C.E. and the 4th century C.E. The treatise (*Nāṭyaśāstra* 35, 47–56) describes two types of drama including different aesthetic flavours (*rasas*) and emotions (*bhāvas*), the delicate (*sukumāra*) and the energetic (*āviddha*), and specify that the delicate type of production, based on *śrīngara rasa* – the auspicious erotic mood – is the favourite of the kings and, therefore, should be produced by women (Iravati 2003; Varadapande 1983).

The auspiciousness attributed to music and its role in auspicious rituals is clearly stated by Bharata who writes that 'in places in which there occur instrumental music and dramatic performance, or song and instrumental music, there will surely never be any kind of inauspicious happening' (*Nāṭyaśāstra* 36, 23–28).[1]

Dance is as auspicious as music (*Nāṭyaśāstra* 4, 267–269) and musical instruments, for their inherent auspicious quality, are even worshipped (*Nāṭyaśāstra* 3, 72–73).

Because of their auspiciousness, the performing arts also took on a special role in the rituals of the temples which flourished from the Gupta period (4th–7th centuries C.E.) onwards and, just like the royal courts, they were meant as reproductions of the heavenly courts. Indeed, temples were replete with beautiful courtesans (*devadāsīs*) performing music, dance and erotic rituals for the gods as clearly stated by the inscriptions in the temples themselves.

Numerous sources, including the diaries of the many travellers visiting India (Brown 2000; Gaston 1981; Kersenboom 1987), testify that the ritual worship through auspicious dance and music offered by a specific group of women – called *devadāsī, māhārī, kalāvantulu* or *vilāsinī* according to the different temple traditions – notwithstanding the hostility of the Muslim and English rulers, was widespread all over India during the 2nd millennium. In fact, in important temples such as those at Madras, Tamil Nadu, and Puri in Orissa, it was practised until the 20th century (Kersenboom 1987; Marglin 1985a).

The idea of auspiciousness as life force embodied by women, kings, music and dance was partially accepted and absorbed, even by Muslim courts, in a quite natural process. The Mughal emperors, for instance, conceived the power of sound in a way very similar to ancient Indian thought. Abul Fazl, in his *Ā'īn ī Akbarī,* enlists the *naqqārkhāna* music ensemble among the ensigns of royalty, as a symbol of imperial power and victory (Abul Fazl 2, 30); the *naqqāra* drum, which they brought from Central Asia, represented the imperial qualities and even the representatives of the emperor were provided with instruments as signs of authority (Brown 2000; Tingey 1994). Akbar's harem hosted more than 5,000 women (Abul Fazl 2, 15) and in Mughal courts the birth of a prince was lavishly celebrated with music and dance, as is clearly shown in various miniatures depicting ensembles of horns, *naqqāra*, cymbals and dancers engaged in producing powerful and auspicious sounds. Female *dhādhis* and *domnīs* musicians and dancers were traditional harbingers of auspiciousness in Mughal life cycle ceremonies and female performers were represented as auspicious symbols in Mughal paintings (Brown 2003).

Performing arts were still considered as auspicious in the 19th century, when courts of rich kings such as Ram Singh II of Jaipur were still full of performers (Bor 1986/87; Erdman 1985). At the court of Sayajirao Gaekwad of Baroda (1875–1939), either an Indian orchestra or a collection of instrumentalists was to be prepared to play during the most propitious moment of the ceremonial lunch, and a woman singer was asked to perform, due to her auspiciousness, not a man (Bakhle 2005: 271).

Courtesans and music were the main symbols of the court/temple culture complex until the 20th century, when a new political and cultural context and the emergence of a Westernized middle class, who found it difficult to accept the ancient world of kings filled with eroticism, caused a vigorous anti-courtesan movement and a ban on the institution of the temple courtesans. However, music and dance, which were synonymous with auspiciousness and crucial elements of worship, reshaped with a strong devotional contour under the 'respectable' frame of classical arts, were chosen as emblems of the renewed ancient Hindu culture.

Rain on the lotus pond

The most ancient version of the origin of the drums, called *puṣkaras*, is presented in the *Nāṭyaśāstra* in the chapter devoted to drums, called covered instruments (*avanaddha vādya*). The invention is attributed to Svāti:

> During an intermission of studies in the rainy season, Svāti once went to a lake for fetching water. He having gone to the lake, Pākaśāsana (Indra) by (sending) great torrential rains commenced to make the world one (vast) ocean. Then in this lake, torrents of water falling with the force of wind made clear sounds on the leaves of lotus. Now the sage hearing suddenly this sound due to torrents of rain, considered it to be a wonder and observed it carefully. After observing the high, medium and low sounds produced on the lotus leaves as deep, sweet and pleasing, he went back to his hermitage. And after coming to the hermitage, he devised the *mṛdaṅga*, and then the *puṣkaras* (like) *paṇava* and *darduras* with the help of Viśvakarman. On seeing the *dundubhi* of gods, he made *muraja*, *āliṅgya* and *āṅkīka*. Then he who was master of reasoning of positive and the negative kind, covered these and *mṛdaṅga*, *dardura* and *paṇava* with hide, and bound them with strings. He also made other drums such as *jhallarī*, *pataḥa* etc., and covered them with hide.
>
> (*Nāṭyaśāstra* 33, 5–13)

While the term *puṣkara* refers to *mṛdaṅga*, *paṇava* and *dardura*, the *Nāṭyaśāstra* is not clear about what instruments are meant by the words *tripuṣkara* or *puṣkaratraya* referred to in subsequent sections of the text. As the *mṛdaṅga* is considered the most important of all the drums and it is described as a set comprising three types of drums (Figure 4.1) – *ūrdhvaka* or the 'uppermost', *āliṅgya* or 'embraced' and *āṅkīka*, or 'held over the hip' – I suggest that the word *tripuṣkara* indicates the three *mṛdaṅgas*, as is confirmed by a wide range of iconographical sources.[2] The group of *mṛdaṅga*, *paṇava* and *dardura*[3] were considered the main members (*aṅga*) of the *avanaddha* category while the others, such as *dundubhi*, *jhallari*, *pataḥa* and so on were considered secondary (*pratyaṅga*). The word *puṣkara* is used to denote also the skins of the three *mṛdaṅgas* while explaining the three different tunings (*mārjanā*) (*Nāṭyaśāstra* 33, 102–105).

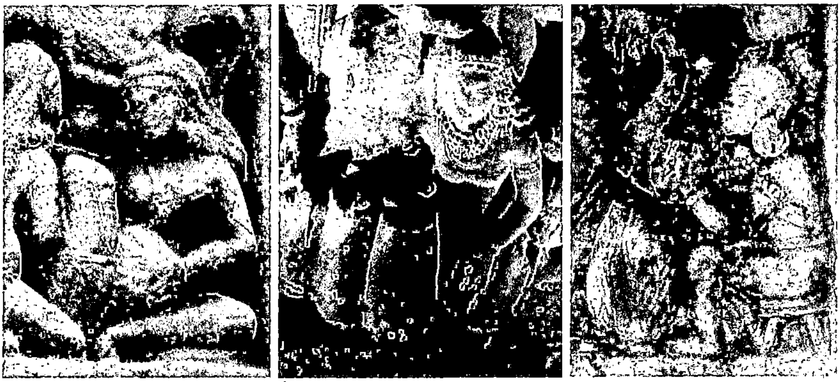

a. b. c.

Figure 4.1 a. Drummers playing the *tripuṣkara*. Detail from the serpent king Mucilinda in his court and his wives around the Buddha, Sanci, 2nd century B.C.E. Photo © Anandajoti Bhikku, www.photodharma.net; b. Detail from Temptations of Mara, Ellora, cave 26, 7th century C.E. Photo © Anandajoti Bhikku, www.photodharma.net; c. Detail from Naṭarāja, 10th century C.E., Bhubaneshwar, Mukhteshwar Temple. Photo by P. Pacciolla.

Puṣkara[4] – together with *abja*, *aravinda*, *kamala*, *nalina*, *padma* and *puṇḍarīka* (Kintaert 2010: 484; Pieruccini 2002: 40) – is one of the most common names denoting a lotus (*Nelumbo nucifera*) flower in Sanskrit literature, and it is different from other species of flowers of aquatic habitat such as water lilies (Kintaert 2010: 486). The lotus flower, which opens each morning, is raised on its stalk up to two metres above the water, while the flowers of water lilies, mostly night-bloomers, generally float on the water's surface. The lotus is a perennial rhizomatous herb whose rhizome or root-like stem 'throws off flowers and leaves at intervals, but there is no branching stem, and the stalk of each flower or leaf rises directly from the rhizome' (Coomaraswamy 2001: 58). Lotus leaves (*puṣkaraparna*) are circular with the petiole connected to the centre of the leaf. The first leaves to emerge out of the water float on the water's surface, while most of the others rise out of the water on stiff green stalks (Kintaert 2010: 489).

Even though in the *Nāṭyaśāstra*'s myth the term *puṣkara* does not denote the flower but the leaves of the lotus (Kintaert 2012: 3; Sathyanarayana 1987: 16;), it seems that the scene described is quite realistic; lotus leaves are circular like drum-skins and those raindrops falling on the leaves of different sizes floating on the surface of water will undoubtedly produce a sound different from that produced by raindrops beating on the many other leaves rising out of the waters.

According to Sathyanarayana – who bases his argument on Abhinavagupta's view – Bharata's version of the origin of the *mṛdaṅga* is 'largely phenomenological and only a little mythical' (Sathyanarayana 1987: 12) because the myth comes out not from metaphysical circumstances but from the simple observation of an acoustical principle: Svāti was inspired to create the *puṣkaras* of different sizes by the sounds produced by the raindrops swept by the wind over the lotus leaves of different sizes. According to Abhinavagupta, Bharata implies the acoustical principle of the inverse relation of pitch with membrane width as well as the observation that loosening the membrane would produce a deep sound while tautening it would give a high note. Since Svāti conceived the pond as the resonator for the lotus leaves beaten by the raindrops, he envisaged also the necessity of a hollow resonator for the membranes in order to produce a deeper sound, while the single or collective, successive or simultaneous beats of the raindrops on the lotus leaves inspired the sage to create a specific playing technique based on different fingerings.

The phenomenological interpretation is interesting and fitting,[5] but I suggest that the most significant aspect emphasized by the myth is the fact that the sound of the rain on the lotus pond is so beautiful that Svāti, fascinated by it and wishing to hear it again, in order to reproduce it, creates the *puṣkaras*. What is particularly stressed in this myth, I argue, is the sonic aspect of the scene and its creative power; it is the beauty of the sound of the rain on the lotus leaves that solicits the creative process in Svāti's mind. What is implicit in the narration is that the sound of the rain on the lotus leaves is procreative or, in other words, auspicious; and since that sound is auspicious, also the sound of the *puṣkaras*, created to reproduce it, is auspicious. Indeed, many times Bharata stresses the auspiciousness and importance of the sound of the *puṣkaras* and *mṛdaṅgas* (*Nāṭyaśāstra* 33, 19–20 and 33, 227).

Looking at the myth as if it were a picture, a miniature or a theatrical scene, a completely different range of information may be evinced. The image resulting from the myth is that of Indra showering rain over a lotus pond, and the most significant elements of it are rain, wind and a lotus pond. These are some of the most important symbols of the Indian mythological and philosophical world and trace back to the goddess Lakṣmī and more, in detail, to the iconography of Gaja-Lakṣmī or of the *abhiśekha* of Lakṣmī, one of the important motifs of ancient Indian art.

Gaja-Lakṣmī

Lakṣmī is a goddess of fortune, prosperity and wealth; she is also referred to as Śrī-Lakṣmī. Lakṣmī is the universal mother of life in her benevolent life-bestowing and life-increasing aspect (Zimmer 1947: 100). Everything good and auspicious such as flowers, banners, beds, gems, fruits, seeds, cows, horses, elephants and married women with their husbands living are believed to be the abode of *Śrī* who is *Mangaḷa* (Sivaramamurti 1982). Both the words *Śrī* and *Lakṣmī* appear first in the *Ṛg Veda*; *Śrī* used as a noun and adjective denoting prosperity, wealth, well-being (Gonda 1969: 176–224) and that which is pleasing to the eye (Coomaraswamy 1929: 175), and *Lakṣmī* denoting a pleasant or auspicious quality. Śrī and Lakṣmī appear as one goddess in the late Vedic *Śrī-Sūkta* hymn, but only in the epics is Śrī-Lakṣmī a concrete goddess associated with victorious kings or gods or with Viṣṇu as her husband.

The goddess is strongly linked to water and particularly to the lotus, which is the most important feature of her iconographic representations. According to Coomaraswamy (1929: 178), there are three main categories of images based on her relationship with the flower: when she holds a lotus flower in her raised right hand (*padma-hastā*), when she is supported by a flower as her seat (*āsana*) or pedestal (*pīṭha*) and when she, surrounded by stems and growing leaves, holds in her hands two of those flowering stems (*padma-vāsinī*). Among these categories, which are often combined in a single representation, the most distinctive is the last one which is never connected to any other goddess or god. Śrī-Lakṣmī is also strongly associated with the *pūrṇa kalaśa*, the vase of plenty, with lotus sprays, a very auspicious symbol of prosperity and abundance, and she is often represented standing on it as a pedestal; the association is such that the 'full vessel' may even have been intended as an aniconic representation of her (Coomaraswamy 1929: 183; Singh 1983: 56). A particular iconography is the so-called Gaja-Lakṣmī, 'Lakṣmī with the elephants', where she is represented seated or standing on a lotus spreading out of the *pūrṇa kalaśa* in a pond-like environment, while two or four elephants, supported by lotus flowers, pour down on her the water coming out of the inverted jars which they hold in their trunks (Figure 4.2). This iconography is called '*abhiśekha* of Śrī' type because she is anointed with water (Coomaraswamy 1929; Singh 1983).

As previously noted, the *Śrī-Sūkta* is the earliest text which eulogizes Śrī and Lakṣmī as a single deity and associates to this goddess all the elements that will characterize the so-called Gaja-Lakṣmī type. In the *Sūkta*, the goddess, considered as an embodiment of wealth and prosperity, seated on a lotus, heavily adorned and holding a lotus with one hand and a Bilva fruit with the other, is delighted by the roar of the elephants (Banerjea 1956: 372; Coomaraswamy 1929: 175; Singh 1983: 16). She has an auspicious character both in Buddhist and Jain literature, where it is among the 14 auspicious dreams of Tisala, the mother of Mahavira. The Purāṇas give numerous descriptions of her different forms and worship and report her origin as being from the churning of the ocean (Kramrish 1928: 107), and various other Sanskrit sources, both literary and philosophical, describe the Gaja-Lakṣmī motif (Coomaraswamy 1929: 175–177; Singh 1983: 22).

Representations of Gaja-Lakṣmī on bas-reliefs, terra-cottas and coins have been common since the 2nd century B.C.E. and are widespread all over India – Bharhut, Sanci, Bodhgaya, Manmodi, Orissa, Ellora, Badami, Mahabalipuram, Khajuraho and so on – on Hindu, Buddhist and Jain monuments. A feature of many renditions of the motif is the presence of *yakṣas* and *mithuna* couples as her attendants.

Gaja-Lakṣmī is an auspicious motif; indeed, all the elements of this iconography are strongly connected with water, rain and fertility. The place where the goddess is being anointed is clearly a lotus pond – which is beautifully carved in unusual detail at Ellora (cave 16) (Figure 4.2) and not only implied as it most often is – and she stands on a lotus which is a symbol of the waters. The *pūrṇa kalaśa*, the vase of plenty, is the most common of all the auspicious symbols adopted by Indian sects. Thought of as an

Figure 4.2 Gaja-Lakṣmī, Kailasa, Ellora cave 16, 6th century C.E. Photo © Ronak Shah.

inexhaustible vessel it is always associated with vegetation, and in art it is represented as a heavily ornamented pitcher full of water out of which spring bunches of lotus buds, flowers and leaves. It is a brimming vessel with its overflowing water, suggested by the lotuses emerging from it. As a life symbol 'it clearly belongs to the order of ideas characteristic of the ancient life cults and fruitfulness' (Coomaraswamy 2001: 63).

The elephant is a symbol of fertility, wealth and abundance and plays an important role in this particular iconography. The relationship of elephants with Śrī is stated in the *Mahābhārata* (13, 11; Gonda 1969: 218), where it is written that she lives in maidens, sacrifices, rain clouds, lakes filled with lotus flowers, royal thrones and elephants. Elephants bathe in the ponds with mud and are called *padmin.*[6] Airāvata, the white elephant, a prototype of the elephant race, is one of the 14 precious objects that arose from the milky ocean along with Śrī herself; he is the vehicle of the god Indra and hence a symbol of royalty. Elephants have a strong relationship with clouds. Indeed, they are endowed with the magic virtue of producing clouds. This special power is hidden in Airāvata's consort name, Abhramu, composed of *abhra*, 'cloud' and '*mu*', to fashion, to fabricate (Zimmer 1947: 106). The association of elephants with clouds and rain explains the existence of the cult around them, which is documented by many texts speaking about festivals held in their honor and where they were objects of worship (Gupta 1983: 11). The word *gaja* derives from the root *gaj* which means to sound or roar (Singh 1983: 14).

Seated on his elephant, Indra pours down rain and the elephant draws up water from the underworld – the Pātāla or the world of the *nāgas* – for Indra to rain (*Mahābhārata* 5, 99). This function of Airāvata shows that he is representative of the same powers and ideas which are embodied in Indra and that the king of the gods is a cloud too. The *Rāmāyaṇa* explains the cycle of water represented by the powers of Indra in a lyrical way. The poet compares the process through which the heat of sunrays draws the water from the oceans to the insemination of the sky and the clouds to pregnant women, containing in their wombs the rainwater that they will deliver, after nine months, during monsoons (*Rāmāyaṇa* 4, 28, 2–3). Thus, rainwater is conceived as the elixir of life nourishing the earth and the crops, and hence producing food for human beings.

The elephants represent water or water condensed in clouds. Hence Gaja-Lakṣmī is a visual representation of the water cycle, and for this reason it can hardly be doubted that in this iconography the elephants, the vessels and waters represent clouds and rain (Coomaraswamy 1929: 183). 'This scene was, no doubt, interpreted as the fertilizing of a female being representing, or connected with, the earth or the fields by rain-clouds; clouds were often represented by elephants, the word *nāga* having both meanings' (Gonda 1969: 220; Singh 1983: 8).

The fact that the scene is a symbolical representation of the fecundation of the earth resulting from Lakṣmī's union with the sky is also confirmed by the already mentioned alternative name of the motif: '*abhiśekha* of Śrī'. The word *abhiśekha* indicates the ritual of coronation of a king by means of water and the hidden symbolical meaning of the rite was that, through it, the gods continued to inseminate the land and the king to ensure its uninterrupted fertility. According to the *Aitareya Brāhmaṇa* (1.3) the waters represent seed and thus the consecrated become 'possessed of seed' (Jain 1997: 69). The king's land is a female (Inden 1985: 33) and he himself is a female too, thus the *abhiśekha* ritual is meant to fertilize the king and with him his land and people. Receiving the *abhiśekha* he becomes a fertile woman.[7]

Some particular meanings of the lotus (*puṣkara*), its leaves and the pond (*puṣkarīnī*) are pointed out by Garzilli in a study on the lotus (*puṣkara*) in the hymns of the *Ṛg veda.* Quoting a few stanzas she shows how a lotus pond (*puṣkarīnī*), beautiful like the dwelling of the gods (Garzilli 2003: 300–303), is compared to a womb and the lotus flower (*puṣkara*) to an embryo (Garzilli 2003: 297); as the lotus grows in the water of the pond, the embryo grows in the amniotic liquid. Analyzing another hymn, on the birth of the poet Vasiṣṭha, she shows that the lotus leaf represents a womb fertilized by a drop of rain – which stands for the poet – indeed like a drop falling on a lotus leaf the gods placed the sage upon it.

Śrī-Lakṣmī represents beauty and for this reason is associated with the lotus pond. She is not visualized as a simple pond, which would fit as a symbol of fertile earth and fertility as well, but as a pond of beautiful flowers sprouting from the mud. She is beauty, she stands for beauty as a source of life and indeed beauty is considered auspicious (Dehejia 2009; Donaldson 1975). She is a representation of the door giving access to life, which in the world of human beings is represented by the female body and particularly by the womb. She is a representation of the procreative powers and beauty of the female body. The many ornaments she wears, like fruits on trees or flowers on a plant, show that she is fertile and underline that fertility goes together with beauty (Dehejia 2009: 24). The elephants are symbols of Indra and clouds pregnant with rain, the elixir of life, semen and of the wind that precedes the rains. Gaja-Lakṣmī, Śrī-Lakṣmī bathed by the elephants, is a representation of the insemination of the earth, the union of sky and earth and the highest *mithuna*, the most auspicious symbol, at the very root of life. The lotus is, at the same time, the child born out of the inseminated mud and the goddess; and, at a universal level, the world.

The cloud-drum

In this section I argue that Gaja-Lakṣmī and the *Nāṭyaśāstra* myth of origin of the *puṣkaras* are two different representations of the same identical scene. They both represent the fertilizing union of sky and earth. The torrential rain poured by Indra, seated on his elephant, over the lotus pond is visually expressed by the cloud-elephants showering water over Lakṣmī, the lotus goddess identified with the lotus pond. Indra, the cloud and the elephant are synonymous images, and Lakṣmī, lotus and the pond are synonymous as well. The sound of thunder and rain over the lotus leaves is the sonic narrative of the myth.

The sound of thundering clouds and rain symbolize the copulation of sky and earth, their conjunction, and hence the voice of the *puṣkaras*, inspired by it and created to reproduce it, had to be similar to that of a cloud showering rain.

The relationship of the *puṣkaras* with the clouds is clearly expressed by Bharata when he says that once the *mṛdaṅgas*, *paṇavas* and *dardaras* had been made, Svāti brought about a similarity of their sound with that of the clouds. Soon, he establishes a further relationship between the instruments and particular clouds specifying that:

> the high sounding cloud named Vidyujjihva gave note to *vāma[ka]*, the great cloud named Airāvaṇa to *ūrdhvaka*, the rain-cloud named Tadit to *ālingya*, the Puṣkara cloud to the *dakṣina*, and Kokila to the *vāma[ka]*, and (the cloud named) Nandi to the drum named *āligya* and the cloud named Siddhi to *āṅkīka*, and Pingala to *āligya*.
>
> (*Nāṭyaśāstra* 33, 276–279)

The dramatic spectacles (*prekṣā*) on stage, had to be started after worshipping the gods and, as it was believed that the clouds were pervaded by spirits (*bhuta*), in order for the performance to be successful an offering had to be made to the spirits (*bhuta*) of those clouds.

The specific features of the sound of the *puṣkaras* are its depth, sweetness and pleasantness, which is due to the tuning paste smeared on the skins (*mārjanā*), and the fact that they produce syllables; indeed, the *mṛdaṅgas* have no harshness of sound like the other drums which do not produce distinct syllables and notes and hence don't need *mārjanā* (*Nāṭyaśāstra* 33, 25–27). The voice of the *mṛdaṅga* is auspicious and the *Nāṭyaśāstra* says that, for the success of the performance, it should be played from the beginning, 'from the tossing of the curtain' (*Nāṭyaśāstra* 33, 227).

The *mṛdaṅgas* were considered extremely important instruments and Bharata makes it clear that the playing of drums is the basis – literally the bed – of the dramatic performance (*Nāṭyaśāstra* 32, 493) and, indeed, held the main position at the centre of the stage. They were so important that they were not allowed to touch the ground, and were placed on a heap of dried cow dung. The drums also had associations with other gods. A long and detailed treatment explains each of the aspects of these instruments and their techniques, as well as the ceremony of their installation on the stage. It establishes the making of three *māṇḍala* with cow dung free from bad smell, assigned to Brahmā, Rudra and Viṣṇu, where *ālingya*, *ūrdvaka* and *āṅkīka* had to be collocated respectively, and the offerings they should receive are also described.

Only after having completed the offering (*dakṣina*) and the worship of the *gandharvas*, could the drums be played. The gods of *murajas* are Vajrekṣana, Śaṅkukarṇa and Mahāgrāmaṇī.

The *Nāṭyaśāstra* specifies that the skins to be used for the *mṛdaṅgas* should be of cowhide (*Nāṭyaśāstra* 33, 250–254). The cow Kāmadhenu came out of the churning of the ocean together with Śrī-Lakṣmī and the elephant Airāvata, and hence was taken to be a representation of the goddess and a symbol of prosperity.

An important association of the *puṣkaras* with the lotus pond is included in the name *mṛdaṅga*; this word is connected with mud (*mṛd*), or the earth fecundated by water, which represents Lakṣmī, and mud is indeed applied on the skins in order to tune them. Bharata writes that '*mṛdaṅgas* are so called because of being made of *mṛd* (earth)' (*Nāṭyaśāstra* 33, 272–274), but explains also that tuning (*mārjanā*) the *mṛdaṅga* should be done by means of earth, and specifies that the blackish earth from a riverbank, which is fine after giving out water, should be used for *mārjanā* because it produces proper notes (*Nāṭyaśāstra* 33, 111–117; Raghavan 1955: 136). The names *mṛdaṅga* and *puṣkara* are linked by the same symbolism, both referring to the wet, fecundated earth and to Sri-Lakṣmī, as mud or lotus coming out of mud.

Thus, these drums are lotuses (*puṣkara*) and, deriving from lotus leaves, they give voice to the wet earth and take sound from mud (*mṛdaṅga*). They are also clouds – and as clouds they thunder or roar – and elephants showering rain. All these elements are symbols of Śrī-Lakṣmī, the goddess of fertility, wealth and prosperity, the most auspicious one, the source of all auspiciousness. Another very interesting aspect linking the drum and the goddess which has to be noted is that just as Lakṣmī is anointed with the water poured by the elephants, the *mṛdaṅga* is anointed by the wet mud smeared on its skins. To play the *puṣkaras*/*mṛdaṅgas* corresponds to evoking the goddess and auspiciousness.

Since it was connected to Indra, the king of the gods, by means of cloud and elephants, the *mṛdaṅga* is strongly associated with kings and kingship too, and, moreover, since it was a representation of Lakṣmī, who was the embodiment of sovereignty (Gonda 1969: 223,188; Marglin 1985a: 181), the drum itself was conceived as a symbol of sovereignty. Indeed, as can be deduced from the abundant references to its presence in royal courts and festivals, its sound was one of the most important elements of the sonic landscape of all the kingdoms (Pacciolla and Spagna 2008).

Another important aspect of the sound of the *mṛdaṅga* is that it reproduces the sound of the *mithuna* of sky and earth and as such is full of procreative power. The creativity of sound and its being like a womb are emphasized in almost all the Indian traditions, from the Vedas to the Upaniṣads, the Purāṇas and Tantras. Words such as *Om*, *vāk*, *śabda*, *dhvani* and *nāda* are almost synonymous, all of them having the meaning of the concept of sound – pure or lettered – as the source out of which sprouts the whole universe. Among the Upaniṣads, for instance, the *Māṇḍukya Upaniṣad* is completely devoted to the explanation of the meaning of the *Om*, 'which is past, present and future', and 'whatever is beyond the three periods of time is also verily *Om*' (*Māṇḍukya Upaniṣad* 1.1). The *Bṛhaddeśī* of Matanga, a treatise on music from the 8th century, refers to *dhvani* as the ultimate origin – *yoni*, womb – of everything (Sharma 1992: 5) and uses the word *nāda* giving to it the same significance and concept. The term *nāda*[8] derives from the root *nād*, to sound, thunder, roar or bellow (Rowell 1998: 44), and shares semantic and phonetic properties with the word *nadī*, or river. The flow and movement of rivers is very similar to that of the growth of the lotus creeper and they have been adopted as similar symbols of the flux of life (Coomaraswamy 2001; Rowell 1998: 45). In Tantra-Yoga contexts the word *nāda*, conceived as a sonic symbol of universal energy, represents the earlier moments of the cosmic manifestation and it is referred to as the *mithuna* of Śiva and Śakti (Woodroffe 1994: 137–138).

Rain of blessings

Up to this point, I have analysed some aspects explaining and justifying the auspiciousness attributed to the *mṛdaṅga* in relation to Gaja-Lakṣmī and the concept of fertility, but there is another very interesting view on its auspiciousness that deserves to be considered. It is again connected to the goddess but deeply rooted in yogic vision and practices. According to this view, Lakṣmī is an auspicious goddess not only because she bestows fertility and wealth, but because she guides spiritual seekers towards awakening (Narayanan 1985: 59; Zimmer 1947: 98).

A clear reference to this double view on auspiciousness is reported by Narayanan in her essays on the Śrī Vaiṣṇava *sampradāya*, where she explains that the members of the sect consider auspiciousness as having two levels, a worldly one, aiming at fertility, wealth and progeny, and a theological one, called *prapatti*, aiming at the attainment of enlightenment (*mokṣa*). The latter, resulting in the meeting of the human soul with Viṣṇu, can happen only through the intercession of Śrī, consort of the god, who acts as a mediator giving to the individual soul the knowledge leading to *mokṣa* (Narayanan 1985: 59). Similar qualities are attributes of the Buddhist *Prajñā-Pāramitā*, a lotus goddess derived from Lakṣmī, considered the essence of the Buddhas, 'the queen of the spiritual kingdom attained through enlightenment (*bodhi*), representing the extinction (*nirvāṇa*) of both individualized consciousness and the cosmic manifold of biological, human, and godly being' (Zimmer 1947: 98–99).

Marglin recognizes a double meaning of auspiciousness too, and identifies it in the opposite worlds of Vrindavan, the realm of the young Kṛṣṇa where human rules have no meaning, representing a transcendent type of auspiciousness, and Dwaraka, the reign of the prince Kṛṣṇa bound to time, where auspiciousness is necessary in order to guarantee sovereignty and health (Marglin 1985a). Similarly, Printchman identifies a dichotomy in the celebrations for the month of Kartika in Benares; according to her, the two faces of Kartik *pūjā* celebrating Kṛṣṇa's *līlā* in Vrindavan and the glory of Vaikunth represent, respectively, the spiritual auspiciousness connected to religious devotion and the worldly auspiciousness sustaining sovereignty (Printchman 2003: 339).

In line with this point of view, I propose an alternative interpretation of the iconography of Gaja-Lakṣmī according to which it symbolizes the human mind entering into *samādhi* and the beatitude (*ānanda*) resulting from that experience: the mind, represented by the goddess, receives from the cloud-elephants a shower of wealth and knowledge. Just like the dark monsoon clouds release the rain which enlivens and inseminates the earth, the mind of the *yogin* completely devoted to the attainment of liberation receives – from a special cloud – a rain of blessings, a pure elixir of beatitude (*ānanda*) which marks the fulfilment of his/her task.

One of the most ancient and authoritative literary representations of this mental process can be found in an extremely interesting *sūtra* of Patañjali's *Yoga Sūtras*, where the sage deals with the ultimate stages of liberation. He writes (IV, 29) that 'having no-interest left even in the Highest-Intellection, there comes from constant discrimination, the trance known as the Cloud-of-Virtue (*dharmamegha*)' (Prasada 1998: 307–308), and Vyāsa, one of the most authoritative commentators of Patañjali, explains it as follows:

> When this Brahmana has no interest left in the Highest Intellection, *i.e.*, desires nothing even from that, then unattached even to that, he has discriminative knowledge ever present, and thus by destruction of the seed-power of potencies, other thoughts are not born. Then does he attain the trance known as the Cloud-of-Virtue.
>
> (Prasada 1998: 307)

Even though among the contemporary scholars there is not a uniform understanding of the concept expressed in this *sūtra* (Rukmani 2007: 131), almost all commentators identified *dharmamegha* with the stage of *jīvanmukti* or complete liberation, and explained the word *dharmamegha*, Cloud of Dharma, as the outpouring of the highest *dharma* and the accomplishment of the very aim of human life; Vijñānabikṣu, the last of the classical commentators wrote, more explicitly, that it had been called so because it rains down the *dharma* which eradicates, without a trace, all afflictions and *karmas* (Klostermaier 1986: 253). Similar views and explanations can be found in two Upaniṣads of the *Śukla Yajur Veda*, the *Paiṅgala* (Aiyar 1914: 49–50) and the *Ādhyātma* (Aiyar 1914: 58).

While the word *dharmamegha* is not so common in Hindu literature (Klostermaier 1986: 253), the concept and idea of rain as an outpouring of blessings is widespread, particularly in literature and visual arts where the granting and receiving of blessings or knowledge are represented as a shower of flowers, having an identical meaning to rain. The Vidyādharas, semi-divine figures, bestow knowledge in the form of a shower of flowers and epics and *kāvyas* are replete with such images.

By contrast, the term *dharmamegha* is prominent in Mahāyāna Buddhism under the theory of the *daśabhūmi*, the ten stages of progress of a Bodhisattva, presented in the text *Daśabhūmikasūtra*, which considers *dharmamegha bhūmi*, also called *abhiśekha bhūmi*, to be the highest. According to the *Milinḍhapañha* the *yogin* should possess five qualities of the rain cloud, and the last and most important one is that as the rain cloud pouring down fills streams, wells, and lakes with water, the hardworking *yogin*, earnest in effort, should open the Rain Cloud of Dharma (*dharmamegha*) to fill the mind of those who are longing for knowledge (Klostermaier 1986: 258; Rhys Davids 1890: 352).

The rain cloud has a particular connection with the Buddha (Kubo and Yuyama 2009: 95) and a very clear example of it is given by the *Lalitavistara*, in which the motive of the rain cloud is associated with the coming of the Buddha and the cessation of afflictions: 'Enveloping like a cloud the world which is scorched by the fire of afflictions, pour down, you hero, like a rain of nectar into the fever of men's afflictions' (Klostermaier 1986: 262).

However, the strong connection of the Buddha with clouds can be inferred from his even stronger association with elephants, an unsurprising aspect considering that he was a prince, and kings are, as already pointed out, from a symbolic perspective, rain clouds. The elephant is an important symbol of Buddha. In fact, his birth was announced to his mother by the dream of a white elephant entering her body, and many stories narrate the previous lives of the Buddha as an elephant or are centred on that animal. Among the many such stories, a very interesting one, the Taming of Nalagiri, narrates how the Buddha tamed Nalagiri – a notoriously dangerous elephant belonging to king Ajatasattu – who had been forced to drink 16 pots of liquor in order to kill the enlightened. The story tells that Buddha was wandering around in Rajagriha, the capital of Magadha, with his followers when, on the order of his cousin Devadatta, the mahouts released Nalagiri onto his path, but the elephant, who had already started running through the streets panicking people, approached the enlightened and listening to his voice calmed down and bent at his feet.

This story has a particular significance because it furnishes an interesting link between the taming of the animal and the yogic practices aimed at controlling the human mind, and traces back to the concept of the *dharmamegha samādhi* and the powers attributed to the *mṛdaṅga-pakhāvaj*. It is the core of Buddhist thought and is intended to show Buddha's control over his mind; indeed, the taming of the mad elephant is meant to demonstrate that the Buddha had completely tamed his mind, and offered an example and a teaching to monks and people.

Both the teaching and the simile had good fortune and spread, as can be inferred from the numerous writings comparing the human mind to an elephant, like the following one from the Theragāta:

> I shall fasten you, mind, like an elephant at a small gate. I shall not incite you to evil, you net of sensual pleasure, body-born.
> When fastened, you will not go, like an elephant not finding the gate open.
> Witch-mind, you will not wander again, and again, using force, delighting in evil.
> As the strong hook-holder makes an untamed elephant, newly taken, turn against
> its will, so shall I make you turn.
>
> (*Vijitasena's verses*, Theragāta vv. 355–357)[9]

The association mind-elephant held strong in Tibetan Buddhism and developed in a meditation practice, called Calm Abiding (*shy-ney*) (Dalai Lama 2001) aimed at fixing the mind on its object of concentration; the meditation, which goes through nine stages, is also visualized in various paintings showing how the monk progressively chases, binds, leads and subdues the elephant-like mind, whose colour accordingly progresses from black to white.

Buddhism elaborated the simile of mind and elephant in many ways, always emphasizing the necessity of its taming through meditative techniques, but it was not exclusive to Buddhism. Indeed, it can be found in many other later Indian traditions. According to Kabir, for instance, 'this body is a *Kajali* forest and the mind is an elephant gone mad, the jewel of wisdom is the goad but few are the Saints who can apply it!' (White 1996: 238) and the Sikh Śrī Gurū Granth Sāhib states that 'the mind is the elephant, the Guru is the elephant-driver, and awareness is the prod (whip)' (www.srigranth.org: 516, line 18).

Hindu Tantric traditions adopted the elephant-mind association too and highlighted the enlightening power of sound in his audible form (*ahata nāda*), as stated by the *Nādabindu Upaniṣad* according to which 'the sound (*nāda*) serves the purpose of a sharp goad to control the maddened elephant – mind (*citta*) which roves in the pleasure-garden of the sensual objects' (*Nādabindu Upaniṣad*, Aiyar 1914: 258), and subtle form (*anāhata nāda*), as argued by the *Haṭha Yoga Pradīpikā* (15th century), which says that 'the mind, like an elephant habituated to wander in the garden of enjoyments, is capable of being controlled by the sharp goad of *anāhata nāda*' (*Haṭha Yoga Pradīpikā*, 4, 91, Sinh 1914: 60).

The utilization of sound (*nāda*) as a special tool for meditation practices is explained in a number of texts and Upaniṣads like the *Haṁsa Upaniṣad*, which recognizes ten stages in the process towards enlightenment and links each one of them to the hearing of a particular sound. The first sound is similar to the word *cini*, the second to *cini-cini*, the third sound is a bell, the fourth a conch, the fifth is a lute (*tantri*) and the sixth is cymbals (*tāla*); the seventh is the sound of a flute and the eighth that of *bherī* (drum); the ninth is that of *mṛdaṅga* and the tenth is that of clouds (*viz.*, thunder) (Aiyar 1914: 215).

As shown in Chapter 3, the *pakhāvaj* tradition, especially the Kudau Singh school, maintains a very strong connection between the drum, elephants and clouds, and has various versions of a legend according to which Kudau Singh tamed a mad elephant with the sound of its *pakhāvaj* (Kippen 2000: 121; Mistry 1999: 77).[10] What is particularly interesting about this is that, notwithstanding the obvious different nuances generated in the story by its telling from mouth to mouth, it still revolves around the themes and ideas which have been analysed above. Indeed, it can be easily seen that the plot of the story is very similar to that of the Taming of Nalagiri: in both cases a mad elephant is tamed by the power of sound, that of the *pakhāvaj* in one case, Buddha's sweet and resonant voice in the other. This sonic feature links both the stories to those traditions that emphasize the role of *nāda* and recognize the sound of the *mṛdaṅga* and that of clouds, or thunder, as crucial to the path to enlightenment; the sound of the *mṛdaṅga-pakhāvaj*, similar to a thundering cloud, has the power to tame the mind.[11]

This story traces the *pakhāvaj* back to its ancient legacy, that of Gaja-Lakṣmī, the goddess of fertility, wealth and knowledge and helps to explain another reason for the auspiciousness of the drum. Its sound is auspicious like the thunder announcing the rain that fertilizes the fields allowing the crops to grow, and it is a harbinger of 'rain of *dharma*' that will shower upon the meditating *yogin* and the knowledgeable musician on the path to enlightenment. As already argued, the sound of the *mṛdaṅga* is a sonic representation of the union of sky and heart, but it represents the merging together of the mind and the object of meditation too, the union of *atman* and *Brahman*, the cessation of duality. In other words, the cessation of the individual mind and its expansion is symbolized by the merging of the two streams of water poured into the goddess, symbolizing the vase of plenty of cosmic energy or the lotus of the heart.[12] The *mṛdaṅga-pakhāvaj* represents the tamed mind, the tamed elephant which becomes the vehicle of the monk in his journey across the rainbow, its thundering sound has a taming power and announces the coming of the blessing rains of *samādhi*.

Thus, the *mṛdaṅga-pakhāvaj* has been associated with rainclouds and elephants in two different ways; on the one hand, like the elephant, it represents the cloud producing auspicious rain fertilizing the earth; on the other hand, it is linked to the mad elephant as representation of the untamed human mind. However, although due to the different symbolical interpretations of the elephant this appears to be contradictory, the two symbolisms are but two sides of the same coin since, as has been seen, the mad black elephant-like human mind, once tamed by the monk or the *yogin* attaining *samādhi*, becomes a white elephant and a nourishing source, a cloud full of rain which, just as a monsoon cloud showers fertilizing water on the fields, starts showering wisdom and bliss into the heart of the *yogin*.

The rain cloud, the white elephant and the *mṛdaṅga* are auspicious symbols of sovereignty and represent the fertilizing power of kingship.

Notes

1 All the quotations from the *Nāṭyaśāstra* in this study are taken from the translation by Ghosh (1961).
2 The list of *tripuṣkaras* and *mṛdaṅgas* carved on the walls of stupas and temples is quite long, some of the more important being those at Khandagiri (2nd century B.C.E.), Bharhut (2nd century B.C.E.), Sanci (2nd century B.C.E.), Amaravati (2nd century C.E.), Mathura (1st century C.E.), Ellora (6th century C.E.), Aurangabad (7th century C.E.) or in those of the Mukteshwar temple (10th century C.E.) in Bhubaneshwar.
3 *Paṇava* was an hourglass drum and *dardura* a vascular drum.
4 The word *puṣkara*, according to the Monier-Williams Dictionary means several things: a lotus, blue lotus flower, bowl, the skin of a drum, water, lake and sky.
5 However, it should be noted that, in the context of a treatise very detailed in describing the *purvaranga*, or the ritual procedures preceding the actual performance, as well as all the others rituals relating to the world of the theatre, a purely phenomenological interpretation of the myth would appear reductive.
6 According to Monier Williams, the word *padmin* means 'spotted as an elephant', 'possessing lotuses' and 'elephant'.
7 The symbolic sprinkling of water serves many other purposes as well. 'A Hindu idol is "enlivened" by the same ritual of sprinkling, and a virgin wife is believed to be ceremonially besprinkled, in the rite of the first night by her husband's ejaculation' (Jain 1997: 69).
8 *Nāda* is the most recurrent in relation to music. It first appears only during the 1st millennium and is mostly connected to Tantra Śakta contexts; the *Nāṭyaśāstra* does not formulate an explicit theory on this point but it is implied and suggested in many ways.
9 Text available at: https://suttacentral.net/en/thag5.9 (Accessed 21 September 2016).
10 Personal communication of Svāmī Ram Kishore Das. See Chapter 3, p. 40 for other versions of the story.
11 A very interesting link to mad elephants and music, in line with the above arguments, is provided in the opening verse of his *Gītālaṃkāra* (1, 1) by Bharata (1st millennium C.E.), who defines music as the puncher (*aṅkuśa*) capable of controlling mad elephants who are the adversaries (Danielou and Bhatt 1959: 3).
12 The lotus of the heart is considered as the seat of highest consciousness.

5 The drum of the King-God

An aspect of the *pakhāvaj* which is particularly important according to Ram Kishore Das is its relationship with kings; he underlined that it was the most important drum of ancient India, remarking that king Arjuna played the *mṛdaṅga* and that it resounded in the courts described in both the *Rāmāyaṇa* and *Mahābhārata*. More than once he told me that having technical command over the drum and the knowledge of its heritage elevated the musician to the status of a king. Ramakant Pathak associated the *mṛdaṅga* with Indra, the king of gods and lord of rains, adding that its sound was sweet (*madhura*) and powerful, and almost all of the *pakhāvajīs* I met connected the drum to the gods Śiva or Viṣṇu, both representative of supreme kingship over the universe. Ancient literature is replete with instances of kings expert in music and having voices thundering like rain clouds or like a drum (Lienhard 1984; Vatsyayan 1968; Warder 1988), and the mythologies connected to Śiva or Viṣṇu provide copious instances in which the dancing gods are associated with thundering drums (Sivaramamurti 1974; Varadapande 1982; Vatsyayan 1968).

Numerous textual sources confirm the connection of kings and gods with drums and clouds that is established and underlined by musicians, but why was the *mṛdaṅga* associated with kingship? Why was it associated with gods such as Śiva or Viṣṇu? What generated this association? When did the *pakhāvaj* emerge as the/a royal drum and a new version of the *mṛdaṅga*? In this chapter, in order to answer these and related questions, I will analyse the concept of kingship as it took shape from the beginning of the 1st millennium, observing its relation with the *mṛdaṅga* in ancient and medieval India. This concept, and the world-view connected to it, have been at the core of the history of Indian culture for about two millennia, moulding the evolution of social organization, philosophical and religious thought and literary and artistic expression.

The picture that I will draw is original. Although mostly based on secondary sources, my argument results from a new approach which synthesizes information from different research fields, and looks at ancient Indian culture and the concept of kingship from the point of view of music and musical instruments. Indeed, the most typical scholarly approach to the concept of kingship has been philosophical or religious (Coomaraswamy 1942; Gonda 1956a, 1956b, 1957a, 1957b; Heesterman 1985), while literary studies have focussed almost exclusively on aesthetical issues (Lienhard 1984; Vatsyayan 1968; Warder 1988). Furthermore, in contrast with the numerous studies on Indian temples, arts and iconography, studies about the archaeology of musical instruments or music iconography are scarce and contradictory (Deva 2000; Krishna Murthy 1985; Prajnanananda 1963; Vatsyayan 1968). Even Pollock's (1996, 2006) ground-breaking studies on Sanskrit and Sanskrit literature, despite illuminating the relationship between politics and aesthetics, do not treat music in detail and, similarly, Ali's (2006) writing on ancient Indian courtly culture does not deepen issues on music.

Synthesizing all the useful information provided by these studies and drawing on my own research on the iconography of Indian music, I will trace the emergence of the concept of the King-God according to the different perspectives of the cults of the two main deities Śiva and Viṣṇu, and of the function and role of the *mṛdaṅga*, conceived as a sonic representation of divine kingship.

The socio-historical context of the emergence of the *mṛdaṅga* as major courtly drum

Numerous literary and iconographical sources testify that in ancient India drums were widespread in many varieties and that they had different functions. The sound of drums was needed during the ritual worship of the Buddha – as shown in the reliefs on the stupas of Sanci and Amaravati – and local deities such as the *yakṣas* (Ahuja 2001; Coomaraswamy 2001; Premlata 1985; Vatsyayan 1968), or to give energy to street performances of acrobats (Auboyer 1965). Ritual drums, such as the *bhumi dundudbhi*, were beaten during the Vedic sacrifices such as the Mahāvrata (Deva 2000; Gonda 1981; Krishna Murthy 1985; Prajnanananda 1956; Premlata 1985) and war-drums, such as the *dundubhi*, the *bherī*, the *muracu* or the *taṇṇumai*, resounded in battlefields (Deva 2000; Gonda 1981; Hart 1975; Krishna Murthy 1985; Prajnanananda 1956; Premlata 1985). Numerous visual sources from archaeological sites such as Chandraketurgarh, Sanci, Bharhut or Amaravati show that various types of drums accompanied and heralded royal processions (Krishna Murthy 1985; Premlata 1985; Srinivasan 2005). Concert drums such as the northern *mṛdaṅga*, *muraja*, *paṇava*, *dardura*, *dindima* or the southern *muḷāvu* and *taṇṇumai* were described or depicted in connection with the performances of dance and drama inside the court (Deva 2000; Hart 1975; Krishna Murthy 1985; Premlata 1985; Vatsyayan 1968), and royal drums such as the *dundubhi* and the *muracu* were conceived as symbols of kingship (Hart 1975; Premlata 1985).

The *mṛdaṅga* is the most frequently represented and mentioned of all drums in literature. By the 4th to 6th centuries C.E., as sanctioned by treatises such as the *Nāṭyaśāstra* and Sanskrit literature, it became the most important instrument, emblematic of art, music and courtly culture, symbolic of kingship and of deities such as Śiva and Viṣṇu.

The first carved representations of the *mṛdaṅga* that we know, belong to a period following the fall of the Maurya empire (185 B.C.E.). The collapse of the empire, which extended to practically the entire Indian subcontinent, was followed by a long period of large-scale regional powers. These included Indic dynasties such as the Śuṅga, the Khāravela, the Sātavāhana, the Vākāṭaka and the Gupta, and the Indo-Greek Kuṣāna and Śaka dynasties. These dynasties were quite eclectic and cosmopolitan, and their commercial, cultural and religious exchanges with Central Asia and China favoured cultural hybridization and the development of new political, religious, philosophical and aesthetic ideas (Clothey 2006; Samuel 2008; Thapar 2002). The city, whose importance increased significantly in this period, was the place where the new cultural and religious syntheses took place.

A major development in this period was the sacralization of kingship and its legitimation in terms of the old Brahmanical texts. Indeed, the new model incorporated elements of the old Vedic-Brahmanical model of kingship, such as horse-sacrifice (*aśvamedha*). The new king, conceived as a god himself and as the preserver of the natural law (*dharma*), was perceived as the personification of wisdom, the epitome of culture and patron of the arts (Clothey 2006; Samuel 2008; Thapar 2002).

A parallel major religious development during this period was the growth of a new kind of idea of the deity, conceived as a transcendental and all-embracing god. This conception was incarnated mostly by Śiva and Viṣṇu, who emerged at the beginning of the 1st century C.E. as high deities associated with royal power. Śiva, whose origin was traced back to the Vedic god Rudra, by the 3rd and 4th centuries C.E. had become an important deity associated with royal power; he was the god of warrior kings and Brahmin sacrifices, and a central figure for the Tantra cults. Viṣṇu, who was a minor deity in late Vedic literature, became a high god and incorporated other deities of clan or tribal origin such as Vāsudeva (Kṛṣṇa) and Saṃkarṣaṇa (Balarāma), and heroes such as Rāma and Kṛṣṇa, who eventually became his incarnations (*avatars*). Rāma, whose story was told in the *Rāmāyaṇa*, was a folk-hero and a warrior, as well as a sacral king. Kṛṣṇa, whose worship was connected to Mathura, a centre of Buddhist art and culture, was a cowherd and warrior. In the *Bhagavadgītā* he appears as the embodiment of the cosmos and the personification of totality as well as the teacher par excellence. Absorbing all these warrior deities, in later Indic tradition Viṣṇu became the deity most centrally associated with royal power and rule.[1]

The new deities required new religious attitudes and ritual practices. Icons representing the gods became the means of worship and a personal relationship was adopted as the main way to approach them. Brahmins, the representatives of the ancient religious tradition of hereditary priestly families, established for themselves ideological supremacy as ritual performers. They largely monopolized the ritual of state and kingship and gradually gained strength in the countryside thanks to the land they received as a gift for their services. Jainism and Buddhism were flourishing. From the Buddhist tree grew the Mahāyāna branch which spread along the trade channels to Central Asia and China. It was during this period that some of India's greatest thinkers and artists, such as the Buddhist philosophers Nāgārjuna and Vasubandhu and the poet Aśvagoṣa, lived and the stupas at Sanci, Amaravati, Bharhut and Nagarjunakonda were erected. Mahāyāna Buddhism proposed a new conception and representation of the Buddha. Indeed, by the 1st centuries of the 1st millennium, the Buddha, no longer represented through symbols but in human form, was thought of as the supreme king.

This period of transition, which lasted a few centuries, culminated with the rise of the Gupta dynasty (c. 320–535 C.E) and the establishment of its empire. The Gupta reign was a period of Brahmanical renaissance, Sanskrit flourished as the language of power and Sanskrit literature reached its peak, but much in the articulation of these times was rooted in the ascetic tradition of the previous centuries, particularly Buddhism (Thapar 2002). Indeed, notwithstanding the fact that the Guptas established Brahmanical Hinduism as the state religion, Buddhism continued to flourish. Tantra cults evolved in Buddhist, Śaiva and Vaiṣṇava contexts. A new vision of the arts and their role was developed, and they became a means for the celebration of the material world and of life itself. The human body was used as the medium through which the sacred was depicted; the body, intended as a micro replica of the cosmos, became the most common way to represent gods (Clothey 2006; Vatsyayan 1983). Within Mahāyāna Buddhism, the Buddha too had human form, as did the new Brahmanical deities. The body, in dance or icons, was affirmed and deities such as Śiva and Viṣṇu were represented as expert dancers (Kalidos 1999).

High culture, associated with the elites at various courts and focused on the aesthetics expressed in creative literature, sculpture, architecture and philosophy, shaped the nobles' life-style. Under the Guptas, the new cultural and religious pattern was further elaborated and spread all over the subcontinent. It is in this context that the *mṛdaṅga* emerged as a major drum, symbol of royal power and kingship.

The sound of the *mṛdaṅga* in the aestheticized life of the courts

The courtly culture which evolved in the Gupta period arose from a complex social reality in which political order, religion, philosophy, ethics, aesthetics and nature were intertwined, and included an ideal of beauty, elegance, refinement, morality, eroticism and political power in an organic whole (Ali 2006). A net of interrelated meanings and metaphors created a world in which beauty and violence, ethics and war, mind/body control and enjoyment, were or were intended to be in perfect balance. Indeed, the specific quality of this difficult balance conferred royal dignity on this culture. Aesthetics played an important role and moulded not only the formal arts but nearly every aspect of the lives of the elite, providing a model for their style of life and their relations (Ali 2006; Pollock 1998). Art provided the people of the court with descriptions and images of ideal beauty and with a series of models through which they could learn appropriate manners. It taught them how to indicate, through words and gestures, their emotions to the different members of the elite according to their position (Ali 2006).

Beauty, elegance and style were striking preoccupations in the lifestyles of the people of the court, and were applied to their bodies, movements, speech, clothing, surroundings and souls. Beauty was considered an auspicious (see Chapter 4, p. 54 and p. 65) virtue since physical beauty signified moral worth and portended worldly success (Ali 2006; Dehejia 2009; Inden 1985; Lienhard 1984).

Poetry proposed metaphors and similes with plants or animals to describe ideal beauty and visual arts gave shape to them through colours and stones. Women had feet like lotuses and thighs shapely and smooth like plantains; their arms were like tendril lianas and their hands like lotuses. The physical beauty of men, which ideally included aspects of masculine strength and feminine delicacy, was also described through similar metaphors. They had lotus-like feet; while long arms were similar to the trunk of an elephant and hands graceful like plant tendrils (Ali 2006; Bhatnagar 2003; Dehejia 2009; Delahoutre 1994; Lienhard 1984; Pal 1983). Ornaments (*alaṃkāra*) were a necessary complement of beauty for women and men and were a sign of auspiciousness.

Similes and metaphors defined not only the ideal beauty of the body, but also its postures and movement, since they were intended as an expression of emotional states and associated with social rank. A firm, inflated posture and elegant, calm and balanced movements were signs of emotional control and high rank; they were explained through a simile forging a link to the elephant's dignity – so people of rank were described as having a slow elephant-like gait. A drooping posture and excessive, jerky and sudden movements were signs of internal agitation and low rank (Ali 2006; Dehejia 2009; Delahoutre 1994; Lienhard 1984).

Physical beauty and bearing had to be complemented by elegant speech, represented by Sanskrit. The central feature of this refined speech, which vernacular languages did not have, was its adherence to the phonetic and grammatical rules set down in treatises on grammar. Sanskrit had the capacity to express minute thoughts and emotions in the most refined way, but had to do it by strictly following the rules of grammar; grammar, in turn, also had an ethical value since its order provided a model of discipline. Indeed, this noble language represented the perfect balance of refinement and vigour, moral strength and delicacy aimed at by kings and the elite of the courts. It was the appropriate vehicle for the expression of royal will and its knowledge was a necessary component of kingliness (Ali 2006;

Dehejia 2009; Pollock 1998). Only those of moral and political worth had access to the universal provenance of refined speech known as Sanskrit.

Music played an important role in the life of the nobility. Like Sanskrit, music balanced elegance and delicacy with respect for the strict rules of its grammar and was one of the major elements of the training of kings and elite men. Literature described kings as accomplished musicians, often playing the *mṛdaṅga*, and patrons of musicians and scholars of music (Ambedkar 1947; Auboyer 1965; Pacciolla and Spagna 2008).

Sexual pleasure played a significant role in the life of high-ranking men and its pursuit was a matter of great distinction among kings who, in their inscriptions, were systematically compared to Kāmadeva, the god of love, in beauty and sexual prowess (Ali 2006). *Śṛngāra-rasa*, the mood of erotic love, was also called the *rāja-rasa*, and since it encompassed numerous subsidiary emotions, it was conceived as the basis for experiencing the self and the world in the most comprehensive way (Ali 2006; Bansat-Boudon 1992a: 360; Rowell 1998: 332). However, self-discipline and mastery over the senses were recommended to men in the court in all their pursuits, including sexual relationships. The texts on polity emphasized that the training of the prince should lead him to master the various elements of his own self since it implied control of mind, and an ordered mind was the prerequisite for success in polity. The important practice of self-discipline required of the prince was called 'conquest of the senses' (Ali 2006: 239).

Bodily gestures and facial expressions were regarded, like language, as being capable of suggestion, as signs of inner disposition. External signs, including voice, colour, eyes, aspect, gestures and movements were conceived as markers of internal states (Ali 2006). Emotions were thematized. Conceived as moments of an ever-changing inner landscape and compared to the natural world they were associated with seasons, atmospheric events and with the animal, vegetal and mineral worlds in a structured network of meanings. Comparison was a compositional means and similes and metaphors constituted a vocabulary of themes and conventions which were common to the various arts. For instance, a thread of elements such as clouds, thunder, elephants, peacocks, dance and drums, including the *mṛdaṅga*, was used to describe different but interlinked situations such as the rainy season and royal or divine figures. The most typical representation of the monsoon included dense masses of dark clouds – which appeared like mountains or flocks of elephants – thundering or rumbling like drums (*mṛdaṅga, muraja, mardala*) and moving peacocks to dance (Bhatnagar 2003; Lienhard 1984; Warder 1988). An instance of such representations is provided by the poet Māgha in his poem *Sisupālavadha:*

> The row of clouds with its fullness of notes, which rumbled (like) the beat of a great many oiled drums (*mārjana mardala*), made the excited flock of sweetly calling peacocks dance.
>
> (Lienhard 1984: 24)

Descriptions of the rain such as this were standard of *kāvya* literature. But the same elements were linked to the idea of kingship and were, therefore, used to create the image of the king and to indicate his qualities. The association of the king with rain was very strong since one of his main duties was to guarantee the rain for the welfare of his kingdom. As he had to bring the rain, he was symbolically represented by the image of a dark cloud full of rain, and was associated with an elephant who, in turn, represented clouds and kingship. Literary and visual arts create the image of the king as having a voice like thunder, and a body, or parts of it, as powerful as an elephant's; even his bearing is described as similar to that of an elephant, showing calm, control, elegance and strength. Booming drums heralded the coming of the king and the monsoon's arrival was described as the arrival of a king in full parade, like in the opening verse of the second canto of Kālidāsa's *Ṛtusaṃhāram*, devoted to the season of rains:

> With streaming clouds trumpeting like haughty tuskers, with lightning-banners and drum beats of thunder claps, in towering majesty, the season of rains welcome to lovers, now comes like a king, my love.
>
> (*Ṛtusaṃhāram* 2,1)

The thundering clouds herald the rains which will refresh and nurture the earth just like the king showers beneficial rain on his kingdom. The numerous descriptions and depictions of divine and earthly courts included the same themes and metaphors used for the rainy season. Indeed, the *apsaras* and the courtesans dance to the rhythm of the thundering *mṛdaṅgas* like peacocks dance hearing the thundering clouds; the king sits on his throne like rain is held by the clouds. The various representations of the king and the rainy season were joyous and auspicious since the rain brings fertility and food and thus enhances life. Thunder announcing the arrival of the rain was a harbinger of fertility, and thus even the powerful voice of the king, deep-sounding like a cloud or a drum (*mṛdaṅga*), was auspicious (Ali 2006; Delahoutre 1994; Lienhard 1984). The king's voice and the *mṛdaṅga* associated with him had the same quality as the thunder.

The *mṛdaṅga* was part of this rich network of metaphors and symbolical connections, included in the thread of similes linked to kingship, rain and auspiciousness; it incorporated all the images connected to the idea of kingship and, at the same time, evoked all of them. Another unique feature emphasized by several literary sources (Deva 2000; Krishna Murthy 1985; Premlata 1985), which made the *mṛdaṅga* fit for kings, was that its voice was not only powerful but also sweet. Thus, it was chosen as the sonic representation of the ideal balance of power and elegance, strength and grace, heroism and command over arts, aimed for by royal figures. The *mṛdaṅga* incorporated and expressed the qualities of the ideal of courtly maleness.

The language of the *mṛdaṅga*, like Sanskrit, was regulated by a set of rules which was presented and explained in the *Nāṭyaśāstra*, and was also linked to dance. Beautiful courtesans dancing elegant and feminine (*lāsya*) dances to the beats of *mṛdaṅga* were an essential element of the court in order to guarantee auspiciousness to the king and his reign (see Chapter 4), and kings themselves performed fierce dances, dances of victory accompanied and regulated by the rhythms of the *mṛdaṅga*, like the dances performed by the paramount gods Śiva and Viṣṇu.

All these features made the *mṛdaṅga* the most important drum of high culture and the sonic emblem of kingship and high gods.

Śiva, the magnification of the warrior king

The Gupta and Vākāṭaka rule came to an end in the early 6th century C.E. It was followed by a period of about two centuries of military adventurism and constant warfare among states which were short-lived and unable to control large areas (Davidson 2002; Samuel 2008). However, the political order conceived as a 'circle of kings' (*rājamāṇḍala*), which had formed the basis of political strategy and diplomatic thinking at the court of Guptas, continued to dominate. It involved a concentric structure of contiguous and overlapping relations of allied kings and enemies. At the apex or centre of the circle of kings, called 'Great King' (*mahārāja*), stood an imperial overlord, or paramount sovereign, with the title of 'Great King over Kings' (*mahārājādhirāja*) or 'Paramount Lord' (*parameśvara*), who was a divinized figure having the status of the supreme deity ruling over smaller gods (Clothey 2006; Davidson 2002).

The process of creation of divine royalty caused a process of 'royalization' of divinity (Davidson 2002; Samuel 2008). The deity started out being conceived and represented as the celestial counterpart of the king, a fact that implied the organization of the divine hierarchies according to the political structure of the time. Local gods worshipped by emerging monarchs took the central position while minor local deities were thought of as their vassals. Deities lived in fortresses, married, received guests, held court, supported poets and were involved in their own divine military activities. Temples, considered to be their palaces, were erected to the main gods to whom an imperial status was attributed (Clothey 2006; Samuel 2008).

War was the domain of Śiva and of fierce goddesses, and in this period rulers turned their interest to their cults in both non-Tantric and Tantric forms. Rudra-Śiva, warrior par excellence, became the celestial counterpart to the warrior king and Śiva, as the Destroyer of the triple city of the demons (*tripurāsuras*), the model for medieval terrestrial monarchs (Davidson 2002). From the 6th to the 10th century C.E., the iconography of the so-called Śiva king of dance (Naṭarāja), in which the many-armed god dances to the rhythms of the three-drum set *mṛdaṅga* played by a musician, spread all over India (Gaston 1981; Sivaramamurti 1974). Epigraphic and literary sources correlate the dance of Śiva with warfare (Sivaramamurti 1974); his is a martial dance, a dance of victory performed over the battlefield after destroying the triple city, or over the body of killed demons. Gajasamhāra, for instance, is the dance that he performs after killing *Gajasura*, the demon elephant, while holding in his hands the skin of the animal.

Śiva dancing his dance of victory over the enemy was conceived as the divine counterpart of the king, the magnified representation of the power of the triumphant ruler performing his dance of victory over his enemies. This idea is particularly evident in South India where, in early Tamil Śaiva devotional hymns Śiva is called, among other names connected to dance, Naṭamāṭiyavēntaṉ, 'King who danced' or Āṭumaracaṉ, 'dancing king' (Sitanarasimhan 2004: 304–305). The overlap between the figure of the king and the figure of the god is manifest at the level of rituals too, since the various Śaiva sects that emerged and spread during the 1st millennium incorporated several elements of the royal ceremonial in their rituals (Brancaccio 2011; Collins 1982; Davidson 2002). For instance, music and dance, which were emblems of royalty and harbingers of auspiciousness and as such played a crucial role in the court, were two of the six forms of worship that had to be performed in the temple according to the sect of the Lakulīśa-Pāśupatas (Collins 1982: 614).

The correspondence of the figure of the king and the god is clearly shown by the fact that the *mṛdaṅga*, symbol of royalty, was the major instrument accompanying the dance of Śiva Naṭarāja. The study of the iconography of the *mṛdaṅga* in ancient India shows the instrument either in court scenes of various types or accompanying Śiva's dance. One of the most frequently carved court scenes (Amaravati 2nd/1st century B.C.E., art of Gandhara 1st/2nd century C.E.) is the so-called great renunciation of the Buddha, an iconographic model which illustrates the moment when the prince decided to leave his palace while his courtesan musicians fell asleep embracing the instruments they were playing. Other specimens depict performances at the divine court of Indra (Bharhut 2nd century B.C.E.), at courts of human kings (Udaigiri, Amaravati, Vidisa 2nd/1st century B.C.E., Mathura 1st century C.E., Pawaya and Sarnath 5th century C.E., Aurangabad and Ajanta 6th/7th century), nāga kings (Sanci 1st century B.C.E.) and demons such as Mara tempting the Buddha (Sanci 1st century B.C.E.).

Reliefs from the 5th to the 13th century, illustrating the god Śiva dancing to the rhythm of the same kind of *mṛdaṅga* represented in the court scenes, are also quite numerous and widespread all over India.

The fact that the *mṛdaṅga* was played both in royal courts and to provide rhythm to the victory dances of Naṭarāja clearly shows that it was a symbol of kingship and an emblem of power and auspiciousness and, at the same time, proves the overlapping of the figure of the king and the god. An interesting aspect differentiating court scenes from the iconography of Naṭarāja is that while in court scenes the king watches the delicate dance (*lāsya*) performed by courtesans for him, the iconography of Śiva represents the god, king of dance, himself performing a fierce dance (*tāṇḍava*) of victory. However, it seems that the two scenes represent, respectively, elegance and strength, the qualities that the ancient ideal king had to be endowed with and were synthesized in the figure of Śiva. Indeed, both dances are connected to Śiva since, according to the *Nāṭyaśāstra*, the god himself performed the dance of victory (*tāṇḍava*) and introduced the delicate style of dance (*lāsya*) performed by the *apsaras* into drama (Bansat-Boudon 1992a; Ghosh 1961; Pande 1996; Vatsyayan 1968).

The dating of the images shows that court scenes precede by many centuries representations of Naṭarāja, that the two typologies coexisted for about three centuries (5th to 8th century C.E.) and that, from the 8th to the 13th century C.E., the *mṛdaṅga* seems to have been carved only in the iconography of Śiva. Indeed, from about the 8th century onward the *mṛdaṅga* drumset was no longer represented in court scenes, but replaced by a single drum called *mṛdaṅga*, *mardala*, or *muraja* which musical treatises of the 2nd millennium still associate with Śiva in various ways. According to the *Saṅgītaratnākara* (13th century), a treatise strongly influenced by Tantric ideas, the five different categories of strokes of the *mṛdaṅga* derived from the five faces of Śiva (Sen 1994: 64), while the Jain text *Saṅgītopanisatsāroddhāra* (14th century) attributed the creation of the *mṛdaṅga-muraja* to the blue-throated god (Miner 1994). The *Saṅgīta Makaranda* of Nārada (7th/11th century) affirmed that the *mṛdaṅga* represented the combination of Śiva–Śakti. According to this source, the right side of the drum, with its deep sound, represented Rudra while the left side, with its high-pitched sound, stood for Umā. Therefore, the sound of the *mṛdaṅga* consisted of majesty and sweetness and bestowed to the listeners boons such as victory in battles or expansion of kingdoms (Vijay Lakshmi 1996: 219).

During the 2nd millennium, the *mṛdaṅga*, with its alternative names *mardala* or *muraja*, appeared associated also with Śiva as an ascetic but still with a high symbolic value. Indeed, Śaiva texts such as the *Haṭha Yoga Pradīpikā* (15th century), the *Gheranda Saṃhitā* (16th/17th century), the *Śiva Saṃhitā* (16th/18th century) and a few *Yoga Upaniṣads*, providing instructions on meditation by means of attention to sound (*nāda*), mention the sound of the *mṛdaṅga* or the *mardala* at the highest stages. According to a story reported by White, Gorakhnāth, one of the most renowned ascetics of medieval India, rescued his guru Matsyendranāth who had got lost in the world of women, by playing a single stroke on the *mṛdaṅga* (White 1996: 236). Interestingly, in Nepal, Śiva is identified with Nāsadyaḥ, the god of music and dance. The Newars believe that Nāsadyaḥ manifests himself in musical instruments and in particular in barrel drums very similar to the *mṛdaṅga*, such as the *khī*, the *dama:khī* and the three-headed joined drum *kwota* that are considered to be his sonic manifestations (Ellingson 1990; Wegner 1992).

Notwithstanding the significant organological changes which happened to the *mṛdaṅga*, at the beginning of the 2nd millennium its association with Śiva was still strong.

The drum giving voice to death

Almost all the *pakhāvajīs* I met reported two main myths relating to the origin of the *mṛdaṅga*, the one written in the *Nāṭyaśāstra*, attributing it to Svāti, and another one according to which the instrument had been created by Brahmā (see footnote 26, Chapter 3) for Śiva. The latter is a popular Hindu legend and narrates that Śiva, after killing the demon Tripura, exalted by his deed, started dancing so furiously that due to his dance, disordered and lacking rhythm, the earth started sliding away and would not stop. When Brahmā realized that the earth was going to be destroyed he panicked and in order to avoid a disaster created the *mṛdaṅga* out of the dismembered body of the demon Tripura and gave it to Gaṇeśa to play. Soon, Śiva started dancing according to the rhythm of the drum and therefore, thanks to the *mṛdaṅga*, the earth was safe again. Clearly linked to this myth, the invocatory verse of Dhanaṃjaya's *Daśarūpa* (10th century C.E.), a treatise on the ten forms of theatre, directed to Gaṇeśa, recites:

> Homage to that Gaṇeśa whose throat, deeply resonant in his excessive frenzy, serves as a drum (*puṣkara*) in the wild dance (*tāṇḍava*) of Śiva, just as the sound of the wildly expanding thundercloud at the dance of the peacock!
>
> (Haas 1912: 1)

A third very interesting and quite ancient myth may be found in the *Saṅgītopanisatsāroddhāra* by Sudhākalaśa (14th century). This Jain musical treatise establishes that, according to Jainism, the drum was born from a conch-shell (*śanka*),[2] ascribing the story to a popular origin. The myth attributes the creation of the instrument to Śiva. According to this myth, Muraja, an *asura* who had previously obtained from Brahmā a boon that he would be slain by none but Rudra, knowing that the god sat in meditation on mount Kailasa, decided to kill him. In order to distract him, he created Madhu, a demon in the form of nectar, but Rudra awoke from his meditation, discovered immediately the real cause of his distraction and slew Muraja, cutting off his head and limbs. Vultures greedy for food ate a little of the demon's body and then lifted it up, but it was heavy and slipped from their beaks, falling on a tree. The ribcage and belly were hollow and covered by skin which, hanging on the tree in the hot sun, dried and started producing sounds from the gusts of wind. Śiva, who was then wandering in the forest, heard these pleasing sounds and, impelled by curiosity, traced them to their source recognizing it as the body of Muraja. He took it and gave a gentle stroke with his left hand generating a pleasing noise which sounded like the syllable *ta*; then he struck it with his right hand and it generated the sound *dhi*. He experimented again with harder strokes of both left and right hands producing the sounds *thom* and *draim* respectively. After some time, the rainy season came and Śiva, at Umā's request, built a hut with three different types of leaves; the two gods were together when the first drops from a new cloud started falling on the leaves of the hut producing such beautiful sounds that Umā asked her husband to create an instrument to reproduce them. Śiva then recalled the slaying of Muraja and the musical instrument which came into being because of it and proceeded to establish the *muraja* drum and its many strokes which he organized into 35 varieties of sound-groups, inclusive of single-hand and double-hand strokes.[3]

At the end of the chapter, Sudhākalaśa writes that while Rudra created the *muraja* out of Muraja's dead body, among human beings the instrument came to be made of hollow wood covered at both ends with stretched leather, bound with leather thongs in *nāgapāśa* (snake noose) knots (*Saṅgītopaniṣatsāroddhāra*, IV, 48–89).

What is unique about Sudhākalaśa's version of the story is that it links the *Nāṭyaśāstra* myth – which is set during the rainy season – with the popular legend, blending their main features: the connection of the *mṛdaṅga* with rain, and it being an instrument closely related to the death of an *asura* and made out of parts of a dead body.[4] Furthermore, this legend testifies the changes which occurred to the *mṛdaṅga* between the last centuries of the 1st millennium and the beginning of the 2nd millennium C.E. Indeed, over that period, it had become a single drum and, in line with new contexts and beliefs, its myth of origin had been changed. It was still the most important drum and it was still auspicious, but its auspiciousness had acquired new reasons and symbols.

According to me, in this myth – and in those connected to it – the auspiciousness of *mṛdaṅga-muraja* lies in the fact that it represents the dead body of an *asura*. It stands as an iconic representation of the god's deed and its sound represents the voice of the subjugated demon; each time the *muraja* is played the killing of the demon is re-enacted and the life force freed by the triumphant god is reinvigorated. To play the drum is equivalent to the chanting of the god's victory (*jay!*) or to the waving of lamps during *ārati* because it represents the victory of light over darkness, of life over death and destruction. In fact, the death of a demon is considered auspicious because it guarantees the elimination of destructive forces through their transformation into life-giving positive ones. The *mṛdaṅga-muraja* also symbolically represents the purified body of the *asura* and thus its sound projects order, gives life and purifies. Moreover, as highlighted in the second myth by the role of Gaṇeśa whose drumming controls the *tāṇḍava* dance of Śiva bringing it back to ordered movements, the *mṛdaṅga-muraja* is capable of controlling the disordered energies deriving from the action of killing and transforming them in auspicious ones. Relating to this particular point, Ravishankar Upadhyay told me[5] that, according to his *paramparā*, the 'true' story of the origin of the *mṛdaṅga* is the one ascribing it to Śiva. Indeed, the god killed the *asura* and made the instrument out of his body, and for this reason the oldest name of the drum was *mṛt-aṅga*, or *mṛit* – death – *aṅga* – part of the body, but later on it was substituted with *mṛdaṅga*, or *mṛd* – clay – *aṅga*. He also added that its sound, capable of spreading everywhere, is pure, *śuddha*, and purifies the environment.

Thus, in my view, the *mṛdaṅga-muraja* has to be considered as alive, as a living being, since it represents a dead being – the *asura* killed by Śiva – which has come back to life in a new purified body – the drum – and as such it symbolizes the secret power of life which regenerates itself through a continuous sacrifice implying death and rebirth. Although usually considered as inauspicious, death is auspicious when sacrificial. The principle of auspiciousness of death is veiled in almost all myths including sacrificial death; indeed, the life force released by the *asura*, representing destructive forces endangering the right flux of life and law (*dharma*), killed by a *deva* becomes the basis of a new life, the source of life of an entire universe. It is for this reason that almost always a drummer accompanies the dances of Śiva in his various iconographies, implying the killing of an *asura*, such as, for instance, Gajāsurasaṃhāramūrti (Sivaramamurti 1974). Due to this purifying and pristine role the drum precedes the other musical instruments, and the sounding of it by Nandi at the commencement of Śiva's dance is a favourite theme in literary descriptions (Sivaramamurti 1974: 7).

One of the clearest demonstrations that death may be auspicious is given by Vṛtra's myth, wherein Indra, slaying the dragon with his thunderbolt and cutting his body into pieces, releases the waters kept by him which then go to fill rivers, lakes and nurture the whole earth (Bansat-Boudon 1992b; Gonda 1981; Wilkins 1913). This myth is also interesting because it highlights the relation between death and the monsoon: Vṛtra may be interpreted, at the same time, as a dragon who releases nourishing waters after being killed by Indra, and as the monsoon cloud which releases refreshing and fertilizing rains. In fact, according to the etymologists (*nairuktas*), Vṛtra was a cloud (Gonda 1981: 95), and Wilkins (1913: 57) considers the battle, which the Vedas describe in detail, as a kind of representation of the commencement of the rainy season and the strong thunderstorms which usually accompany this change of the seasons. The rainy season plays a particular role in the Hindu calendar as it is considered the time when Viṣṇu retires to sleep, leaving the earth in the power of demons, and the four months (*caturmāsa*) of the monsoon are considered inauspicious, as they represent *pralaya*, the cosmic deluge; most of the agricultural activities are carried out during these four months which also encompass some of the major ritual festivals (Gonda 1969; Vajracharya 2013). The rainy season is an ambivalent period as the monsoon may nurture the dry earth ensuring the continuation of life, but may also become a flood and destroy everything. Rituals and festivals reflect this ambiguity. *Dīpāvali*, for instance, is dedicated to Yama and death but it is also the festival of the new year, while *Rakṣā bandhana* and *Durgā pūjā* stress the destructive aspect of the monsoon and symbolize disorder followed by dramatic reordering. As the gods have followed Viṣṇu in his sleep, the demons are particularly numerous, the borders between the living and the dead vanish and the dead are thought to be very close (Gonda 1969). 'The rainy season represents a ritual break in the annual cycle, the time of cosmic reversals and commencement afresh' (Zimmermann 1987: 58).

The fact that this particular season of the year represents the *pralaya* seems to be implied even in *Nāṭyaśāstra*'s myth which tells how Svāti was going to the pond during the rainy season, when Indra's rain 'commenced to make the world one vast ocean' (*Nāṭyaśāstra* 33, 6). It means then that the creation of the *tripuṣkaras* happened in a 'moment' out of time, out of human time – more precisely in a moment between death and rebirth, and this agrees with the symbolism of the *muraja* myth. The drums, then, represent the ambiguity and the power of *pralaya,* which is a time of destruction and recreation, death and rebirth.

These elements allow us to read Sudhākalaśa's story in a new light and to consider its plot even more interesting and coherent; it connects the killing of Muraja and the making of the drum with the sound of the first rain of the monsoon falling upon the leaves of Śiva and Umā's hut. Thus, what seems to be a simple but efficacious blend of two different stories has a deep coherence. The two myths are linked, and this is confirmed by the strong similarities between Indra and Śiva (Sivaramamurti 1974: 81). Both gods are slayers of *asuras* and destroyers of the *Puras.* Indra dances enveloping the earth with his glory, bestowing prosperity (*Ṛg Veda* 5, 33, 6) and removing the veils of ignorance (Hopkins Washburn 1916: 248; Sivaramamurti 1974: 82–83); Śiva dances out of joy and victory and represents the victory of the true self over the ego, of knowledge over ignorance (Sivaramamurti 1974: 83). Indra killing Vṛtra with his *vajra* is analogous to Śiva Naṭarāja or Gajāsurasaṃhāramūrti and the sound of the thundering *mṛdaṅga* is auspicious because it marks the beginning of a new cycle, new seeds coming with rainwater.

Thus, the new myth of *muraja,* in its various versions, is deeply rooted in the past and strongly connected to the Svāti myth through Indra. The king of gods plays an important role in *Nāṭyaśāstra*'s myth where he is called Pākaśāsana, an epithet having two meanings: 'crop controller', hence god of rain and fertility (Hopkins Washburn 1916: 242), and 'punisher of (the demon) Pāka', this leads back to the concept of Indra as a god of battles and slayer of Vṛtra. The two faces of the god are inextricably intertwined because killing the dragon with his thunderbolt he releases the waters kept by Vṛtra and gives new life to the earth.

The intricate web linking different symbols and myths seems to be logical and coherent, showing the depth of the conceptual background of the *mṛdaṅga* and justifying its high status.

Viṣṇu-Kṛṣṇa, the righteous king and the *bhakti* cults

The model of Kingship offered by Viṣṇu with his two main incarnations, Rāma and Kṛṣṇa, was different from the one represented by Śiva. Although

Viṣṇu and his incarnations were warriors too, they evolved from different cults and sects. Indeed, while Śiva maintained a dangerous and potentially destructive persona due to his connections to Tantra cults, Viṣṇu represented the incorporation of the Brahmanical model of the wise king who had to provide protection – to Brahmans and ascetics in particular – and welfare to his kingdom (Gonda 1969; Pollock 1984). Since the king was a god and incorporated the divine essence, even in this model of kingship the figures of god and the king overlapped. The coincidence of the two functions led to the shaping of new ritual practices of worship conceived as replicas of the royal routine and ceremonies.[6]

The devotional approach (*bhakti*) to Viṣṇu, conceived as a personal god, arose during the 6th century C.E. in South India as the new way towards the attainment of liberation, providing the possibility of participating in the ultimate in a simple form. Combining the previous paths of wisdom (*jñāna*) and action (*karma*), it conceived the deity in human form and established a direct and loving personal relationship with him. Worship, the divine service, was called *sevā*, service. It was considered as the ultimate representation of *bhakti* since *bhakti* was pure and selfless love for God and it was through service (*sevā*) that love could be fulfilled (Thielemann 2002: 89).

Both *bhakti* and *sevā* were important concepts in medieval royal courts. Hierarchical order in the court was based on the relationship between servant (*sevāka*) and master (*swāmin*), and at the top of the hierarchy was the king in front of whom all were servants (Ali 2006: 104). Those men who took refuge in a king received a livelihood from him and performed for him various works denoted by the term *sevā*. The most important quality among the many virtues the royal servants were expected to have was loyalty, usually denoted by the terms *bhakti*, 'devotion', or *anurāga*, 'affection' or 'attachment' (Ali 2006: 105). *Sevā* and *bhakti* were rewarded with a bestowal of favour and grace, the chief mechanism for the redistribution of wealth and power among subordinates.

Viṣṇu was represented by an icon made sacred by priests who ritually invoked the deity's presence in it. The icon, considered as a living manifestation of the god and treated as if it were a king, was housed in a temple representing his divine palace where his devotees could go to see and to be seen (*darśana*) by him. The daily worship in Vaiṣṇava temples promulgated by *Pāṇcarātra Āgama* literature (3rd/6th century C.E.) (Gonda 1969; Thielemann 2002) followed and still follows the division of the day into eight consecutive periods (*aṣṭayāmasevā*) determined by the daily routine in the life of Kṛṣṇa. The standard worship (*pūjā*) performed in temples includes different 'honour offerings' (*upacāra*) to the deity, such as food, water, fresh leaves, sandalwood perfume, incense, betel nuts and cloths.

In courts, the particular acts performed in order to please, gratify and convey respect to another person of high rank were denoted by the term *upacāra*, a word which included gestures and words of respect and acts such as presentation of water and food, gifts of ornaments, clothes, incense or flowers and offerings of dance and music. The goal of the men attending the court was to gain a viewing (*darśana*) of the king.

Music and dance played a crucial role in Vaiṣṇava cults and particularly in Kṛṣṇa cults. The *Bhāgavata Purāṇa*, the principal text of Vaiṣṇava theology, provided precise indications about how art forms had to be included in the ritual service. It clearly stated that 'one should worship the Lord with perfumes, flower-garlands, unbroken grains of rice, incenses, light and food offerings. Having greatly honoured him with hymns and songs of praise, (one should) bow to the Lord' and 'individually or together with others (he should arrange), on festive days, processions and great feasts with song, dance, etc., as done by mighty kings' (Thielemann 2002: 37).

Kṛṣṇa, an incarnation of Viṣṇu, who represented the ideal king and the model of righteous kingship, was himself a king. He was a dancing king (Naṭarāja) and like Śiva performed his warrior dance (*Kāliyamardana*) on the head of the snake-demon Kāliya after having killed him (Kalidos 1999). Medieval poets often described this deed of the blue god evoking the presence of the *mṛdaṅga* by mentioning the syllables (*bols*) indicating its strokes. Sūrdās, one of the main saints and poets of the medieval India belonging to the Puṣṭimārg, wrote that Kṛṣṇa, dancing on the head of the serpent Kāliya, 'with his feet – *thei, thei* – sounds out the rhythm of the deep *mṛdaṅga* drum' (Hawley 2009: 68). Kṛṣṇa, called *Meghśyam* (Varadapande 1982: 17) because of his skin, dark blue like a cloud full of rain and associated with rain and monsoon, is usually depicted wearing a crown decorated with peacock's feathers while dancing like a peacock with the *gopīs* (Varadapande 1982).

Since Kṛṣṇa was a king and a warrior, it is not surprising that the images and symbols associated with him, including the *mṛdaṅga*, encompass all the metaphors of the Sanskrit courtly literature connected to kings and nobles. The deep link between Kṛṣṇa and the *mṛdaṅga* is particularly highlighted by Vaiṣṇava drumming traditions developed during the 2nd millennium in sects headed by saints such as Namdev, Vallabhācarya, Śaṅkaradeva and Caitanya, who played an important role in the spread of the *mṛdaṅga* as the main drum of temple music. Since these founders settled in various areas of India, the *mṛdaṅga*, which by the turn of the 2nd millennium had become a single barrel drum, took slightly different shapes and alternative names having a local character. Thus, for instance, in regions such as Maharastra, Rajasthan, Uttar Pradesh and Punjab it was called *pakhāvaj*, in north-eastern regions such as Manipur and Assam it was called *puṅg* or *khol*, and in Bengal *khol*. All of these sects attributed to the drum a high symbolic function and an important role in their rituals in which music was attributed with having a highly spiritual value (Bandopadhay 2010; Graves 2009; Jhaveri and Devi 1989; Jones 2009). The Assamese *khol* is the most important musical instrument in the rituals of the followers of Śaṅkaradeva. The Vaiṣṇavas of Manipur consider the *puṅg* as the most auspicious instrument and a personification of Kṛṣṇa. The two membranes of the *puṅg* are the two eyes of Kṛṣṇa and the black colour applied to the wood represents his dark complexion. Musicians touch it only after purifying themselves, wearing fresh clothes and with a meditational attitude, and reciting the prayer to the *mṛdaṅga* (*mṛdaṅga Gayatri*). Gurus believe that while playing particular compositions on the *puṅg* they create the idol of Kṛṣṇa and instil life into it (Bandopadhay 2010: 169; Jhaveri and Devi 1989: 8). According to the Vaiṣṇavas of the Gauḍīya sect of Caitanya, the *khol* is a form of Baladeva, the elder brother of Kṛṣṇa, and an alternative manifestation of the flute. Indeed, while the flute was the instrument of Kṛṣṇa in his cowherd incarnation, the *khol* was his favourite instrument when he came to the earth as Caitanya (Graves 2009: 62). Before touching the drum musicians chant a Sanskrit invocation: 'Salutations to Caitanya, the son of Jagannātha. Salutations to the *mṛdaṅga*, endowed with the quality to evoke thousands of sweet *rasas*. Repeated salutations to Baladeva' (Graves 2009: 62). The Mahārājas of the Vallabhācarya Puṣṭimārg told me that they consider the *pakhāvaj* as an embodiment of Kṛṣṇa and its sound as the sonic form of Viṣṇu. The *pakhāvaj*, a very important instrument in the music of the Vārkarī sect founded by Namdev in Maharastra, is considered as the repository of the ancient tradition (Jones 2009).

The cluster of metaphors and symbols which had been attached to Viṣṇu and Kṛṣṇa in particular found a unique form connecting music and visual arts during the 2nd millennium in the context of the *rāgamālā* (Dallapiccola and Isacco 1977; Dehejia 2009; Gangoly 1935). *Rāgamālās* are miniature paintings representing the musical modes (*rāgas*) and were intended as an aid for the musician to meditate on the specific mood of a *rāga*. Kṛṣṇa was a major character of *rāgamālā* iconography and was particularly identified with *rāga megha* or *megh-malhār*, and *rāga vasant*. *Megha* means rain cloud and, in fact, the *rāga megha* is associated with the rainy season and believed to bring rain even during drought if correctly sung (Sharma 2007). In these paintings Kṛṣṇa, dancing under the rain or a cloudy sky, is flanked by women dancing and playing a barrel drum, often a *mṛdaṅga*. This particular *rāgamālā* allows us to see and appreciate the overlap between the figure of the king and the god as well as the cloud as a symbol of kingship. As argued by Vajracharya

> although in the later period many *rāgas* became associated with the cult of Kṛṣṇa, originally they had nothing to do with the god and the cult. An early depiction and description of *megha* makes this clear. For instance, in a fifteenth-century illustrated Nepali manuscript of *rāgamālās*, the personified cloud is depicted in the midst of a cloudscape, and in the Sanskrit verse given in the illustration he is identified with Megharāja 'the king cloud'. This original identity was already lost at the beginning of Rajput painting. In the *rāgamālās* from around 1605 this musical mode is called "Megharāga", cloud *rāga*. He is depicted there as a dancer flanked by two female musicians although he has not yet been identified with Kṛṣṇa.
> (Vajracharya 2003: 165)

Vaiṣṇava cults adopted the rituals and ceremonials belonging to royal courts, including the sensuous offerings of dance and music and their secular traditions (Haberman 2001; Subramaniam 1980). However, while they put themselves in line with the royal tradition, they adjusted it in order to be consonant to their religious views (Haberman 2001) and in the process they made of poetry and performing arts the best spiritual means capable of joining the individual soul with God. Thus, for instance, from a devotional point of view, the symbolical association of Kṛṣṇa with the monsoon rain cloud that relieves the unbearable heat of the hot season was interpreted as the relief brought by the vision of Kṛṣṇa that douses the fire of separation from the beloved. In a similar way, the peacock dance performed by Kṛṣṇa manifested his happiness at seeing the *gopīs* after having been separated from them all day, hence his happiness at seeing his devotees. Even the erotic mood (*śṛngāra-rasa*), the *rasa* of the kings, was transmuted by the Vaiṣṇava philosophers, first of all by Jayadeva in his *Gītagovinda*, and became the metaphor for the attraction of the devotees for their beloved god (Whitney Sanford 2008). *Kīrtana*, the singing of the praises of God, was elected as a perfect means to fulfil union with the divine, the ultimate objective of human life. Combining the auspicious words of the divine greatness with the energy of the musical sound had the capacity to arouse the sentiment of intense loving devotion (Thielemann 2002: 85), 'through singing the praises of the lord, He is brought to life in the heart of the singer, and divine passion is evoked' says the *Bhakti-Sandarbha* 269 (Thielemann 2002: 82; Widdess 2013: 190).

While in ancient India music and dance were conceived as forces energizing the king (see Chapter 4, pp. 56–57), musicians sang to strengthen him in his deeds on the battlefield and the drum of Śiva was an icon of power, in Vaiṣṇava traditions of the 2nd millennium music becomes a perfect spiritual means for the devotee who, while singing, remembers the sacred deeds of his beloved god and in this way meets him in his/her heart. Music is no longer *śakti*, power, but *bhakti*, devotion. While the *mṛdaṅga* played for Śiva was made out of the body of a killed demon (*asura*) and its sound represents his auspicious purifying voice, the sound of the *mṛdaṅga* played for Viṣṇu represents the body of the god and its sound reproduces his auspicious voice.

Notes

1 Female tribal or folk deities entered the theistic pantheon as goddesses. They would reach the status of high deities but only later on.

2 *Śanka*, the conch-shell, is one of the emblems or treasures of the universal monarch (*cakravartin*) identified with Jina, the founder of Jainism.

3 Two later versions of Sudhākalaśa's legend are reported by the *Mṛdaṅgalakṣaṇam* (16th century), an unpublished treatise by unknown author, and by Cikkabhūpāla (*Abhinavabharatisārasaṅgraha*, 16th century). According to the first source Viṣṇu – and not Śiva – created the *muraja* out of the dismembered body of the demon and gave it to Nandikeśvara to accompany the dance of the blue-throated

6 From *mṛdaṅga* to *pakhāvaj*

In the previous chapter I argued that the *mṛdaṅga* synthesized and included in its body and sound the qualities of the ideal nobleman and the specific features of the high gods. It was a war drum, and its sound guided Śiva's and Kṛṣṇa's dances of victory against demons, and at the same time had a delicate (*lāsya-madhura*) and fertilizing voice, required to guide the dances and the drama played for kings in their courts. It was a drum producing both heroic and delicate emotions, strength and elegance, power and eroticism, and for these specific qualities it had been elected as the drum for the ideal king in his earthly and divine representations. In this chapter I will follow the organological development of the *mṛdaṅga* during the 2nd millennium until its identification with the vernacular drum *pakhāvaj* in the Mughal period. I will conclude the chapter arguing that the evolution of the *mṛdaṅga* is the result of its deep relationship with kingship and godship over almost two millennia, as well as of a process of Sanskritization which has more than once transformed vernacular (*deśī*) drums into the courtly (*mārga*) *mṛdaṅgas*, and the *pakhāvaj* into the *mṛdaṅga*.

The multiplication of *mṛdaṅgas* and the emergence of the *pakhāvaj*

In spite of the strong hold of the symbolical world and the metaphors attached to the *mṛdaṅga* conceived as the sonic representation of kingship, as already argued, by the 8th century C.E. the model of the *mṛdaṅga* set, which had dominated for several centuries as representative of kingship, had been replaced in royal courts – in both Śaiva and Vaiṣṇava contexts – by regional barrel drums having new names attached to the ancient one, *mṛdaṅga*.

It is quite difficult to identify conclusively what the *mṛdaṅga* was during the first half of the 2nd millennium. While the ancient *mṛdaṅga* set, notwithstanding the difference in dimensions evident in its carved renditions in different areas of India, was described by literary sources and represented in visual arts with a great degree of homogeneity, the single barrel drum *mṛdaṅga* emerging with the new millennium cannot be recognized as a drum with precise features. Furthermore, *mṛdaṅga* was no longer the only name used to denote the main courtly drum but, according to treatises such as the *Saṅgīta Makaranda* (7th/11th century), the *Saṅgītaratnākara* (13th century), the *Saṅgītopanisatsāroddhāra* (14th century) or the *Saṅgīta Dāmodara* (15th century), *mardala* and *muraja* were alternative names for the instrument. The same treatises provide different descriptions of the features and sizes of the body[1] and the skins of the *mṛdaṅga*, and agree only on the presence of a tuning paste which, applied to the membranes, would make the drum sound like a thunderbolt. There was not even total agreement on the ingredients of the application plastered on the skins, or whether it had to be applied to both heads. Neither was it stated whether the paste was permanent like the modern black pastes or reapplied wet and fresh (Dick 1984d: 695). This application is not visible in sculptures or in the many paintings, in which drummers are most often drawn from the front with their hands placed over the skins.

The *Saṅgītaratnākara* mentions the *mṛdaṅga* in the section describing the ensemble (*vṛnda*) including singers, flutists and *mṛdaṅga* players. Similar ensembles were often carved on the walls of temples in the 1st centuries of the 2nd millennium, some of them including flutes and almost all including barrel drums and hour-glass drums (*paṇava*) (Deva 2000; Vatsyayan 1968). However, while the hour-glass drums are very similar in design and size and seem to correspond to a precise category, barrel drums show considerable variance in typology and size. Some of them are bulging at the middle and look like *āṅkika*, the drum of the ancient *mṛdaṅga* set which was placed horizontally on the floor – although they appear to be strapped to the waist of the musician with a cord; others are cylindrical drums having no relationship to the *mṛdaṅga*. Confirming such variance in typology, in Kerala, the *miḻāvu*,[2] a huge pot drum providing the music for the ancient Sanskrit theatre known as Kūṭiyāṭṭam, was named *mṛdaṅga* in medieval texts (Rajagopalan 2010) and represented in murals as the drum providing the rhythm to the dance of Śiva (Sivaramamurti 1974).

The name *mṛdaṅga* appears in some poetical works but it is often not clear whether the writers are using it as a poetical theme or whether they are referring to a precise instrument – and in the latter case, what drum was called by that name. For instance, in his *Kitab I Nauras*, Ibrahim Adil Shah (1556–1627) mentions the *mṛdaṅga* (*mirdang*) in a song devoted to *rāga bhairava* represented as Śiva (Ahmad 1956: 130). Considering the familiarity of the Muslim ruler with classical Indian poetical imagery (Delvoye 1993: 11), it is not surprising that he associated the *mṛdaṅga* with Śiva, and hence his reference cannot be considered to be to a precise musical instrument but rather as an adherence to a poetical canon.

Numerous literary and visual sources show that during this period certain regional varieties of drum had become even more important than the *mṛdaṅga*. Indeed, for instance, in the *Saṅgītaratnākara*, the barrel drum *deśī paṭaha* receives more extensive description than the *mardala* and the most extensive exemplification of drum syllables (Powers 1984:

696; Miner 1994: 318; Nijenhuis 1977). In a similar way, the Pārśvadeva's *Saṅgītasamayasara* provides a detailed description of the technique of the *paṭaha* and just a brief list of the strokes of the *mṛdaṅga*, and an early Persian treatise on Indian music such as the *Ghunhyat al Munya* (14th century) includes descriptions and drawings of the *parah* (*paṭaha*) and other *deśī* drums such as the *hurkā* (*huḍukka*) (Nijenhuis 1977; Sarmadee 2003) and the *pakhāvaj*.

The changing features of the *mṛdaṅga* during the first half of the 2nd millennium parallel the historical context. Indeed, in this period marked by continuous warfare, new Hindu kingdoms emerged and various Muslim dynasties such as the Turkic-Persian Khiljis (1290–1320) and Tuglaqs (1320–1413), the Sayyids (1414–1451), the Afghan Lodis (1451–1526) and the Turkic-Mongol Mughals (1526–1707) established their power over the subcontinent. In these centuries of transition the invaders slowly settled in India, increasing their interaction with Indians, and absorbing aspects of Indian culture and religion while, at the same time, many aspects of Indian culture changed and adapted to the new context (Asher and Talbot 2006; Trivedi 2010). Sufis, the Muslim mystics, entered Indian territory and settled in the subcontinent interacting with the Hindu mystics (*bhaktas*) and ascetics (*nāths*) and by the meeting of these mystical paths new ones emerged, like, for instance, that of the Sikhs founded by Guru Nanak (Trivedi 2010). New regional societies were established and new regional styles emerged involving all the sectors of human culture and arts (Asher and Talbot 2006; Miner 1994; Trivedi 2010). Music and musical instruments of Turkish, Persian and Central Asian origin entered India brought by Muslim invaders and were assimilated into the Indian system (Malkeyeva 1997; Trivedi 2010; Wade 1998).

Out of this period of transition in which Turkish, Persian, Central Asian and Indian cultures merged producing new regional syntheses, a new barrel drum, a regional instrument called *pakhāvaj*, slowly emerged as the main drum gaining, by the time of the reign of Akbar, a high reputation (Greig 1987) and incorporating the heritage of the *mṛdaṅga*. *Pakhāvaj* was a vernacular term and similar terms including the word *āuja* or *āvaja* were used quite commonly to denote musical instruments. According to the *Saṅgītaratnākara*, *aḍḍāvaja* – 'half-*āvaja*' – was the alternative name for the *deśī pataḥa* and professional percussionists referred to the hour-glass drum *hudukkā* as *āvaja* (Dick 1984e: 21; Sathyanarayana 1994: 15), while the *Saṅgītopanisatsāroddhāra* mentioned instruments such as *āuja*, *khandāuja*, *pakhāuja* and *pattāuja* adding that they were appropriately named in vernacular in accordance with their position with respect to the body of the performer (Miner 1994; *Saṅgītopanisatsāroddhāra* 4.92).

The very first description and depiction of the *pakhāvaj* may be found in the *Ghunhyat al Munya* (14th century) where it appears as an hour-glass drum having pasted over its skins a mixture of flour and ash and producing several syllabic sounds (Sarmadee 2003). It had a high status in those days since the same treatise, in the section devoted to instrumental music (*vādya prabhandas*), mentions two kinds of compositions specific for the *pakhāvaj*.

About two centuries later, Abul Fazl, in his *Ā'īn ī Akbarī* (16th century), describes the then most important concert drum (Greig 1987: 492–494) *pakhāvaj* as a barrel drum with

> a thick shell of wood shaped like a myrobolan and hollow. It is over a yard in length and if clasped round the middle, the fingers of the two hands will meet. The ends are a little larger in circumference than the mouth of a pitcher and are covered with skin. It is furnished with leather braces which are strained, as in the *naqqarāh* or kettle-drum, and four pieces of wood, under a span in length, are inserted (between the shell and the braces) on the left side and serve to tune the instrument.
>
> (Blochmann and Jarrett 1894, vol. 3: 70)

The *pakhāvaj* was played by two specific groups of musicians, the *kanjaris* and the *naṭwas* (Blochmann and Jarrett 1894, vol. 3: 70). The men of the *kanjari* group played the *pakhāvaj*, the *rabāb* and the *tāla*, while the women, who were also called *kanchanīs* and were the major courtesans of the Mughal society, sang and danced (Bor 1986/87; Brown 2003). The *naṭwas* were male singers and dancers who played the *pakhāvaj*, the *rabāb* and the *tāla*.

Although mentioned in various medieval Sanskrit treatises as a vernacular drum, the *pakhāvaj* (*pakhṣāvaja)* was, for the first time, identified with the *mṛdaṅga* by the *Nartananirṇaya* (Sathyanarayana 1994: 15). This treatise on dance written by Puṇḍarīka Viṭṭhala for Emperor Akbar, includes a chapter devoted to the *mṛdaṅga* in which the drum is described in minute detail. According to Puṇḍarīka Viṭṭhala, the *mṛdaṅga* was four spans in length, measuring 60 inches in circumference at the middle in the region of the belly, and the right and left apertures measured 11 and 12 inches respectively (Sathyanarayana 1994: 169). It was placed against the waist of the musician and held there by means of a cotton or silken ribbon (Sathyanarayana 1994: 171). The treatise also provides important detail on some aspects of the crafting of the drum and its parts that can only be found there (Sathyanarayana 1994: 278), such as the fact that the heads were multilayered. Indeed, it says that three skins were fixed to each aperture and that the middle portions of the inner and the outer skins were cut off – in the form of a lotus leaf – on both the membranes (*Nartananirṇaya* I, 29–30). Once the membranes were bound to the body of the drum, the right hand one was plastered with flour mixed with iron powder – hence the paste was black – while a mixture of boiled rice, wood-ash and wheat-flour was applied to the left one. This information is quite interesting in relation to the general development of the skin-making technology and is particularly useful for an understanding of the evolution of the multilayered skins of the contemporary *mṛdaṅga* type. The *Nāṭyaśāstra* does not say explicitly that the skins of the ancient *mṛdaṅga* were multi-layered, and since it describes in detail other aspects it seems probable that they had a single skin. Other important treatises featuring a section devoted to instruments (*vādyā adhyāya*) either do not say whether the *mṛdaṅga*, the *mardala* or the *muraja* had composite heads (Dick 1984d: 695), or specify, as the *Saṅgītaratnākara* does, that they had single thick skins. By contrast, regional drums such as the *deśī paṭaḥa* are described as having a second, upper skin, called *uddalī*, which must have been cut in the centre since two distinct strokes were produced by striking the two different skins (Dick 1984e: 21). These aspects suggest that during the 1st centuries of the 2nd millennium the multiple-layer skins of regional origin and the tuning paste, which was the pre-eminent mark of the *mṛdaṅga* types, had been joined producing a new type of membrane.

Miniature paintings represent another significant source for the study of the drum although miniatures depicting the *pakhāvaj* are scarce in Mughal paintings (Greig 1987: 494; Vatsyayan 1982: 117; Wade 1998: 90), which by contrast abound in representations of *dāire*, *daf* and *naqqarāh*, suggesting that they were by far the most common drums in Muslim courts. According to Greig, since it was never depicted in ensembles including instruments peculiar to Middle Eastern music, the *pakhāvaj* was used solely in Indian music (Greig 1987: 515). Two interesting miniatures from the late 16th century depict the *pakhāvaj* being played to accompany dances performed in front of royal figures. One of these paintings comes from the *Akbarnāma* (1590–1595) held at the Victoria and Albert Museum[3] and it is known that the dances are performed in front of Akbar himself. In the other painting, held at the Cleveland Museum of Art (ca.1600) (Figure 6.1), there is no mention of the identity of the royal figure watching the dances. In both miniatures, which provide different perspectives of the *pakhāvaj* player, the drum, held at the waist of the standing musicians supported by a strap, appears quite big. The right skin with a black spot and the wooden blocks inserted under the leather braces are clearly visible in the painting at the Cleveland Museum of Art.

The most interesting image of the *pakhāvaj* I have been able to find is a Mughal miniature (ca.1650) held at the Freer Gallery of Art (Figure 6.2) depicting two women seated on a terrace surrounded by female attendants. The scene takes place in the women's quarters (*ḥarīm*) and the drummer is a woman.

The *pakhāvaj* featured in this painting, from the dimensions of the body, the skins, the distribution of the leather straps and the general appearance, seems a very close representation of the contemporary drum. This painting, by distorting the view of the drum as if it was seen through a concave mirror, allows us to see the two membranes very clearly and shows, from the perspective of the music researcher, the most striking detail: on the skin of the *pakhāvaj* on the left-hand side is clearly painted the flour paste which is also given a three-dimensional aspect. The only thing which is not visible in this miniature is whether the skins or the heads are multi-layered.

Figure 6.1 Grotesque dancers performing, c. 1600, Subimperial Mughal. Colour on paper. Andrew R. and Martha Holden Jennings fund 1971.88. The Cleveland Museum of Art.

However, considering the meticulous description provided by the *Nartananirṇaya* a few decades before and given the fact that it seems to match with the painting in many respects, we may suppose that the *pakhāvaj* had already adopted complex heads. This image shows that by the 17th century, at least in some parts of the Mughal empire, the *pakhāvaj* had already completed its process of organological development, becoming the drum which is still played in contemporary India.

If the descriptions provided by the *Ā'īn ī Akbarī* and the *Nartananirṇaya* testify that the *pakhāvaj* was a very important drum under the reign of Akbar, evidence from other sources shows that it was still an elite drum during the reign of Aurangzeb (1658–1707). Indeed, according to Brown, under the reign of Aurangzeb musical connoisseurship and patronage had become an important signifier of noble (*mirzā*) status, and the *pakhāvaj*,

Figure 6.2 Two women with attendants on a terrace (left) and detail (right), ca. 1650, Mughal. Freer Gallery of Art, Smithsonian Institution, Washington, D.C.: gift of Charles Lang Freer, F1907.213.

which was of such high prestige that the Mughals believed that the legendary *dhrupad* singer Nayak Bakhshu played it (Delvoye 1990: 98; Sanyal and Widdess 2004: 50), had become the emblem of the ideal masculinity of the Mughal elite. 'Masculinity was synonymous with the public display of power and control over knowledge, over material commodities, over women and people of lower status, and over oneself' (Brown 2003: 125); it was defined in opposition to all things feminine since womanhood meant lack of social power and 'to be controlled, not merely by men, but by the irrational whims of the lower self' (Brown 2003: 296). Since masculinity was synonymous with power, even men of inferior social status were considered to be similar to women. Music and musical instruments were gendered as masculine and feminine too. Only the most prestigious of those classes of musicians whose genres and instruments were gendered masculine were permitted to enter the elite's musical space (*meḥfil*), since they would enhance *mirzā*'s masculinity while musicians who belonged to the vulgar space of the *bazār*, or the female space of the *ḥarīm*, were unequivocally excluded as 'effeminate'. At the top of the list of musicians were the *kalāwants*, the primary exponents of the *dhrupad*, the most prestigious vocal genre, and the two most venerated instruments, the *vīnā* and the *pakhāvaj*, who were of masculine gender (Brown 2003; Sanyal and Widdess 2004). At the bottom of the list were the *dhādhis* and the *bhānds.* The *dhādhis* were players of the *dholak*, a small cylindrical drum, and the *khanjari*, a small frame drum, both of which signified the low-status world of the *bazār* and were associated with weddings and women's music. Furthermore, not only did the *dholak* and *khanjari* represent women's music and female space, but the male *dhādhis* accompanying female musicians subordinated themselves to women. The *bhānds*, were a homoerotic community of Muslim male dancers who played the *dhol* and danced in the *bazār* (Brown 2003).

In order to preserve his masculinity, the noble Mughal (*mirzā*) had to maintain distance from the worlds of women and the lower classes. For this reason, the *dhādhis* were contrasted unfavourably with players of the more masculine *pakhāvaj*, who traditionally accompanied the high-prestige *kalāwants* in their performance of the masculine *dhrupad* compositions (Brown 2003).[4]

The *pakhāvaj* had incorporated the heritage of the ancient *mṛdaṅga*. However, in the process, the balance of masculinity and femininity – strength and elegance, power and softness – which was the ideal of the male elites of ancient India and was represented and expressed by the *mṛdaṅga* and its sound, got lost. Under the Mughals, where the masculine–feminine dichotomy was rigid, since masculinity meant high social status and control over oneself and others, while femininity meant low social status and subjugation, the *pakhāvaj* was considered to be the emblem of pure masculinity, devoid of any touch of femininity.

The model of the pure masculinity of the *pakhāvaj* based on the Mughal ideal is generally maintained by contemporary musicians who affirm that the main character of the drum is its vigorous and heroic mood (*vīra rasa*). Although a few of the *pakhāvaj* players I met say that the drum may convey other *rasas* as well, Dalchand Sharma is the only one who has developed his own theoretical view and playing style on the basis of the ancient Indian model, and argues that the *pakhāvaj*, like its ancestor *mṛdaṅga*, has to convey different *rasas*, not only the heroic one (see Chapter 7, p. 123).

However, according to iconographic sources, the contexts in which the *pakhāvaj* was played were not limited to the male Mughal noble elite space (*meḥfil*), but it was also played by women. Numerous Mughal, Rajasthani, Deccani and Bengali miniatures, as well as paintings from Uttar Pradesh, show both men and women playing the *pakhāvaj* in ensembles accompanying dances performed for kings and Mahārājas. Furthermore, the *pakhāvaj* was also, at least occasionally, played in women's quarters; the Mughal miniature at the Freer Gallery of Art (Figure 6.2) provides a beautiful instance of such utilization, and at least some later paintings from Golconda (ca. 1720)[5] and Murshidabad (ca. 1760)[6] at the Victoria and Albert Museum represent very similar situations.

In most of the miniatures from the 17th to the beginning of the 19th century representing music and dance scenes in royal courts, the ensembles include *pakhāvaj*, cymbals, a kind of *tānpūrā* or the *rabāb* and a female dancer.[7] From the beginning of the 19th century onward, the *pakhāvaj* is replaced by the *tablā*, almost exclusively played by men, and the string instruments are replaced by the *sārangi*.

The *pakhāvaj* was also played in temples. It accompanied Sikh devotional singing (*gurbani kīrtan*) and had been adopted as the main drum and symbol of Kṛṣṇa by the followers of the Puṣṭimārg. The sect, which emphasized the religious function of aesthetics and had strong relationships with the Mughal emperors and the Mahārājas of Udaipur, played an important cultural role from the 16th to the 19th century. Indeed, numerous Mughal, Rajasthani and Deccani miniatures and *rāgamālās* depict the *pakhāvaj* played by Kṛṣṇa's lovers, the *gopīs*, to provide rhythm to his dances, and while celebrating Holi. The *pakhāvaj* is the main drum of all miniatures associated with Kṛṣṇa and is represented until the 21st century, but while in paintings of royal courts it is most frequently played by women, in those portraying actual temple worship it is exclusively played by men.

Being the most important drum of the imperial courts as well as a symbol of Kṛṣṇa, the *pakhāvaj* was adopted in numerous courts and temples of Northern and Central India, and in the Deccan. It even reached Nepal, where it is called *paścimā*, a name probably meaning 'from the West' or Delhi,[8] and Assam, where it was introduced during the reign of Ahom kings by musicians who learnt to play it in Delhi (Barthakur 2003).

From *mṛdaṅga* to *pakhāvaj* and vice versa: making the *deśī mārga* and the *mārga deśī*

A very interesting aspect which comes out of my research on the heritage of the *mṛdaṅg-pakhāvaj* is the strong interrelation of the dichotomic categories of sacred-secular and *mārga-deśī*. As discussed in the previous pages, from the 1st centuries of the 2nd millennium, the *mṛdaṅga* represented, at the same time, the realms of the sacred and the secular: it was the symbol of the ideal noble warrior masculinity and the emblem of the highest gods of the Hindu pantheon. It was a drum of power, a drum of victory, giving expression to warrior strength and divine auspiciousness. It was the drum of the King-God and as such it was also associated with Sanskrit, the language of the Vedas and the gods, but also the language of earthly power, the language of kings. The *mṛdaṅga* itself 'spoke' Sanskrit[9] since, according to the detailed description of the technique provided by the *Natyaśāstra*, each drum stroke of the *mṛdaṅga* produced a letter of the devanāgarī alphabet.[10] Indeed, in the chapter on drums (*avanaddha vādya*), Bharata specified that while the sounds produced on the chordophones and aerophones were of the nature of musical sound, *svara*, those produced on drums were of the form of letters, *varṇas* (Chaudary 1997: 63; Ramanathan 2003: 54).[11]

Sanskrit was a sacred language and anything associated with it was guaranteed an aura of antiquity, purity and high status. It was the instrument by which all elements of a changing landscape could be linked to the Vedic tradition. Indeed, the *mṛdaṅga* represented the emblem of the royal world and the drum of the highest god; it was the model of the perfect drum, but it became such a drum only after being associated with Sanskrit. It was a highly refined instrument with a well-structured grammar and complex language, but it was a drum, and drums were also strongly linked to tribal life and non-Vedic cultures (Bahattacharya 1999; Hart 1975) – the *sāman* chant did not make use of *tālas* and drums such as the *dundubhi* were occasionally used in ritual – thus it needed to be linked to Sanskrit in order to be introduced into the new Brahmanical world and to fit in with the new model of kingship which was developing in the centuries following the fall of the Maurya empire. Providing it with a myth of origin and linking it to Sanskrit and Brahmanical culture, the *Natyaśāstra* sanctioned the raising of the *mṛdaṅga* to the highest status. According to the treatise, these highly refined drums not only spoke Sanskrit but their music was equal to Vedic recitation (Natyaśāstra 33, 23–28). The *trisāma*, for instance, a purely instrumental composition (Ramanathan 1999: 354–355) corresponding to *sāman* chanting, was played by drums at the beginning of the drama to welcome the gods, 'as the syllable *Om* is pronounced at the beginning of the four Vedas' (*Natyaśāstra* 33, 221–226). The *Natyaśāstra* represents the culmination of a process of refinement, sacralization and incorporation of tribal and non-Vedic art forms in the context of Vedic culture, and the ultimate establishment of the *mṛdaṅga* as main drum. The treatise itself claims that theatre developed from the Vedas and popular festivals such as Indra's Flagstaff (Raghavan 1956; Bansat-Boudon 1992a), and according to Paulose 'Bharata refined the crude stage, confined it to well-built halls and prescribed a grammar for performance. Just like Panini refined the Sanskrit language from various vernacular languages (Prakrits), Bharata culled out from popular forms an elegant performing style' (2014).[12]

Tribal gods and cults had been incorporated into the Brahmanical world through the elaboration of new mythologies which linked them to Vedic deities, and similarly tribal and folk performing arts were polished, refined and structured in the framework of a strong grammar in order to be fit for the new political and social order. Thus drums, which were highly representative of tribal culture, were introduced into the Brahmanical world and by the time of the *Natyaśāstra*, one of them, the *mṛdaṅga*, had been reshaped and elevated as the main one, raised to the highest status and legitimated through its association with Sanskrit.

The *mṛdaṅga* and the Sanskrit language were so intimately linked that they underwent a very similar process of evolution. According to Pollock, Sanskrit inscriptions (*praśasti* or praise poems) eulogizing royal elites – which start to appear at the beginning of the 1st millennium inscribed on rock faces, pillars, monuments and copper-plates – together with *kāvya* (written literature), *mahākāvya* (courtly epic) and *nāṭaka* (epic drama), are evidence of the inauguration of a new cultural formation in which Sanskrit had become the language for the public literary expression of political will. Indeed, 'previous to this Sanskrit culture appears to have been restricted to the domain of liturgy and the knowledge for its analysis' (Pollock 1998: 10), while the languages used for the inscriptions were almost exclusively Middle-Indic dialects, called Prakrit. Pollock argues that the spread of political Sanskrit from North India happened with extraordinary speed and over a vast space including, with a striking simultaneity, not only the Indian subcontinent but also Burma, Thailand, Cambodia, Laos, Vietnam, Malaysia and Indonesia. In a millennium, extending from the 2nd up to the 12th century, it produced a globalized cultural formation characterized by a homogeneous political language of poetry in Sanskrit along with a range of other cultural and political practices, such as temple-building or city planning, which the elites could perceive to be part of a common Sanskrit culture. However, around the beginning of the 2nd millennium, throughout South Asia, the Sanskrit cosmopolis came to an end and writers turned to the use of vernaculars for literary and political expression. It was not only a shift of language but the adaptation of a transregional code into a regional one. Indeed, writers appropriated a Sanskrit aesthetic and a range of literary models into their languages and even produced new versions of the Sanskrit epics re-localizing them in their regions. According to Pollock, to understand this process, which is the most important cultural change in the medieval world, it is necessary to look at the role of the court and the presence of a new cultural logic where the aesthetic was central, or to consider 'some new self-fashioning through the vernacular distinction of persons and places' (Pollock 1998: 32), more than to local religious movements against Brahmanism as is most often affirmed.

The evolution of the *mṛdaṅga* followed the same pattern as political Sanskrit; iconographic and literary evidence clearly shows that it was the main drum in royal courts almost everywhere in India where Sanskrit was adopted as cosmopolitan language, and also in South-East Asia either in court ensembles or accompanying the dance of Śiva. Even the diffusion of regional varieties of *mṛdaṅga*-type barrel drums paralleled the spread of the vernaculars described by Pollock. In the process of making the *mārga* (global) *deśī* (local), the *mṛdaṅga*, the cosmopolitan drum, became the model which inspired the creation of new drums having a local character but incorporating symbolic, linguistic and organological elements of it. The *mṛdaṅga*, like Sanskrit, represented the way (*mārga*) to be followed (Pollock 1998: 21), for the sophistication of its language and grammar and its capability to express minute emotions, and at the same time indicated a precise heritage strictly connected to court aesthetics and culture; it was the archetype of the perfect Hindu royal drum.

While the ancient *mṛdaṅga* set was the refined version of tribal and folk drums, the new *mṛdaṅga* was a single barrel drum whose features changed according to the different regions which had incorporated the heritage and the language of the ancient one. In other words, while the ancient *mṛdaṅga* had been raised to the highest status by being associated with the Sanskrit, vernacular drums had been elevated to royal status through the appropriation of the heritage and the main aspects of the ancient *mṛdaṅga*. In this passage the drum was no longer a precise instrument but a symbol encapsulated in the name *mṛdaṅga*, and the name *mṛdaṅga* itself became a seal of purity and tradition, a means of Sanskritization.

The term Sanskritization was introduced by the anthropologist Srinivas in the context of a study on the tribal population of the Croogs of South India, to describe a process by which lower castes gradually adopted characteristics of higher-caste Sanskritic culture in order to raise their social status (Srinivas 1956).[13] Over the course of time the term has assumed different meanings (Babiracki 1991; Srinivas 1956; Staal 1963). I adopt it here – concerning the relationship of Sanskrit with the *mṛdaṅga* – to indicate a process of synthesis and incorporation of models of a dominating culture into those of an emerging one as a procedure of legitimation.[14] A clear representation of this process is provided by a victorious king taking the royal insignia and the sovereign apparatus of the defeated enemy as main booty since they incorporate his power: they are not empty symbols but concrete embodiments of power. There are several instances of this praxis, the most extreme being explained by Hart, who writes that, according to Sangam literature, the flesh of the slain king was ritually cooked and eaten by the winner in order to control and subdue the power unleashed on the death of his rival (Hart 1975: 88). In other cases, the victorious king took the royal drum of the defeated king – a procedure which was practised even by Mughals as explained by literary sources and shown by miniature paintings (Wade 1998). The same practice is also shown by several Indian myths – like the already examined ones relating to the creation of the *mṛdaṅga* by Śiva – and images where a god or a goddess, such as Śiva or Durga, kills a demon in order to control his energy and utilizes it to give birth to and nurture a new cycle. To cook the flesh of a defeated enemy, to adopt the royal symbols and to absorb some crucial aspects of the culture of a decaying kingdom means to subdue them, to tame them and to legitimize, through them, a newly established political order. While an emerging empire such as that of the Guptas had to incorporate numerous cultures, cults and languages – since it had to control numerous different people – and to create a symbol capable of synthesizing all of them and, at the same time, of representing a new established power, the small regional kingdoms re-emerging from the fall of the Gupta empire reinterpreted its main symbols and power emblems in their own way as means of legitimation. Thus Sanskrit and the *mṛdaṅga*, which under the Guptas were emblematic of kingship and royal power, were adopted by the new dynasties of kings to legitimize their reigns. The inclusion of Sanskrit metaphors and images into regional poetry and the medieval vernacular versions of the Sanskrit epics are instances of a process of incorporation and legitimation.

Similarly, the regional drums replacing the ancient *mṛdaṅga* but taking its name are clear instances of new kings asserting their power and legitimizing it by identifying their drums with the ancient symbol of power through its name, *mṛdaṅga*.

The expedient of adopting a name intended as the 'soul' of something is perfectly in line with the Indian tradition where the name not only represents but is the intrinsic deepest nature of the named (Gonda 1963; Woodroffe 1994). Thus, to give a name means to attribute a quality, a soul. This view explains and justifies theoretically the continuity of the tradition of the *mṛdaṅga*, in spite of its changing body: the name *mṛdaṅga* includes and indicates the qualities and the powers of the ideal royal drum, rather than referring to the specific features of its body.

The global–local dichotomy has been described and defined by music treatises through the terms *mārga* and *deśī* and, interestingly, the same terminology is adopted in texts on Sanskrit literature (Pollock 1998). *Mārga* indicated the structured ancient ritual tradition, while *deśī* indicated the regional patterns which emerged during the second half of the 1st century (Nijenhuis 1974; Pollock 2006; Rowell 1998; Sanyal and Widdess 2004). As pointed out by Lath, the *Bṛhaddeśī* (7th–8th century C.E.), the first musicological text to employ the terms, described *deśī* music as 'that which women, children, cowherds and kings sing out of love and pleasure in their own regions' (Lath 1988: 45), and specified that the *deśī* was called *mārga* when it was structured through *ālāpa*, and the other sections included in *mārga* music. Thus, according to Matanga, *deśī* was the music of both peasants and kings and had a twofold path: it was *deśī* when it was played without precise rules and it became *mārga* when it was bound to a well-defined structure and musical theory (Lath 1988). However, the definition of these words changed over time; later treatises such as the *Saṅgītaratnākara* (13th century) or the *Saṅgīta Darpaṇa* (15th century) provided explanation of the terms based on a spiritual interpretation, and used *mārga* to mean the music leading to liberation and *deśī* to mean the vernacular music of the various regions (Coomaraswamy 2004; Greig 1987; Pande 1996; Sanyal and Widdess 2004). By mid-17th century Mughal India, the term *mārga* had taken on several meanings implying divinity and universality, associations with an imagined South as origin of the tradition, association with Sanskrit and Sanskrit treatises on music, with antiquity, authenticity, authority and alignment of music with theory. *Deśī*, by contrast, had become representative of the local context of the North, the current practice of musicians and with modernity and newness (Brown 2003; Bush 2010).

The *dhrupad*, the most valued style of music of the Mughal period provides interesting evidence of the Sanskritization of a regional musical form. Indeed, it had a *deśī* origin but, since it had absorbed the main features of the earlier forms, was soon raised to the status of *mārga* music (Sanyal and Widdess 2004: 47), and, to further reinforce its position, outstanding masters such as Nayak Bakhshu were supposed to have contributed to its creation.

The emergence of the *pakhāvaj* as main drum and its incorporation into the complete cluster of ideas associated with the ancient *mṛdaṅga* – in one word its heritage – provide further evidence for the process of making the *deśī mārga*. As already argued, although highly esteemed by the Mughal noblemen for its masculine voice conceived as representative of their ideal heroic character, the *pakhāvaj* was a *deśī* instrument played by specialized groups of professionals. In order for it to be officially sanctioned as the main Indian drum[15] of the period, the *deśī pakhāvaj* was identified with the *mārga mṛdaṅga*, since the name *mṛdaṅga* meant antiquity and purity of tradition. The necessity to establish this connection – in the Mughal period – between a vernacular instrument and the most representative drum of the Hindus can be explained by the fact that, even in that cultural epoch, processes of Sanskritization were at work, involving the discovering of ancient Indian history and culture (Butler Schofield 2010; Bush 2004; Truschke 2012). According to Brown, aspects emphasized by musical treatises of the period such as – among others – the location of a golden age in the past, in Sanskrit and in the South, and the re-connection of contemporary practice with that of the Sanskritic past, are clear markers of an ongoing process of Sanskritization (Butler Schofield 2010: 495).

The Sanskritization of the *pakhāvaj* clearly explains why contemporary *pakhāvaj* players trace their instruments back to ancient India, and provides an explanation for the interesting – although often partial and simplistic – information that they report. The Mughal period can be identified as the cradle of the *pakhāvaj* – the new *mṛdaṅga* of Northern India – and its reconstructed heritage. Indeed, even though based on ancient Sanskritic sources, such a heritage derived from the Mughal elites' interpretation of the ancient Indian past. Their view was obviously marked by the cultural trends of their period and the specific socio-historical context. In other words, the *pakhāvaj* inherited the heritage of the ancient *mṛdaṅga* as the Mughal elites perceived it, and their interpretation constituted the root of the new tradition and established new links with the ancient past. An obvious sign that the information provided by the contemporary players comes from the Mughal period is that, as already noted, almost all of them, agreeing with the view of the Mughal elite, consider the *pakhāvaj* as a purely masculine and heroic instrument, while in ancient India the *mṛdaṅga* was conceived as a 'hermaphrodite' instrument including both masculine and feminine aspects (see Chapter 5, p. 80).

Interestingly, during almost the same period, the *pakhāvaj* went through a parallel process of Sanskritization, but while the first Sanskritization had a political character – since it recognized the drum as a courtly warrior instrument – the second one was markedly religious. Indeed, the *pakhāvaj* was also adopted by Vaiṣṇava sects worshipping their god as a King-God. An example of this is the Puṣṭimārg of Vallabhācarya, where again it was traced back to the ancient *mṛdaṅga*, although in this case connected to its function of symbolizing the highest deity. Thus the *pakhāvaj* absorbed – in its new contexts – the two functions of the ancient *mṛdaṅga*, becoming a symbol of both sacred and secular power.

The process of Sanskritization involved not only music but also literature and languages. The veneration and imitation of Sanskrit also brought a remarkable innovation in the development of Brajbhasha poetry as supraregional literary language in 16th and 17th century India (Bush 2004). Indeed, Brajbhasha, the typical language of the Braj area of North-Western India, now recognized as 'the language of the gods', a designation which before had always been used for Sanskrit, absorbed several images from Sanskrit literature (Bush 2010).

The 19th century was another crucial period in this process of continuous changes. A quite important phenomenon was the so called Indian Renaissance, when Indian nationalists – who intended to contrast the British interpretation of India's history – reconnected, once again, their culture to the ancient golden age of the glorious Indian empires and to Brahmanism (Thapar 1978).[16] Music, identified as one of the most important features of Indian culture and Hindu spirituality, was one of the main points in the agenda of the nationalist movement; conceived as a means to attain liberation, it was traced back to the *Sāma veda* and linked to the Vaiṣṇava *bhakta* cults (Bakhle 2005; Jones 2014). While the instruments played by Muslim musicians underwent a process of Sanskritization which could allow them to be included into the newly fashioned world of Hindu/Indian 'classical' music (Bakhle 2005), the *pakhāvaj*, which had already been identified with the ancient *mṛdaṅga* in the Mughal period and was linked to divine kingship, Vaiṣṇava cults and saints, was immediately included as a Hindu instrument with spiritual qualities.

Contrasting with the 19th century *pakhāvaj* players and founders of the schools such as Kudau Singh and Nana Panse, who were considered as almost legendary figures with a high spiritual profile, contemporary *pakhāvaj* players, although conscious of the important role attributed to the *pakhāvaj* in the past, hold the low status of accompanists in the musical society of the present day (see Chapter 3).

In this ever-changing scenario generated by the local–global dichotomy, or *deśī mārga*, instability and relativity appear as the stable aspects of a continuous flow of changes and re-elaborations of ideas and forms.

Notes

1 Dick even notes that according to the *Saṃgītaratnākara* the body of the *mardala* was slightly waisted while the commentators defined it as a barrel drum (Dick 1984d: 695).
2 The Sanskrit version of the name *miḻāvu* or *muḻāvu* is *murava* or *muraja* (Raghavan 1955). Thus, even the name brings us back to the *mṛdaṅga*.
3 Picture, available at: https://collections.vam.ac.uk/item/O9302/akbar-painting-kesav-kalan/ (Accessed 21 July 2016).
4 The association of the *dholak*, *dhol* and *khanjari* to the low-status world was such that some *dhādhis* took up higher-prestige instruments such as the *pakhāvaj* to raise their status and eventually became accompanists to the higher-prestige *qawwāls* (Brown 2003).
5 Picture, available at: http://collections.vam.ac.uk/item/O405413/painting-unknown/ (Accessed 21 July 2016).

6 Picture, available at: http://collections.vam.ac.uk/item/O88043/painting-unknown/ (Accessed 21 July 2016).

7 A few Mughal miniatures portray a group of women musicians, including a *pakhāvajī*, playing for male dancers in the women's quarters.

8 Matthias-Gert Wegner personal communication, 4 July 2018.

9 The most famous association of drum and Sanskrit was established by the *Maheśvara Sūtras*. These aphorisms (*sūtras*), found at the commencement of the Pāṇini's *Aṣṭādhyāy* (6th–4th century B.C.E.), the authoritative treatise on Sanskrit, are said to have been produced by the drum strokes of the *damaru*, the hour-glass drum shaken by Śiva at the end of his furious (*tāṇḍava*) dance (Danielou 1987; Deshpande 1997; Shulman 2005), the same dance which he performs to the rhythm of the *mṛdaṅga*. Śiva, the King-God, had invented Sanskrit and the *mṛdaṅga* and both were symbols of earthly kingship. However, the association of drums and words was not new even in the Vedic texts since, as argued by Malamoud, the rhythm produced by the stones pressing of the Soma stems over the earth drum (*bhumi-dundubhi*) were already associated with the recitation of hymns in the *Śatapatha Brāhmaṇa* (Malamoud 2005).

10 According to the *Natyaśāstra* (33: 40), the *mṛdaṅga* produces 16 letters of the devanāgarī alphabet – k, kh, g, ṭ, ṭh, ḍ, ṇ or dh, t, th, dh, m or ya, r, l and h – each one of which may be combined with the various vowels.

11 The association of drum strokes with letters is also strongly emphasized by the Kashmiri philosopher Abhinavagupta, according to whom drums were tuned to a definite pitch (*svara*) in order to minimize their syllabic structure (Ramanathan 1999: 44).

12 Text, available at: http://kgpaulose.info/index.php/from-the-press/12-articles/41-theatre-classical-and-popular (Accessed 21 July 2016).

13 This is for instance the case of the *pakhāvaj* players of the Vārkarī sect who started studying the repertoire of the classical *dhrupad pakhāvaj* in order to raise the status of their style, labeled as vernacular, and their own social status (Jones 2009).

14 The term Sankritization is adequate for this interpretation since classical Sanskrit itself, as its history shows, evolved from a dialect of the old Indo-Aryan and included elements of Prakrit languages (Staal 1963: 271).

15 The *naqqara* was already a symbol of power for Muslim rulers. It was one of the Mughal emblems of royalty and the defeated king had to give his drum to the winner as a sign of defeat (Wade 1998; Tingey 1994).

16 This process has been spoken of as classicization instead of Sanskritization since it was mostly inspired by the concept of classical music imported by the British (Bakhle 2005; Jones 2009; Subramaniam 2006a).

7 The Nathdwara *gharānā*

Playing the *pakhāvaj* for Nāthjī

In the previous two chapters, drawing on iconographic and textual sources, I have analysed the historical and organological evolution of the ancient *mṛdaṅga*, the drum of the King-God, until its identification in the Mughal era with the vernacular *pakhāvaj*. I have argued that, notwithstanding the significant changes the body of the drum had gone through during the first half of the 2nd millennium, the name *mṛdaṅga* still stood as an emblem of kingship and the supreme gods, and that various Vaiṣṇava sects had adopted different vernacular versions of it as a ritual drum to worship the King-God Kṛṣṇa. In this chapter I will focus on the Puṣṭimārg, one of the most important of such sects. The study of the Puṣṭimārg is particularly interesting since it allows the researcher to analyse the role of music in worship and the function of the *pakhāvaj* in a cult based on a King-God. At the same time, it provides important information on the recent history and development of the *pakhāvaj* in general. Furthermore, it sheds light on the analysis of the solo recital presented in Chapter 9.

Vallabhācarya and the Puṣṭimārg

According to various sectarian and non-sectarian historical sources, Vallabha, the son of Telegu Brahmin parents, was born in 1479 in a forest near to the modern city of Raipur and received his education studying Sanskrit, the Vedas and their auxiliaries in Benares (Gaston 1997: 44; Saha 2007: 303; Tapasyananda 2004: 1). When he was 11, after his father passed away, he undertook a pilgrimage of the whole of India which he later repeated twice more. There are few historical records of Vallabha's life while the literature of the sect records numerous miraculous phenomena associated with him. During his second pilgrimage, while travelling in Kṛṣṇa's childhood home of Gokul, located in Braj, Vallabha received, from Kṛṣṇa himself, the *Brahmasambandha mantra* (*Śrī Kṛṣṇaśaraṇam mama*, Lord Kṛṣṇa is my refuge) – a sacred formula which purifies devotees and makes them fit to pursue a devotional path – together with the instruction to administer it. He was also told by Kṛṣṇa that the icon on Mount Govardhan worshipped by local residents under the name of Devadamana was his *svarūpa*,[1] the form where he resides, and as such should be venerated. Vallabha renamed it Govardhananāthjī, established a shrine and reorganized the rituals performed by the local communities according to his view (Saha 2007: 304). The first person initiated to the new faith was Dāmodara Dāsa, Vallabha's close companion, and this event is generally regarded as the founding of the sect.

In the new form of religiosity established by Vallabha the devotee would live a householder's life based on devotion to the Supreme Lord Kṛṣṇa and purified by his divine grace (*puṣṭi*) (Saha 2007). The complete reliance on Kṛṣṇa's grace explains why Vallabha's community came to be known as Puṣṭimārg, or the Path of Grace. He affirmed that all the members of the Puṣṭimārg had to establish a personal relationship with Kṛṣṇa for their spiritual growth (Saha 2006) and proposed that the relationship between the god and his devotee was to be maintained through a process called service, or *sevā*, entailing the dedication of one's material wealth to Kṛṣṇa and the worship of his images. It had to be performed as a spontaneous expression of love for him if one wanted to experience the joy associated with his boundless grace.

When Vallabha died in 1531 the leadership of the Puṣṭimārg community, which consisted of both men and women from diverse social and economic backgrounds, fell to Vallabha's elder son Gopīnāth (1512–1543), who was soon succeeded by his younger brother Viṭṭhalnāth (1515–1585). Viṭṭhalnāth established the major geographical centers and temples of the new religion at Govardhan and Gokul, spread its doctrine and interpreted it to the rulers and kings of the time, thereby increasing the wealth and prestige of the sect. He concentrated the leadership in the hands of his seven male descendants and this led to the formation of the 'Seven Houses' of the Puṣṭimārg which were based upon the principle of male primogeniture (Ho 2006: 108; Saha 2006: 227). They inherited the exclusive right to initiate disciples into the community and were given custody over various images of Kṛṣṇa. The most important of these, Nāthjī, was entrusted to Viṭṭhalnāth's eldest son, who was the head of the sect designated as Tilkayāt. Viṭṭhalnāth's frequent association with the Mughal and Rajput aristocracy led him to design the major temples of the sect as palaces, which he called *havelīs*, named after the Rajasthani princely palaces. Decorated with exquisite paintings, enriched with gold and silver accoutrements of the deity, and providing an atmosphere similar to the secular palaces of Rajput princes, the *havelīs* were intended to communicate the regal splendour of the deity and at the same time the aristocratic position of the other ruling leaders of the lineage who were, indeed, called Gosvāmīs (lord of the cows) or Mahārājas (Great King). Another important aspect of Viṭṭhalnāth's legacy was the institutionalization of the practice of *sevā* and the making of it a royal ritual including visual arts, music and culinary arts (Ho 2006: 79).

A further important contribution to the development of the sect and its cult was provided by Gokulnāth (1551–1640), Viṭṭhalnāth's fourth son. He was a leader, proselytizer and prolific writer, and he was the one who chose the local language (Brajbhasha) as the principal mode of religious instruction, and crystallized through his writings the practice, style and devotion of the sect. Indeed, while Vallabha, Gopīnath and Viṭṭhalnāth had written their theological treatises in Sanskrit, Gokulnāth started regularly instructing his followers in the vernacular Brajbhasha, a language which had already been adopted by the eight major poets (*aṣṭachāp*) of the sect because it enabled the devotees to understand the songs (Gaston 1997: 56).

The religious and social influence of the sect increased significantly during the 16th century in the Braj area – and in Gujarat, where it was supported by wealthy merchants – to the point that the Mughal emperors issued a series of edicts assuring to it the perpetual property of the villages around Govardhan and Gokul (Ho 2006: 78; Richardson 1979: 36; Saha 2006: 228). However, the political instability of the Braj area, and the iconoclastic zeal of the Emperor Aurangzeb (1658–1707) who banned the worship of Kṛṣṇa in Mathura and threatened to destroy the temples in 1668 (Gaston 1997: 50), forced the community to move, along with the image of Nāthjī, to Rajasthan where it took shelter under the Rajput kings. In 1672, the then king of Mewar, Rāj Siṃh, granted to the Tilkayāt a fiefdom, and the icon of Nāthjī was installed in a temple (*havelī*) in a town which was renamed Nathdwara, literally the gateway (*dwārā*) of the lord (*nāth*) (Gaston 1997: 51; Saha 2006: 228). The relationship of the sect with the Mewar royal house was fruitful for both sides and durable, since it lasted at least until the 19th century.

The organization of the sect and the temple went through significant changes after independence. Indeed, in 1959, with the so called Nathdwara Temple Act – which is still in force – the Rajasthan government entered into the temple's administration with the right to appoint members to the Puṣṭimārg board from all over the country and to control the valuables and the properties of the temple. Significant new changes have been continuing over the last few decades, since the spread of members of the sect throughout the world has led to the building of new temples, while new technologies and the internet have provided the Gosvāmīs with new ways of promoting their religion and personal work. It was on YouTube that I came across several videos of the solo *pakhāvaj* recitals that Wagdish Gosvāmī and Harirai Gosvāmī had uploaded on their channel,[2] and again through their site that I have been able to contact them and their father, Kalianray Mahārāja, leader of the second house of Nathdwara.

Śrī Nāthjī, the King-God and his worship

Situated in southern Rajasthan, a few miles away from Udaipur, the town of Nathdwara hosts the temple (*havelī*) of Nāthjī where the most important *svarūpa* of Puṣṭimārg is enshrined. It represents Kṛṣṇa at the age of 7, with his left arm raised above his head in the act of lifting Mount Govardhan

(*Govardhandharan*) to protect the denizen of Braj from a storm sent by Indra, and his right hand closed in a fist and resting on his hip. Indeed, the icon is based on the myth according to which Kṛṣṇa challenged and defeated the Vedic king of gods Indra.[3]

Made from a large black stone of about 137 cm in height (Ambalal 1987: 49), the idol has several animals – two cows, a snake, a lion, two peacocks and a parrot – and a few human figures, representing the inhabitants of Mount Govardhan, engraved on it.[4] The icon rests on a lion throne (*simhāsana*) placed on a cloth with the same name, flanked on either side by a kind of long round pillow called *takiya*. As has already been noted, it is not a symbol of the god but his very being; it is a *svarūpa*, a form of the living deity. This is also a reason why in Puṣṭimārg there are no temples as such but *havelīs*, or palaces, in which he resides in his several forms corresponding to his various *svarūpas*. The term *havelī* indicates the traditional palaces of the princes of Rajasthan, and the *havelī* of Nāthjī at Nathdwara is the court of a divine child-king cowherd who is worshipped and treated according to royal etiquette. The entire activity of the palace and the town revolves around his daily routine marked by eight main moments (*darśana* – from the Sanskrit verbal root *dṛś*, to see), in which he offers himself to the sight of his devotees and, at the same time, blesses them with his sight. He is offered sumptuous dishes, fine and rich clothes, and the compositions of the *aṣṭachāp* are played by an ensemble including singer, *tampūrā* or harmonium, *sārangi*, *pakhāvaj* and cymbals (*jhānjh*).[5]

As already noted, this procedure of worship was institutionalized by Viṭṭhalnāth who thought it necessary to evolve the austere form of worship established by his father – Vallabha at first used to offer cooked grains to the deity and later included the offering of music (*kīrtans*) by Kumbhandās – into something much more elaborate and even lavish, which could be better followed and understood by his contemporaries.[6] Viṭṭhalnāth centred the worship on music (*rāga*) and food (*bhoga*) offerings, and emphasized the importance of dressing the King-God richly and adorning him with precious jewels and gems (*śṛingāra*). This procedure of worship was intended to communicate to the devotee and the other kings that Śrī Nāthjī was at the same time an earthly king and a god, a King-God (Richardson 1979: 26).

The main aim of worship through service (*sevā*) is to arouse a particular emotion or state of mind (*rasa*) in the devotee, with the most important *rasa* being love for God, or devotion (*bhakti*). According to Vaiṣṇava systems, the service may be done in three forms, with body (*kāyika*), with wealth (*vittaja*) or with mind (*mānasa*); in Vallabha's sect the service with body and wealth has taken the form of serving the god in images, since they are conceived as his very being. God reveals himself in the form of the icon to receive the loving adoration of his devotees, and the worship offered to him is not symbolic but a real loving care for the most honoured and beloved one. Although the main *svarūpa* of Nāthjī is the child-raising Mount Govardhan, many other aspects or events of the life of Kṛṣṇa are recalled in songs and artistic representations produced at Nathdwara. The most common depict him playing the flute surrounded by his lovers (*gopīs*) in the groves of Vrindavan, with his friends or dancing a victory dance on the serpent Kāliya. They are meant to remind the devotee that he has to be approached and worshipped with different emotions. Kṛṣṇa as child (Bāla Kṛṣṇa) and Kṛṣṇa the youth require the devotee to approach with the emotional attitude of the mother Devaki and the stepmother Yaśodā, or the lover Rādhā, respectively. Both forms of devotion are based on love, but the one requires the loving affection of a mother for her child (*vātsalya*), while the other involves the erotic and romantic love (*śṛingāra*) for the lover. The aspect of Kṛṣṇa as a child is the most popular object of love and service in the Puṣṭimārg and parental love and devotion (*vātsalya*) is the most favoured;[7] in Nathdwara most of the worship rituals centre on Kṛṣṇa's needs and the main priest (*mukhiyā*), acting on behalf of the devotee, mimics the daily tasks of Yaśodā (Gaston 1997: 54; Tapasyananda 2004: 34).

An extremely interesting and unique aspect of the Puṣṭimārg *sevā* highlighted by Ho (2006: 188) is that, while most other sects propose the withdrawal of the senses from the world, it involves all the senses and emotions in full force in order to obtain *nirodha,* liberation. The world of Kṛṣṇa, who is the manifestation of the entire spectrum of emotions and its cause, has to be lived with the senses at their major capability, including sex, which he enjoys with his many lovers (*gopīs*). He is a King-God and his world, which is an expression of fully lived life and fully activated senses, brings to mind the model of ancient kingship which he represents as an incarnation of Viṣṇu. Similarly, the circle of Mahārājas, who are vassals of the paramount lordship represented by Nāthjī, recalls the ancient *māṇḍala* of kings proposed by the *Arthaśāstra,* in which subordinated kings were just called Mahārājas (see Chapter 5, p. 81) and, at the same time, it recalls the hierarchical organization of the Mughal empire. Another interesting fact which has to be noted – again connected with kingship and court culture – is that the adoption of Brajbhasha as the main poetical language and substitute for Sanskrit, as well as the association of the *pakhāvaj* with Mughal courts and with the court of Nāthjī, happened during the same period. The poetic language adopted by poets in the court of the emperor resounded also in the court of the King-God, and the sound of the drum which was played for the kings and nobles resounded for the king of the universe too. As has already been noted, the sound of the *pakhāvaj* is considered as the sonic form of Viṣṇu, hence of Kṛṣṇa (see Chapter 3, p. 44 and Chapter 5, pp. 89–90), and the instrument plays, or at least played, an important role in the ritual as is demonstrated by the presence of eight different *pakhāwajs* in the temple. *Meghnād,* the *pakhāvaj* thundering like a rain cloud (*megh*), is the most important and venerated among them. It is a festival instrument and, according to Purushottam Das, it was played together with the other instruments during *Rājabhoga darśana,* when Śrī Nāthjī was marked with a *tilak* on his forehead. Measuring two feet in circumference, with the right- and left-hand heads of 12 and 14 fingers respectively, it is said to have been donated by a devotee who had looted it from a Mughal camp (Gaston 1997: 110).

The role of music and aesthetics in the cult of Puṣṭimārg

The *Bhāgavata Purāṇa* (8th–10th century C.E.) lists listening to (*śravanam*) and singing the praises of the lord (*kīrtanam*) as the first and the second fastest methods for attaining liberation, and the worship and the service of an icon (*arcanam*) as the fourth (Ho 2006: 155; Thielemann 1999).[8] Puṣṭimārg attributes the highest efficacy to worship (*arcanam*) and then lists singing the praises of the lord (*kīrtanam*), but always associates the two practices. Indeed, music (*rāga*), together with food (*bhoga*) and ornamentation (*śṛingāra*), is a constant element of ritual service (*sevā*). The presence of these elements in worship is exoterically justified by the fact that Nāthjī takes pleasure in the finest aspects of life and the best quality items, and esoterically explained by the fact that he is considered a perennial enjoyer (*bhogi*) of pleasure whose appetite is insatiable (Ho 2006: 155). Both the interpretations explain the aesthetic approach of the *sevā* which involves all the senses through the offering of food, material objects, music and the arousing of emotions in the devotee by listening to the stories of the god and by taking care of him with extreme love.

The deep understanding and utilization of aesthetics in Puṣṭimārg *sevā* and the association of specific *rāgas* with songs suggests a connection with the Sanskrit poem *Gīta Govinda* composed by Jayadeva (12th century CE) (Ho 2006). They also suggest the influence of classical aesthetics – from the *Nāṭyaśāstra* to Abhinavagupta – which both Vallabhācārya and Viṭṭhalnāth were knowledgeable about, as clearly shown by their writings on the experience of Kṛṣṇa and *rasa* (Ho 2006; Redington 1990). All the elements present in the ritual are invested with feelings – including poetry and music which are inherently filled with emotions (*rasa*) – by establishing relations with episodes of Kṛṣṇa's life or associating each element to him with the aid of imagination. While offering sweets to Kṛṣṇa the devotee enjoys imagining his enjoyment; while imagining the passionate relationship of Kṛṣṇa with a girlfriend (*gopī*), the doer of *sevā* visualizes himself/herself as that girlfriend since the more one is able to imagine that world the nearer one is to it. Indeed, *gopīs* are the primary model of imitation in general Vaiṣṇava and Puṣṭimārg theology in particular (Krishnakinkari 2012: 19). Becoming Kṛṣṇa's companion and lover the devotee is able to 'enjoy' Kṛṣṇa; it is the highest goal of the followers of the sect who aim at *nirodha*, the state of forgetfulness of the world and complete addiction to Kṛṣṇa.[9]

The ritual of *sevā* by means of objects, acts and imagination creates emotional states which are meant to replicate the divine world of Braj in the social-historical reality in which the service takes place. Continuous practice gradually leads the devotee to transcend the disjunction of the two realities and, eventually, to attain the state of *nirodha* where he/she sees everything as Kṛṣṇa (Ho 2006; Redington 1990). The devotees perform *sevā* in order to participate in the divine games (*līlā*) of Kṛṣṇa; thinking of what Kṛṣṇa would play, eat and dress today they recreate the world of the divine Braj on a daily basis. The same activities take place whether in one's home or at a temple, but whereas the devotee generally performs service alone, a retinue of *sevāks* (those who serve) perform the worship in the temple according to a liturgy scheduled on the basis of the time of the day, season of the year and type of divine play. *Kīrtans*, based on the same time principles, following an established set of *rāgas* and *tālas*, and detailing the precise timing of the activities of the eternal world punctuates every moment of the liturgy, and as highlighted by Ho, 'temple singers avow that time is accurately shown in *rāga* because from the text alone, it may not always be clear which meal Kṛṣṇa is taking, and when' (Ho 2009: 36).

Kīrtans range from short to extensive poems. Short poems (*pada*) may intend to create a moment of rapture or yearning, or to present brief genealogies of the Vallabha lineage. They may be intensely charged with emotion and feelings or provide detailed descriptions of a major festival. Singing and listening to the qualities of the divine (*śravanam*) are the two complementary parts of *sevā* since, as Vallabha himself explains, sounds and songs elevate mundane actions to a divine level: 'renounce attachment to other activities, perform Kṛṣṇa's service, and listen to and sing his praises with love; from this the seed of devotion will be augmented' (Ho 2006: 184). Music activates the imagination of the devotees while they perform *sevā* and helps them to participate in the life of the cosmic world of Kṛṣṇa. It gives presence to and enlivens the cosmic moment in its full emotional power. Vallabhācarya elaborates a theology for singing song in service affirming that together they bring about the state of liberation in this lifetime (*nirodha*).

It has to be noted, however, that, although it is still considered as a spiritual path by leaders of the sect such as Gokulotsav Mahārāja (*The Hindu* 3 September 2009), the importance of music in worship has declined over the last few decades and, consequently, the job of temple musician (*kīrtankar*) at Nathdwara has almost lost its role (Gaston 1997: 185). Furthermore, due to a decline in the living conditions afforded to musicians, some of them have even become reluctant to teach their art to their children. The dwindling of interest for the hereditary profession already reported at the end of the 1970s by Jindel (1976: 162) is confirmed by Verdia who wrote that at the beginning of the 1980s musicians were full-time employees but, like other service (*sevā*) providers, they were paid exclusively in kind, most usually through food offerings (*prasāda*). He commented on the status of the temple musicians writing that, while art has been patronized by the temple, musicians have not been honoured properly, and thus they need to engage in other activities, usually concerned with some aspect of the temple, to increase their incomes (Verdia 1982: 94). In line with Verdia, Gaston reports that musicians received *prasāda* as remuneration for their service and, to increase the small amount of cash they received from the temple, they used to keep part of the food offering for themselves and sell the rest (Gaston 1997: 176).

Thus, the depth and theoretical subtleties of the aesthetic approach contrast with the concrete living situation of the musicians who, notwithstanding their important role in the daily ritual activities, feel that they are not adequately respected and remunerated for their work, with the result that very few of the younger generation of temple musicians are now ready to continue with the tradition. Indeed, although some of them, such as Keshav Kumavat – Prakash Kumavat's son – know many songs in the repertoire and play the *pakhāvaj* proficiently, presently, almost exclusively elderly musicians play regularly as service (*sevā*). However, *havelī saṅgīt* may be easily heard in the markets near the temple, where numerous shops play loud recordings of the octogenarian Vitthaldas Bapodara and the very few other musicians who are striving to keep the tradition of Puṣṭimārg *kīrtan* alive.

The family of Purushottam Das

The community of musicians at Nathdwara is composed of three different groups which can be distinguished according to the place in which they perform: the band of the Tilkayāt's personal bodyguard, which plays outside the temple, the musicians playing in the *naqqārkhāna*, and the *kīrtankars*, who play inside the temple.

The band of the Tilkayāt's personal bodyguard performs during ceremonial occasions and includes 16 musicians who play trumpet, clarinet, euphonium, alto-horn, circle bass, large and small tubas, a large bass drum and kettledrums (Gaston 1997: 149).

The musicians of the *naqqārkhāna*, which is located above the main gate of the temple, play daily at regular intervals to announce *darśana* and continue until it is closed; the ensemble includes five *shahnāī* players, and three drummers who play *naqqāra*, *dhumsa* and *ḍhol*. These musicians learn the music and inherit their post from their fathers (Gaston 1997: 149).

The *kīrtankars* are the most numerous and important of the three since they play in the innermost part of the temple, in front of Nāthjī. This group includes singers, players of *vīnā*, *pakhāvaj*, *sārangi*, harmonium and *jhānjh*. Their main duty is to play daily during *darśana*, when the deity is prepared and when he is eating, but they also play during festivals and other special ritual occasions. Each temple has a head musician, *kīrtankar mukhiyā*, who decides which songs will be sung in the temple and co-ordinates the music; he is highly regarded and receives additional remuneration for his responsibility. The post of musician in the temple is hereditary and thus the family heritage has a particular value. Gaston (1997: 138) reports that during the 1980s the *kīrtankars* who were in service in the temple of Nathdwara belonged to seven families which included tailors, makers of decorative objects, building contractors, farmers and, among the younger generation, medical doctors, teachers and businessmen. Six among these families belonged to the community of Kumavat and one to the Brahmin community. The Brahmin family and one Kumavat family traced their origin to Braj and the other five were of Rajasthani origin. While the Kumavat families intermarried, the Brahmins remained separate, and in general the three different groups of musicians did not intermarry.

The family of Purushottam Das belongs to the Kakatya group of *kīrtankars* of Rajasthani origin. The status of the members of this lineage was quite different from that of all the other musicians playing in the temples of Nathdwara. They started their career as court musicians and after only a few generations settled at Nathdwara as temple musicians invited by the Tilkayāt, and they always had a special relationship with the Tilkayāts who granted them permission to leave the temple to play again in princely courts, and at a later stage to play on the concert stages and teach in national institutions.

Another unique feature of this musical tradition is that two of its members, Ghanshyam Das and Purushottam Das, documented its history and repertoire in two books, the *Mṛdaṅg Sāgar* (1911) and the *Mṛdaṅg Vādan* (1982) respectively. However, these materials are problematic. The *Mṛdaṅg Vādan* includes a significant number of compositions in different *tālas* providing their *cakras* (diagrams), but reports only a short history of the family. By contrast, the *Mṛdaṅg Sāgar* is more detailed in the telling of the history and includes a huge quantity of compositions, but has been written in an old Rajasthani dialect that is almost incomprehensible for a modern reader.

Mistry provides an outline of the history of the family which she reports – without mentioning any reading difficulties – is taken from the *Mṛdaṅg Sāgar* and the interviews with Purushottam Das and some artists of Nathdwara (Mistry 1999: 108). Interestingly, in the chapter on Nathdwara she includes the history of two other traditions which she calls 'The second *paramparā* of Nathdwara' and 'The third *paramparā* of Nathdwara'. Mistry writes that 'The second *paramparā* of Nathdwara', according to Mulchand, an old representative of that tradition, was founded by his great grandfather Ranchhod Das, expert *pakhāvaj* and *sitār* player, who moved from Vrindavan to Nathdwara, where he settled as temple musician, and was continued by his son Dev Kishen, grandson of Parmananddas, and by himself and his brother Ratanlal (1999: 108). Gaston (1997) mentions Mulchand saying that he was a senior musician, who played both harmonium and *pakhāvaj* in the temple of Śrī Nāthjī and mentions also his brother Ratanlal but does not speak of a school.

Mistry's 'third *paramparā* of Nathdwara' indicates the heritage of the Mahārājas of the temple of Vitthal Das – the second house of Vallabha's lineage – started by Gosvāmī Govind Raiji Mahārāja, chief of the Vallabha sect and expert *sitār* and *pakhāvaj* player, and followed by five generations of descendants, including Gosvāmī Devki Nandan Mahārāja, Gosvāmī Krishna Rai Mahārāja, Gosvāmī Giridhar Lal Mahārāja, and his three sons (1999: 109). The three brothers, besides being leaders of the sect are expert musicians and two of them, Gosvāmī Gokulotsav Mahārāja and Gosvāmī Devki Nandan Mahārāja are famous as concert performers too, the former as a *khyāl* and *havelī saṅgīt* singer, the latter as a *pakhāvaj* player.[10] The two sons of Gosvāmī Kalyanray Mahārāja, the elder of the three Mahārāja brothers, are continuing the tradition. Harirai and Wagdish Gosvāmī, whom I met with their father in their palace at Nathdwara, are expert *pakhāvaj* players.

The most detailed narration of the history of the family of *pakhāvaj* players is provided by Gaston in an article first published in the *Dhrupal Annual* 1989 as 'The Hereditary Drummers of the Śrī Nāthjī Temple: The Family History of Pakhāvajī Guru Purushottam Das' (Gaston 1989).

Mistry and Gaston provide two different versions of the beginning of the family's history.

According to Mistry, the *Mṛdaṅg Sāgar* says that the *paramparā* was started at Amber by Dadaji Tulsidas (Mistry 1999: 96) and it prospered under his grandson Haluji – Haluji becoming such an excellent *pakhāvajī* that two estates, one at Amber and the other at Jaipur, are still named after him as '*Halujiki pol*' (Mistry 1999: 97). Other members of the family were brilliant *pakhāvajīs* but the tradition took a new path during its fifth generation with Rupram (Mistry 1999: 97).

According to Gaston, the history of the musical tradition told by the *Mṛdaṅg Sāgar* begins in the early 17th century when three brothers were forced by the circumstances of war to leave their village near Jaipur and live as wandering devotional musicians. After some time, one of them, Halu, found a post at the court of Amber and later had two sons, while the other had no children. Only one of the two, Chabaldas, had children and his descendant Rupram, after four generations, was still court musician at Amber when the capital was moved to the newly founded city of Jaipur in 1727 (Gaston 1997: 243).

From Rupram onward, the histories provided by Mistry and Gaston coincide.

Invited by the rāja of Jodhpur, Rupram joined his court in 1735[11] and stayed there as a respected musician for many years also serving his successors. A significant detail reported by the *Mṛdaṅg Sāgar* and emphasized by both Mistry and Gaston is that Rupram was a 'master of *tāṇḍava parans*' (Gaston 1997: 244) and Rāsalīlā (Mistry 1999: 97). This is particularly interesting since it suggests the presence of compositions similar to the contemporary *stuti parans* in the repertoire of the *pakhāvaj* during the 18th century.

In 1769 he had a son, Vallabhdas, and trained him on the *pakhāvaj*. According to the *Mṛdaṅg Sāgar*, Vallabhdas also received some training from Pahar Singh, another good *pakhāvajī* who was in residence at the court of Jodhpur (Gaston 1997: 244; Mistry 1999: 98).[12] Vallabhdas took over his father's post as court musician from 1790 to 1802, when he accepted the invitation of the Tilkayāt Giridhar to leave Jodhpur for Nathdwara. In 1820, invited by the Gaekwad, Vallabhdas, after having asked his teacher Pahar Singh to take over his place in the Śrī Nāthjī temple, moved to Baroda and stayed at his court for four years before going back to Nathdwara to settle there permanently at the age of 55 (Gaston 1997: 249). He had three sons, Chaturbhuj, Shankar and Khem. Chaturbhuj moved to Udaipur, Shankar was employed at the temple after his father's death, and Khem, who lived in a joint family with his brother, started working on the *Mṛdaṅg Sāgar* (Gaston 1997: 249; Mistry 1999: 98). While Shankar was a brilliant *pakhāvajī* and his playing was greatly appreciated and guaranteed him honours and gifts from Mahārājas, both religious and secular, Khem engaged himself in the study of old books that were available in his time in order to progress in the art of music (Gaston 1997: 251; Mistry 1999: 99). However, he did not complete the writing of the *Mṛdaṅg Sāgar* before he died, and the task was accomplished by his nephew Ghanshyam, Shankar's son, to whom the book is attributed.

In 1876, the Mahārana of Udaipur invited Shankar to take part in the wedding of one of his relatives in Kishangarh (Gaston 1997: 254). Shankar with his son Ghanshyam and his brother Khem set out from Nathdwara, but on the way to their destination they were caught in a heavy storm and both the brothers fell ill and shortly afterwards Khem died. The tragedy hurt Shankar so much that he became depressed and, accompanied by his family, went on a religious pilgrimage. On his return from the trip, which lasted six months, his son Ghanshyam was married to Ramibai. Shankar died in 1893 and Ghanshyam was appointed as his father's successor at the Śrī Nāthjī temple by the Tilkayāt Govardhanlal. Although he completed the work started by his uncle Khem and is considered the author of the *Mṛdaṅg Sāgar*, he did not provide details about his own life (Gaston 1997: 258; Mistry 1999: 98).

Additional information on the more recent family history is provided by the *Mṛdaṅg Vādan*. Purushottam Das began his musical training at the age of 5, but his father Ghanshyam died when he was still very young. He himself stated that his main teaching aid, besides the instructions received from his father, was the music recorded in the *Mṛdaṅg Sāgar*. At the age of 15, as many other musicians used to do, he started playing in the Śrī Nāthjī temple and learning accompaniment (Gaston 1997: 261), and when he was 18 he spent one month at Udaipur to study with Parasuram, a singer at the Gokulchandramaji temple who, together with his three brothers, had studied *pakhāvaj* with Purushottam's grandfather, Shankar. In the same year, he also had the opportunity to study *tablā* with musicians of different *gharānās* who had gone to Nathdwara to perform for the Tilkayāt (Gaston 1997: 262).

In 1932, Purushottam Das took the post of *pakhāvajī* of the Śrī Nāthjī temple which was designated as the hereditary tradition of his family. He held the post until 1957, when, recommended by Nazir Aminuddin Dagar who had just heard him on the All India Radio, he was invited to teach at the Bharatiya Kala Kendra at New Delhi. By the end of the 1970s Purushottam Das joined the Kathak Kendra of New Delhi where he taught until 1981, when, at the age of 74, he retired from there and returned to Nathdwara. He died at Nathdwara on the 21st of January 1991.

The history of the family tradition demonstrates that many Mahārājas had a keen interest in music, and that the Tilkayāt maintained substantial political power and exerted considerable influence on the musicians of Nathdwara. It shows that the relations among resident musicians at Nathdwara and visiting performers was good and useful. It also sheds light on the procedures of transmission of knowledge among musicians and how they changed over time. Gaston highlights that both Ghanshyam and Purushottam Das emphasized that their only teachers were their fathers (Gaston 1997: 258). It seems that Ghanshyam never taught anyone else, whereas Shankar taught at least four other students, the brothers Parasuram, Ramnarayan, Gangadas and Tikamdas, who played at the temple in Udaipur. The family connection remained since Tikamdas's daughter Gulab was married to Purushottam Das. However, as underlined by the many mentions of their relations in the *Mṛdaṅg Sāgar*, Vallabhdas had received some training from Pahar Singh, a brilliant musician belonging to a different tradition, and similarly Purushottam Das received some training from other *pakhāvajīs* too, although only from those belonging to the same tradition, and – in addition – he received *tablā* lessons. Gaston rightly observes that since the *Mṛdaṅg Sāgar* had been his main aid in training and most of the pieces notated in the book are intended for solo *pakhāvaj* recital while most of the music played today at Nathdwara is as accompaniment to the *havelī saṅgīt,* it may be questioned whether the compositions included in the book correspond to the repertoire of Ghanshyam Das or Khem, or were a compilation of a variety of compositions which might not have been part of their repertoire (Gaston 1997: 261). If this were the case, it would mean an important change in the transmission of the family heritage and, significantly, that the solo repertoire of the family would be quite recent. However, it has to be observed that members of the family had been playing at the court of Jaipur and Jodhpur before Vallabhdas decided to move to Nathdwara, and he himself had been court musician and had inherited at least a part of the tradition of Pahar Singh. Even Shankar had been travelling and playing both for Mahārājas and kings, and thus it is plausible that they had a rich repertoire for solo even though they did not play it in the temple. This might have also been the reason why they decided to notate their solo repertoire, since fewer opportunities to perform it would have caused its loss. Furthermore, they had always been in contact with the numerous visiting musicians playing for the Tilkayāt and thus they might have had the opportunity to increase their repertoire.

A very interesting aspect of the history of this lineage of musicians is its being in a continuous process of change. It started as a family tradition of musicians (*paramparā*) playing in the courts, then it moved to the temples, remaining a familial hereditary profession, and finally it left the temple and became a school (*gharānā*). While Vallabhdas had brought the tradition into the temple, Purushottam Das inaugurated a new phase in which the knowledge belonging to a single family of professional musicians became open to any student. Indeed, Purushottam Das taught not only his grand-nephew Prakash but many others as well, at the school in Nathdwara and at the Bharatiya Kala Kendra and the Kathak Kendra at New Delhi. With him the repertoire of the *pakhāvaj* played for Nāthjī went out of the temple and the style spread among his many students and from them to many others. Purushottam Das transformed his family lineage (*paramparā*) into a school (*gharānā*) and thus the special aspects of the tradition and its repertoire, which had been the exclusive knowledge of a single family for several generations, became the shared knowledge of a wide community of people.

One of his most accomplished disciples at the Bharatiya Kala Kendra, the one who helped him in the writing of the *Mṛdaṅg Vādan*, was Bhagavat Upreti, a humble and gentle man, and a retired university lecturer, who told me he had not undertaken the career of professional musician since he does not belong to any music family. Totaram Sharma is another brilliant student of Purushottam Das. Awarded the Sangeet Akademi Award in 2012, he is famed for adding new dimensions to the art of Rāsa Līlā. He trained his son Radheshyam and his nephew Mohan Shyam Sharma, a well-known accompanist of the Dagar family, and among many other students, Dalchand Sharma, presently the foremost representative of the Nathdwara *gharānā*, both as soloist and as accompanist.

Pandit Dalchand Sharma and my research

I met Dalchand Sharma (Figure 3.2a) for the first time at the University of Delhi, where he has a post as staff musician. I introduced myself and my research on the *pakhāvaj*'s heritage and he soon started telling of his numerous travels and concerts in Europe, in Frankfurt, Rome, Milan and Venice. After that he asked me who I had studied *pakhāvaj* with previously and when I mentioned Svāmī Ram Kishore Das he said that he was a good musician and that they esteemed each other. Then he spoke with feeling of the relation between *tālas* and *rasas* and explained his view on the *pakhāvaj*; he said that each *tāla* has its own *rasa* and that, even though most of the *pakhāvajīs* think that *vīra rasa* is its main *rasa*, the *pakhāvaj* is a melodic instrument. To demonstrate what he was arguing, he recited numerous compositions giving detailed definitions of different kinds of *bols* such as, for instance, the forceful *dhet*, played with the right middle finger and ring finger, and the soft *dhet*, played with the forefinger alone. He proudly defined himself as a *pakhāvaj* devotee but added that in his youth he studied also *tablā*, *havelī saṅgīt* and acting, and affirmed that all these experiences and knowledge combined to allow him to understand, appreciate and produce the many shades of the *pakhāvaj*'s sound. He said that the Indian *tāla* system is based on the specific character of the cycle and not on the number of its beats; *jhaptāla*, a ten *mātrās* cycle, for instance, has a calm flow similar to the calm gait of a woman or to that of an elephant, which he showed me with skilful movements of the body simulating the oscillations of the animal's trunk. *Jhaptāla*, he argued, blends *śṛngāra* and *bhakti rasa*, evoking at the same time erotic and devotional feelings. By contrast *sūltāla*, which also counts ten *mātrās*, has a completely different character, being a fast cycle associated with Śiva and expressing heroic feeling (*vīra rasa*). Excited by his passionate way of conveying his ideas and knowledge, I asked many questions which he was ready to answer and, after one hour of conversation, we agreed to meet again in his house.

Dalchand Sharma was the first of 15 *pakhāvajīs* who I met during two different fieldwork trips, but his respect for the *pakhāvaj*, his kind behavior and his way of looking at things and music with critical attention soon convinced me that he was the right person to try to collaborate with. I intended to interview various representatives of the different *gharānās* to collect their histories and a description of their repertoire through a presentation of their typical solo *pakhāvaj* recital, but my main aim was to concentrate the research on the language of a single *gharānā* and to work together with a knowledgeable and articulate musician.

During our next meeting, I explained my research project to Dalchand Sharma. He immediately agreed to collaborate and then, in order to introduce himself better, started telling his life story.

His youth had been very tough; he came from a simple Brahmin family and had left home at a young age to learn music. He studied at Vrindavan under the *guruśiṣyaparamparā* system. His first guru was Baba Jivan Das who taught him vocals and *tablā* but, after that teacher's sudden death, he devoted himself to the *pakhāvaj*, an instrument for which he felt a stronger inclination, studying under the guidance of Pandit Totaram Sharma. Later, he had the opportunity to receive training from Purushottam Das himself. His training had been very strict; he told me with great simplicity and sincerity that he was allowed neither to ask any specific questions to his guru nor to be taught any particular composition. During those years of hard work and study he did not have a proper diet; he often used to have very small and simple meals and, in fact, according to him, the lack of proteins and vitamins had stunted his physical growth. However, his eagerness to learn was such that despite that difficult situation he engaged three times in *cillā*, a 40-day long practice consisting of eight hours of uninterrupted playing in order to develop *siddhis* (powers). He explained 'it is only God's grace if a tiny man like me can play an energetic and heavy instrument such as the *pakhāvaj*'. After the hardships of his youth he started a brilliant career soon becoming a leading exponent of the *pakhāvaj*, both as a soloist and as accompanist, and receiving numerous important awards.

Dalchand Sharma is a sweet and determined man, respectful of the tradition but aware of the new musical trends of contemporary Indian society and the risk of the *dhrupad pakhāvaj* tradition disappearing. With his many students, he adopts a flexible and open form of the traditional teaching system and, in order to share and spread the fascinating aspects of the *pakhāvaj* heritage, he delivers lectures on the drum and its *tālas* from the point of view of the aesthetics of emotions, *rasa siddhānta*. His approach to the drum is based on *rasas*. He was keen from our very first meeting to highlight that the beauty of the *pakhāvaj* results from *rasas*, more than from mathematics; indeed, even his *layakārīs* are built on a very fine control of dynamics and *rasas*. According to him, each *tāla* has been designed to project a specific *rasa* or a blend of *rasas*; it has its own character and associated emotions. His music is entirely based on *rasa siddhānta*, or the art of producing the right *rasa* in the proper way and at the right moment. He argues that there are various *rasas* and each *rasa* may take several forms. Using *vīra rasa*, the heroic mood, as an example to explain his vision, he argues that it is very often conceived and played as a combination of *bhayānaka* (the fearful) and *vīra rasa*, producing the same emotion which arises from watching wrestling. By contrast, on the basis of the approach of his tradition and cult, he associates *vīra rasa* with Kṛṣṇa and Rāma; according to him it has to express their character, hence energy, strength and power, but, of course, beauty as well. In other words *vīra rasa* has to convey an idea of regality, including vigor and refinement. In a similar way, he argues that even *śṛngāra-rasa* may take several forms. It represents conjugal love, it has a romantic mood but, according to its tradition, it refers to the love of Rādhā and Kṛṣṇa, and hence should not have any kind of vulgarity and should also include *bhakti rasa*. Similarly, *bhakti rasa* – the main *rasa* of *havelī saṅgīt* – should not be dramatically exhibited, but should convey pure devotion, like that sprouting from the poems of Mīrā and Sūrdās. According to him, only two *rasas* cannot find expression in music, and they are *bhayānaka* the fearful, and *hāsyarasa*, the comic. These may, however, be experienced by the audience at a concert when a musician is having serious problems or appears ridiculous.

While explaining his ideas on *rasas*, Dalchand Sharma underlined the importance of music and *rasas* in Puṣṭimārg and clearly pointed out that his approach had been strongly influenced by his being a member of the Nathdwara *gharānā* and a follower of the Puṣṭimārg. He explained that the careful attention to the *rasas* typical of his *gharānā* resulted from the strong aesthetic approach to *sevā* and the necessity for a musician to try to meet the needs and taste of Nāthjī. However, he stated clearly that his knowledge of the *pakhāvaj*'s history and language resulted also from his own research on

Indic religions, Sanskrit treatises, Brajbhasha literary tradition, from his conversations with the elders, and his observation of nature. According to him, classical music or *śāstriya saṅgīt* – including the *dhrupad pakhāvaj* – represents a spiritual path, since it is played for God as a form of prayer. It is mostly based on *bhakti rasa* and has to be respected as a sacred art; it cannot be performed with the sole aim of earning money or to entertain. He argues that the spiritual aspects of Indian classical music can also be seen in its strong relationship with nature, which he underlines by mentioning not only well-known associations such as those of *rāgas* and seasons, but also the connections of some compositions in the *pakhāvaj* repertoire with the rhythm of rain or with the flow of a river.

The philosophical and ritual importance attributed by the founders of the Puṣṭimārg to *rasas* has clearly deeply influenced the aesthetic approach of the school and, in particular, Dalchand Sharma's style. By contrast, the religious ideology of the sect does not seem to be a major feature of the Nathdwara *gharānā*. Bhagwat Upreti, the student of Purushottam Das who actually wrote the *Mṛdaṅg Vādan* under his dictation, told me that, although he was like a family member of his guru, he visited Nathdwara and the temple for the first time during the 2000s, to accompany his daughters who had been awarded a scholarship for research on *havelī saṅgīt*. He also told me that the teaching of Purushottam Das at the Bharatiya Kala Kendra was centred on music and that, while he provided his students with very clear explanations of the various features of his style, he very rarely spoke about his belief.[13] Although Dalchand Sharma considers music as a spiritual path, he does not identify it with the Puṣṭimārg of which he is a follower; his students belong to various religious beliefs – including Islam – and nationalities, and, as several of them told me, they are attracted to study with him for his personal approach to the playing of the *pakhāvaj*. Indeed, I have met at least two *pakhāvaj* players belonging to different *gharānās* who had become his students to comprehend and imbibe his ideas and technique. Prakash Kumavat, grandnephew of Purushottam Das and employee of the temple of Nathdwara, was the only one who spoke of music and *pakhāvaj* from the perspective of the Puṣṭimārg.

Coming into close contact with such a knowledgeable and sensitive musician as Dalchand Sharma – with whom I have had numerous intense conversations on the *pakhāvaj* and its players in contemporary India, on its heritage, its language and the solo repertoire – induced me to deepen my study of the Nathdwara tradition in its many aspects and its unique quality of being born to please the King-God Nāthjī through a sensitive use of *rasas*. It provided me not only with details about a particularly interesting *gharānā* but also with insights into how a court-based pre-colonial model has adapted its aesthetic approach to suit the contemporary cultural context of modern-day India. It also provided me with a further instance of the process of continuous change that has occurred to the *mṛdaṅga* (2nd century B.C.E.–2nd century C.E.) from its birth until its transformation into the *pakhāvaj* (15th–17th century). Indeed, the Nathdwara *gharānā* represents well the last part of that process, the moment when the *pakhāvaj* leaves the courts and temples and moves to the new performing contexts and the new audiences of the 20th and 21st centuries.

Notes

1 The physical form of a Kṛṣṇa icon is defined by Puṣṭimārg members as *svarūpa* (form) since it implies immanence, whereas the most conventional term *murti* (image) indicates representation (Ho 2006: 119).
2 Video, available at: www.youtube.com/user/shrivithaleshmandal (Accessed 21 July 2016).
3 The story is told in the *Bhāgavata Purāṇa* (8th–10th century C.E.), in the *Mahābhārata* and the *Harivaṃśa* as well.
4 www.pushti-marg.net.
5 The percussion instruments (*pakhāvaj* and *jhānjh*) are prohibited when the deity is awakened from his sleep (*maṅgalā* and *utthāpana*) or put to rest (*śayana*) (Thielemann 2001: 410).
6 Text, available at: www.pushti-marg.net/pushti-history1.htm (Accessed 26 November 2016).
7 Two other ways to relate with Nāthjī included in the worship are to approach him as a friend (*sakhyabhāva*) or as a servant with his master (*dasyabhāva*).
8 The complete list includes: (1) hearing (*śravanam*) the names and stories of Viṣṇu, (2) singing his praises (*kīrtanam*), (3) remembering and meditating on him (*smaraṇam*), (4) serving his image (*pādasevanam*), (5) offering worship to him (*arcanam*), (6) prostrating to him (*vandanam*), (7) dedicating one's action to him (*dāsyam*), (8) cultivating friendship with him (*sakhyam*) and (9) dedicating one's entire life and being to him (*ātmanivedanam*) (*Bhāgavata Purāṇa* 7.5.23).
9 In Puṣṭimārg, liberation is not considered as the actual union or mergence into God, like in other sects.
10 Also Gaston (1997: 70) and Ho (2006: 46–47) mention them as excellent musicians.
11 According to Mistry (1999: 97), Rupram was born in 1735.
12 The fact that Ghanshyam Das acknowledged in the *Mṛdaṅg Sāgar* that part of the family knowledge did not came from family members is striking and highlights Pahar Singh's importance for the family.
13 Interview held on 10 March 2013.

8 The repertoire

In this chapter, on the basis of the information collected in numerous interviews and conversations with *pakhāvaj* players of various schools, I will describe the repertoire of the solo *pakhāvaj* tradition. Presenting their main features and compositional methods, I will argue that some kinds of composition are intended to stimulate, through association, visual images in the mind of the listener – being strongly linked to visual arts and Sanskrit poetry. Furthermore, I will argue that ideas and symbols connected to the ancient *mṛdaṅga* are still present in the repertoire of contemporary *pakhāvaj* playing and help us to understand some of its main features. Although I was introduced to the visual and narrative content of certain compositions in the repertoire by Ram Kishore Das and have discussed them with Dalchand Sharma, the interpretation of the multiple levels of the compositions and their relationship with Sanskrit literature which I provide in this chapter result from my own research based on a multidimensional approach.

The *pakhāvaj*: facets of its language and playing styles

As argued in Chapter 5, the *pakhāvaj* is a speaking drum and its repertoire includes several *bols* (syllables). The set of four *bols* ***tā, din, thun, na***, is often considered as the very foundation of learning and, as such, is taught during the first lessons. However, the *bols* representing the foundation elements of the language of the *pakhāvaj* are actually seven, including five for the right hand (***tā, ta, ṭadin, na***) and two for the left hand (***ga*** and ***ka***) (Figure 8.1) (Das and Das 1977; Dick 1984d: 698), and one (***dhā***) produced by playing together the right hand ***tā*** and left hand ***ga***.

Although this set of single syllables has been adopted by all the schools, each one of them uses it in its own way. Indeed, there is no precise correspondence between the syllables and the strokes, and there may be different associations according to the schools, at times varying from composition to composition. An instance of this fluidity of correspondence – shared at least by the Kudau Singh and Nathdwara schools since it has been explained to me both by Ram Kishore Das and Dalchand Sharma – may be given by the syllable ***ka***, which usually denotes the closed stroke on the left hand,

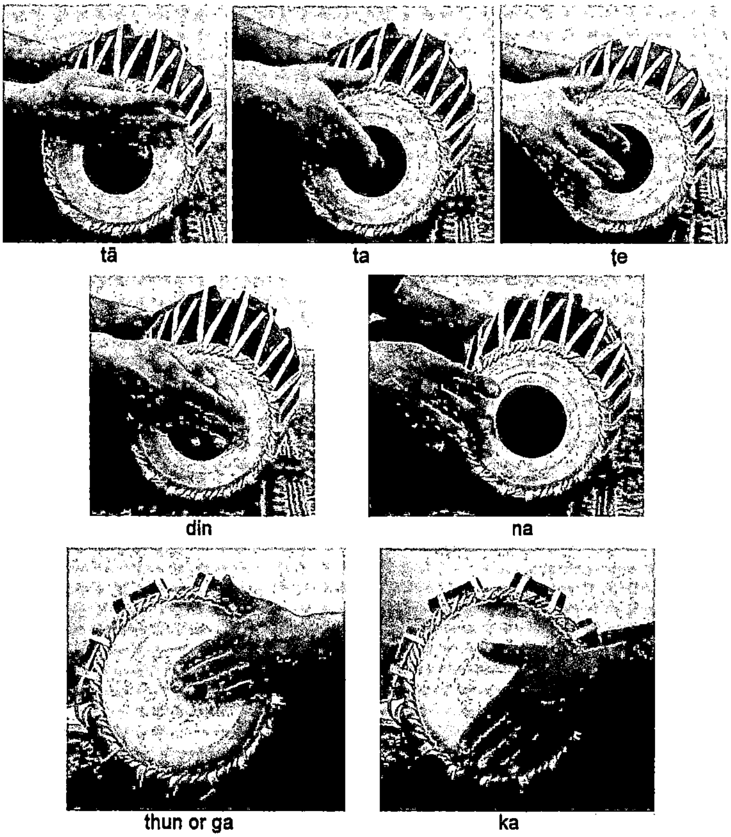

Figure 8.1 The seven main strokes of the *pakhāvaj*.
Photo by L. Spagna.

but when included in strings such as ***dhumakite takiteta ka-kite***, stands for the syllable ***tā***, indicating a resonating stroke of the right hand. In this case, as in others, the clarity and expressivity of the vocal recitation takes precedence over slavish adherence to fixed correspondence between syllables and strokes. Another instance of a similar inverted correspondence between *bols* and strokes is given by the use by the Kudau Singh school of the compound ***thunga*** which is played in exactly the opposite way to how it is written: the *bol* ***thun***, corresponding to the resounding stroke of the right hand on the *siyāhi*, is played as ***ga***, the resounding stroke of the left hand, and the *bol* ***ga*** is played as ***thun***.

At present, the *pakhāvaj*'s repertoire is strictly linked to the following set of *tālas*:

Cautāla 12 beats
| dhā dhā | din tā | kiṭe dhā | din tā | kiṭe taka | dhādi gana |
X 0 2 0 3 4

Dhamar tāla 14 beats
| ka dhe te dhe te | dhā – | ge ti ṭe | ti ṭe tā – |
X 2 0 3

Jhaptāla 10 beats
| tā gege | din din tā | tā tiṭa | kata dhadi gana |
X 2 0 3

Sūltāla 10 beats
| dhā dhā | din tā | kiṭe dhā | kiṭe taka | dhādi gana |
X 0 2 3 0

Tivra tāla
| dhā din tā | kiṭe taka | dhādi gana |
X 2 3

Interestingly, the 16-beat *tīntāla* does not always figure in the list of today's main *tālas*. According to Dalchand Sharma, *tīntāla*, which is still the most important in the Nathdwara tradition and is called, for this reason, *mūla tāla*, the root *tāla*,[1] was gradually dismissed from the main set of *dhrupad tālas* because of its increasing importance in the *tablā*'s repertoire and the consequent need felt by the *pakhāvajīs* to clearly demarcate the two traditions. Indeed, although the *tālas* of the *tablā* are associated with the gait of animals such as the horse (*tīntāla*), the camel (*jhaptāla*) and the peacock (*kaharvā tāla*) (Vir 1977: 23–26), they are mostly intended as time frames, while the *tālas* of the *pakhāvaj* are thought of as structures with precise associations and features, and expressing specific ideas. Ram Kishore Das associated them with deities – the fast seven-beat *tīvrātāla* to the warrior god Kartikeya, the nine-beat *candrakiṛa tāla* to the moon, the ten-beat *Rudra tāla* to Śiva, the severe 12-beat *cautāla* to the warrior and ascetic god Rāma, and the joyful 16-beat *tīntāla* to Kṛṣṇa and his dances. In a similar way, but without establishing any association with gods, Dalchand Sharma emphasized that each *tāla* is connected to a specific *rasa* (see Chapter 7, pp. 122–123).

However, the list of *pakhāvaj tālas* is not limited to the most important mentioned ones and includes, for instance, cycles such as the 14-beat *Brahmātāla*, the 15-beat *gajajhampā tāla*, the 18-beat *Lakṣmītāla*, the 19-beat

Sarasvatī tāla, the 20-beat *Kṛṣṇa tāla* and the 25-beat *Indra tāla*, some of which have been popularized by Rāja Chatrapati Singh in his solo concerts and recordings.

Each *tāla* is characterized by a set of fixed *bols* called *ṭhekā* (support). The concept of *ṭhekā* was introduced into the art music system during the 19th century in the context of the *tablā* (Chaudary 1997: 149; Clayton 2000: 53; Kippen 2006: 77: 3) and was adopted by the *pakhāvaj*, but in a different way. Indeed, as noted by Dalchand Sharma, the structure of the *dhrupad tālas* is maintained by claps and waves of the hands of the singers (Clayton 2000; Kippen 2006) and their *ṭhekās* do not show the concept of stressed (*bharī*) and unstressed (*khālī*) beats, which is an important feature of the *tablā*'s *ṭhekās*.

There are no major differences in repertoire between *pakhāvaj* schools and anyway these differences pertain to the approach to the sound of the drum rather than to the grammar or the main classes of composition, which are usually called *paran*, *relā* and *jhālā*. The only exception is represented by the Punjab school which, according to Baldeep Singh, also includes other kinds of compositions such as, for instance, *kafki* and *langar*.[2] Even though musicians attribute to some compositions a significant antiquity, due to the lack of sources of information it is very difficult to establish whether there are extant pieces composed before the 19th century.[3] Some pieces, at least at present, are included in the repertoire of almost all of the schools; one such is the *samā paran* (ex. 8.1). Other compositions appear in the repertoire of more than one school but in slightly varied versions.

One of the most common stylistic differences between schools mentioned by musicians themselves was that the Kudau Singh style adopts a vigorous and powerful approach, while the Nana Panse style is delicate, and the Nathdwara balances them both (see Chapter 3, p. 41). Notwithstanding these stylistic differences, since it is generally conceived as a masculine and energetic drum, the *pakhāvaj* is very often played from forte to fortissimo.

It is also common knowledge among musicians that specific *bols* and patterns are like the signature of a school. Vigorous *bols* such as ***gran***, ***klang***, ***takka***, or ***thunga*** are typical signs of the Kudau Singh school, while strings of soft *bols* like ***dhātrekedhe tetedhetre kedhetete*** denote the style of the Nana Panse. According to Baldeep Singh, a unique feature of the Punjab school is the use of a handclap as a special stroke.[4] The *bols* ***dhenanaka*** are a very distinctive feature of the Nathdwara; another feature of this school are the *bols* ***kiṭetaka dhadigana***, both because they include syllables and sounds different from the most recurring *pakhāvaj's* cadential formula ***ṭiṭetaka gadigana***, and for their playing technique. As explained to me by Dalchand Sharma and Bhagawat Upreti, the *pakhāvajīs* belonging to the Nathdwara's school do not play – as those of the other schools do – two consecutive resonating ***ga*** in the pattern ***gadigana***, but rather play the *bols* ***dhadigana*** as ***gadikana***; in other words, they play only one ***ga***, the first one, and replace the second one with a ***ka***. They claim they do it for aesthetical reasons, in order to avoid the excess of bass resonance produced by two ***ga*** played one after the other.[5] A similar aesthetical motivation, the need for clarity of sound, explains the playing of the ***ka***, the first beat of the *dhamar tāla*, not as simple ***ka***, as is usually done, but together with the resonating ***tā*** of the right hand. These stylistic features differentiate the schools and explain the presence of specific compositions in the repertoire of each of them.

Compositional types

The repertoire of the *pakhāvaj* includes three main classes of composition, the *paran*, the *relā* and the *jhālā*. The *paran* is by far the most important one and encompasses a set of subvarieties. The meaning of the word *paran* is obscure. It appears in the *Saṅgītaratnākara* by Śārṅagadeva (13th century) with the meaning of filling the gap (Caudhury 2000: 83), in the *Rāgadarpaṇa* by Faqirullah (17th century), where it indicates a cadential pattern establishing the *sam* (Kippen 2006: 86) or the *sam* itself (Sarmadee 2002: 282), and again as a cadential pattern in Willard's *A Treatise on the Music of Hindostan* (1834). According to Sarmadee (2002: 282), the term *paran* is not based on any Sanskrit word and has no relation with the Persian word *parand* (flying bird) either, although he does suggest that it may be derived from a *deśī* word (2002: 282). Gottlieb derives the word *paṛhan* from the Hindi *paṛhnā*, meaning to read, to recite (Gottlieb 1977: 218). Ranade derives the word *paran* from the term *parṇ*, which means in Hindi a 'leaf' (Ranade 2006: 155), while Kippen links the word etimologically to the Persian *par* implying a 'wing' (Kippen 2005: 199).

As a musical form the *paran* is quite open and inclusive. It has no restrictions relating to the strokes (*bols*) that can be used, generally needs two or more *tāla* cycles to be completed and may or may not include a *tihāī*, a short cadential composition repeated three times. Several concepts related to the *tāla* and *pakhāvaj*'s terminology and compositions do not find a clear and unequivocal definition either by musicians or in books. This is true also in this case; indeed, in some cases the various schools do not define the different classes of *parans* in the same way and they may be interpreted differently by each of them. Ashok Ranade (2006) provides the most detailed description of *parans*, which he lists in 12 types on the basis of:

- The structural pauses within the composition.
- The association with a descriptive content.
- The affinity to a particular *tāla*.
- Their being inspired by specific movements.
- Their dance orientation.
- The special sound effects that they are designed to create.
- Their relation with special playing techniques.

- Their being inspired by other already existing *parans.*
- Their relation with the tempo of the *tāl.*
- Their structural complexity.
- Their being designed to provide accompaniment.
- Their being minor *parans* (Ranade 2006: 155–163).

The classification provided by Ranade is undoubtedly illuminating yet redundant. I argue that the list may be significantly reduced and that the *parans* may be distinguished on the basis of two main principles expressed by the names which they have been attributed with: a specific structure or a descriptive content. These categories, as will be seen in the following sections, include all the others and represent the main principles of composition.

Parans as structures based on geometrical figures

The first category of *parans* includes compositions characterized by a specific structure expressed by their name, which associates them to geometrical figures. The main terms distinguishing the many varieties of *parans* are *samā, srotogatā, gopucchā, mṛdaṅga* and *pipīlikā.*[6] These terms have been used in musical treatises to denote the various typologies of the *yati,* the structure of *laya* or the rhythmic arrangement of units of slow and quick speed (Chaudary 1997: 55; Clayton 2000; Rowell 1998), and are applied to distinguish *parans* on the basis of their rhythmic organization (*laya*). Notwithstanding the identity of names, there is not always uniformity in the definitions of these compositions which are sometimes described in contrasting ways; the following descriptions have been provided to me by Dalchand Sharma.

The class of *samā parans* (ex. 8.1) includes those compositions in which the rhythmic organization (*laya*) remains constant from beginning to end and the *bols* are grouped in units of 2, 4, 8 or 16 strokes of equal duration. The line is the geometrical figure associated with the *samā yati* (Sen 1994: 137) and it may be associated with the *samā paran* class too, due to its regular flow. An instance of this typology, structured in groups of four *bols,* is the following one in *cautāla,* a cycle of 12 beats.[7]

Example 8.1 *Samā paran, Cautāla* 12 beats

dhāgetiṭe x	dhāgetiṭe	tāgetiṭe 0	tāgetiṭe	kredhākite 2	dhāgetiṭe
dhadigana 0	nāgetiṭe	katitetā 3	ginadhāge	kiṭetaka 4	dhadigana

This composition, which is one of the most played even in solo performances of musicians from different schools, is also considered as a *sāth paran,* another very common typology in the repertoire of the *pakhāvaj. Sāth* means 'with, together', and thus *sāth paran* seems to refer to a category of composition mostly used for accompaniment (*sāth saṅgat*). According to

Ranade, *sāth* is 'a pattern of rhythmic sound-syllables running full time distance of a *tāla* cycle from *sam* to *sam*' (Ranade 2006: 165), while Kippen suggests that the *ṭhekās* which are now associated with their *tālas* were simple *sāth parans* (Kippen 2006: 169).

The class of *srotogatā parans* includes those pieces whose pace – 'like the flow of a stream (*srota*)' (Chaudary 1997: 55) – is fast at the beginning and slows down at the end, while *gopucchā parans* – 'with tail of a cow' (Chaudary 1997: 55) – are those *parans* which flow slowly at the beginning but increase in speed, becoming very quick at the end. This class of *parans* is a favorite of the Natdhwara school, and provides the structure of numerous pieces such as the *paṛāl* (Audio 8.1), which I notate here in the following way (ex. 8.2) in order to highlight its shape.

Example 8.2 *Paṛāl*, *Cautāla* 12 beats

tā-tā-tā-tā-tā-kiṭakiṭataka di-di-di-di-di-kiṭakiṭataka tu-tu-tu-tu-tu-kiṭakiṭataka na-na-na-na-na-kiṭakiṭataka
tā-tā-tā-kiṭakiṭataka di-di-di-kiṭakiṭataka tu-tu-tu-kiṭakiṭataka na-na-na-kiṭakiṭataka
tā-tā-kiṭakiṭataka di-di-kiṭakiṭataka tu-tu-kiṭakiṭataka na-na-kiṭakiṭataka
tā-kiṭakiṭataka di-kiṭakiṭataka tu-kiṭakiṭataka na-kiṭakiṭataka
tā-----di- ----tu--- --na-----

The *mṛdaṅga parans* are so called because their rhythmic movement reproduces the double truncated conical shape of the body of a *mṛdaṅga*, thus gradually increasing their speed and then slowing it down until the end, while those *parans* having an irregular flow, increasing and decreasing the speed freely, fall into the class of *pipīlikā parans*.

Other pieces based on a particular form are, for instance, those called *ārohī avārohī paran* by Dalchand Sharma and *ulṭī paran* by Ranade – from *ulṭā*,[8] inversion, reverse. As suggested by the names, these pieces are built on a mirror-like structure which goes forwards until its middle and then reverses in the manner of 'abcd-dcba', like an ascending (*āroha*) and descending (*avāroha*) scale (ex. 8.3/Video 1, min. 18.20–19.25).

The typical structure of this kind of composition may be better visualized if notated in the following manner (ex. 8.3).

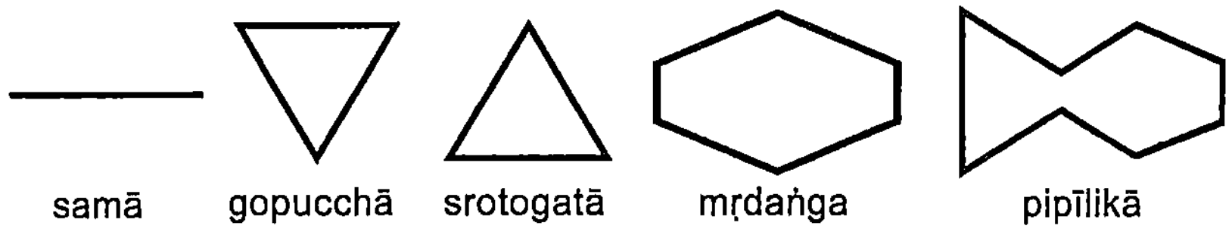

Figure 8.2 The shape of *parans* associated with the five *yatis*.
Drawings by P. Pacciolla.

Example 8.3 *Ārohī avārohī paran*, *Dhamār Tāla* 14 beats

tā-kiṭetakadhadiganadhā- - -
tā-kiṭetakadhadiganadhā-dhā- - -
tā-kiṭetakadhadiganadhā-dhā-dhā- - -
tā-kiṭetakadhadiganadhā-dhā-dhā-dhā- - -
tā-kiṭetakadhadiganadhā-dhā-dhā-dhā-dhā- - -
tā-kiṭetakadhadiganadhā-dhā-dhā-dhā-dhā-dhā- - -
tā-kiṭetakadhadiganadhā-dhā-dhā-dhā-dhā-dhā- - -
tā-kiṭetakadhadiganadhā-dhā-dhā-dhā-dhā- - -
tā-kiṭetakadhadiganadhā-dhā-dhā-dhā- - -
tā-kiṭetakadhadiganadhā-dhā-dhā- - -
tā-kiṭetakadhadiganadhā-dhā- - -
tā-kiṭetakadhadigana

More complicated structures are those featuring the typology of the *cakradār paran*. While a *tihāī* is a pattern of a few beats (*mātrās*) or *vibhāgs* repeated three times, the *cakradār paran* is a composition including a *tihāī* repeated three times in its entirety in order to conclude on the first beat (*sam*) of the *tāla* at its third repetition (ex. 8.4 and 8.5). The word *cakradār* means 'circular' (Ranade 2006: 167) and the composition is characterized by a series of threefold repetitions, thought of as circles of different dimensions.

Example 8.4 *Cakradār paran*, *Tintāla* 16 beats

x dhāgetiṭe	dhāgetiṭe	tāgetiṭe	tāgetiṭe	2 kredhākite	dhāgetiṭe	dhadigana	nāgetiṭe
o katitetā	ginadhāge	kiṭetaka	dhadigana	3 dhā- dhā-	dhā-kiṭe	takadhadi	ganadhā-
x dhā- dhā-	kiṭetaka	dhadigana	dhā-dhā-	2 dhā	-		

* The sections coloured in grey in each example indicate the *tihāīs*.

Example 8.5 *Cakradār paran*, *Jhaptāla* ten beats

x dhāgetiṭe	dhāgetiṭe	2 tāgetiṭe	tāgetiṭe	kredhākite
o dhāgetiṭe	dhadigana	3 nāgetiṭe	katitetā	ginadhāge
x kiṭetaka	dhadigana	2 dhā	kiṭetaka	dhadigana
o dhā	kiṭetaka	3 dhadigana	dhā	dha-di-
x ga-na-				

The *farmāiśī paran* is a complex kind of *cakradār* where mathematical calculations play an important role. *Farmāiśī* means 'requested' and this kind of composition was played to satisfy a patron's request for something impressive. Although explanations differ in certain respects, all are similarly based on the idea that a specific part of the *tihāī* has to fall on the first beat of a cycle (*sam*) in each of its three repetitions. According to Dalchand Sharma, who provided me with ex. 8.6, a *farmāiśī paran* is defined by the position of the *bol* ***dhā*** in the *tihāī*: the first time the drummer plays the *farmāiśī* the first ***dhā*** of the *tihāī* falls on *sam*, the second time the second ***dhā*** of the *tihāī* falls on *sam*, and the third time the third ***dhā*** of the *tihāī* falls on *sam*.

Example 8.6 *Farmāiśī cakradār paran*, *Cautāla* 12 beats

x dhāgetiṭe	dhāgetiṭe	o tāgetiṭe	tāgetiṭe	2 kredhākite	dhāgetiṭe
o dhadigana	nāgetiṭe	3 katitetā	ginadhāge	4 kiṭetaka	dhadigana
x dhā	kiṭetaka	o dhadigana	dhā	2 kiṭetaka	dhadigana
o dhā	tiṭetiṭe	3 katitetā	ginadhāge	4 kiṭetaka	dhadigana
x dhā	kiṭetaka	o dhadigana	dhā	2 kiṭetaka	dhadigana
o dhā	-	3 -			

Similarly, the structure of *kamālī paran* or *kamālī cakradār paran* is not unambiguous, although all the definitions agree that its main feature is the fact that specific ***dhās*** of the composition should fall on the *sam*.[9] Dalchand Sharma defines the *kamālī* as a composition having a nine ***dhās*** *tihāī* and a structure more complex than the *farmāiśī*. Indeed, the particularity of the *kamālī paran*, which is again based on the position of the *bol* ***dhā*** in the *tihāī*, is that the first time the drummer plays the *kamālī* the first of the nine ***dhās*** of the *tihāī* falls on *sam*, the second time the second ***dhā*** of the nine ***dhās*** of the *tihāī* falls on *sam*, the third time the third ***dhā*** of the nine ***dhās*** of the *tihāī* falls on *sam* (ex. 8.7).[10]

Example 8.7 *Kamālī cakradār paran*, *Cautāla* 12 beats

x dhāgetiṭe	dhāgetiṭe	o tāgetiṭe	tāgetiṭe	2 kredhākite	dhāgetiṭe
o dhadigana	nāgetiṭe	3 katitetā	ginadhāge	4 kiṭetaka	dhadigana
x dhā	kiṭetaka	o dhadigana	dhā	2 kiṭetaka	dhadigana
o dhā	tiṭetiṭe	3 katitetā	ginadhāge	4 kiṭetaka	dhadigana
x dhā	kiṭetaka	o dhadigana	dhā	2 kiṭetaka	dhadigana
o dhā	tiṭetiṭe	3 katitetā	ginadhāge	4 kiṭetaka	dhadigana
x dhā	kiṭetaka	o dhadigana	dhā	2 kiṭetaka	dhadigana
o dhā	dhadi	3 gana			

Another interesting typology of *parans* are the *joṛās*. *Joṛā*, a word which means 'pair, couple, twin' (Ranade 2006: 141; Dalchand Sharma, January 2012) is a slightly modified version of an already existing piece. To create new compositions from existing material is a very common practice among *pakhāvajīs* and it may present several degrees of differentiation and complexity. As can be evinced from the analysis of the previous examples, most of the *parans* share their main section which is represented by the *sāma paran* (ex. 8.1) and have been composed on the basis of the same thematic material. Starting from a nucleus represented by the *sāma paran* (ex. 8.1), various new compositions have been created by linking different materials – from a few beats to long *tihāīs* – which give to it a completely new structure and form. The variety of these materials is quite wide and includes a pattern, a phrase, a *tihāī* or a section of a longer composition based on a *tāla* different from that with which it will be linked; a phrase from a composition in the12-beat *cautāl*, for instance, may be easily incorporated into a piece in the 14-beat *dhamar tāla* as well as in the ten-beat *jhaptāla.*

Example 8.8 *Paran, Jhaptāla* 10 beats

dhāgetiṭe x	dhāgetiṭe	tāgetiṭe 2	tāgetiṭe	kredhākite
dhāgetiṭe o	dhadigana	nāgetiṭe 3	katitetā	ginadhāge
kiṭetaka x	dhadigana	dhā-dhā- 2	dhā-kiṭe	takadhadi
ganadhā- o	dhā-dhā-	kiṭetaka 3	dhadigana	dhā-dhā-

When Ram Kisore Das taught me the above-notated *cakradār* in *tintāla* (ex. 8.4) he explained that it was a two-cycle *paran* with *tihāī* in *jhaptāla* (ex.8.8) which had been transformed into a *tintāla cakradār* by adding two extra beats.

A more detailed analysis shows that other strata of materials have been combined to create this piece (ex. 8.4). Indeed the *jhaptāla paran* (ex. 8.8) is constituted by the *sāma paran* in *cautāla* (ex. 8.1), to which has been linked a *tihāī,* which starts from the last two beats – ***kiṭetaka dhadigana*** – of the composition in order to make it fit into the structure of the two cycles of a ten-beat *tāla,* such as *jhaptāla.*

The same compositional procedure based on linking units is also a common characteristic feature within the previously mentioned *farmāiśī paran* and *kamālī cakradār.* If we divide the *kamālī cakradār* (ex. 8.7) into its main constituent parts, we see that it is composed of two blocks, the *sāma paran* in *cautāla* and the nine-***dhā*** 30-beat-long *tihāī* which taken alone or linked to another composition of ten or 20 beats would fit a ten-beat *jhaptāla* or a *sūltāla.* The *bols* ***dhā – dhadi gana*** are the bridging element needed to transform the two compositions into a new one having a completely new structure and form.

Ram Kishore Das told me that it was a common practice to create new compositions by linking beats, patterns or phrases to an already existing one, and that the same process was carried out during improvisation, assimilating in this way improvisation to composition. According to him, the procedure of improvisation, which he called *vistār* or *upaj*, was mostly based on the rhythmic elaboration (*layakārī*) of specific *mātrās* and *vibhāgs* in a composition. For instance, the last four *bols* of the *sāma paran* in *cautāla* (ex. 8.1) may be replaced by similar ones played at double speed (*dugunī laya*).

Rhythmic elaboration (*layakārī*) may be applied to the entire piece which may be played at a different speed (*laya*), such as triple (*tigunī*) or quadruple (*caugunī*) that which is set as the base speed. Due to this practice, Ram Kishore Das requested me to study several *parans* at different *layas*. I was taught numerous patterns and solutions like these and, at the same time, encouraged to elaborate alternative possibilities. I understood that the wide range of possible variations are mostly learnt and memorized during training and the process of improvisation consists mostly of the creation of new strings of precomposed and already known *bols* or chains of compositions.

A few years later, Dalchand Sharma confirmed the procedure, adding some specific features of his school. Using the word *prastār*, for improvisation, he explained that the elaboration of a piece (*paran prastār*) does not modify the entire composition – some *bols* may be replaced by similar ones, for instance, ***dhet-dhet- dhetedhete*** may be used in place of ***dhagetete dhagetete*** – but only some aspects of it, mostly the *tihāī*. Dalchand Sharma said that the same procedure is applied even to *relās* and *jhālās*, while describing a different methodology of improvisation for the *madhya lay ka prastār* or *ṭhekā ke prastār* where the *bols* of the *ṭhekā*, or particular compositions based on them, are used to create a rich spectrum of rhythmical variety and fluctuation of *laya*.[11]

Parans as prayers

The second category of *parans* includes pieces whose main feature is to describe a character, who may be a god, a king or hero, an animal, an atmospheric event, an object or a situation. Although they are all descriptive and their main aim is to draw a picture of a deity or to tell a story, they adopt two different ways. Some of them intertwine *bols* and lexical words while others create images exclusively by means of the words (*bols*) of the *pakhāvaj*. *Gaṇeśa paran*, *Śiva paran*, *Durga paran*, *Hanumān paran* and so on, which are prayers or praises of deities and fall into the sub-category of the so called *bol* (word) *parans*, *stuti* (eulogy) *parans* or *vandanās*, have been composed by intertwining *bols* and lexical words. This is the most characteristic among the various typologies of *pakhāvaj*'s compositions; it blends the Sanskrit or Brajbhasha words of a prayer (*stuti*), describing a god/goddess and his/her powers and features, with the different syllables used to denote the various strokes of the drum. While any *paran* may be spoken and then played according to the drummer's wish, this class is always first spoken and then played. The following *Śiva paran* (ex. 8.9) was taught to me by Ram Kishore Das.

The *paran*, built on equal division of the *mātrā* into three (*tiśra jāti gati*), is organized in two parts. The first one, composed by lexical words in Sanskrit and Brajbhasha describing the god, his attributes and qualities, includes only a few *bols* adding colour and verve to it, or, as in the case of the ***bols dhimike dhimike***, it evokes the sound of the *ḍamaru* drum. The second part, the *tihāī*, starts just after the words of the prayer invoking the god as the most excellent *mṛdaṅga* player and coherently includes exclusively *bols* of the drum in order to show his mastery.

Example 8.9 *Śiva paran*, *Cautāla* 12 beats

x Cha-tra	pati-	o jagata	pati-	2 de-va	pati-
o mahā-	de-va	3 tagaratak--	terekiṭetak--	4 dhereṭetak–	galei
x muṇ-ḍa	mā-l	o śobhita	hea	2 candra	bhā-la
o dhā-kiṭetaka	dhumakiṭetaka	3 dhimike	dhimike	4 damaru	bajāte
x vighna	harate	o daridrā	dhu-kh	2 du-r	karata
o terekitetak–	tānadhā	3 sarada	hi	4 dharata	dhyāna
x guṇijana	sabhā	o karata	gāna	2 muṇijana	sabhā
o dharata	dhyāna	3 e	sajānā	4 patimṛ	daṅga
x rāja	bajāte	o {dhā-kiṭataka	dhumakiṭataka	2 dhā-kiṭataka	dhumakiṭataka
o dhā	dhā-kiṭataka	3 dhumakiṭataka	dhā-kiṭataka	4 dhumakiṭataka	dhā
x dhā	dhā-kiṭataka	o dhumakiṭataka	dhā-kiṭataka	2 dhumakiṭataka}	[dhā-dhā-
o dhā	dhā-dhā-	3 dhā	dhā-dhā-]	4 (dhā	dhā)
dhā					

Great emperor, Lord of the world, Lord of the gods, Mahādeva, you wear a garland of severed human heads which looks beautiful and shining like the moon; you play the ḍamaru, subdue difficulties and move away sorrow and poverty. Always absorbed in meditation, you are the most proficient singer and the most skilled in meditation among all the *sādhus*. Lord of the ornaments, you are the king of the players of the *mṛdaṅga*.[12]

Indeed, it is a very interesting composition for the beautiful arrangement of the 19 ***dhas*** – in particular the one falling on the first beat of the last cycle which breaks the symmetry of the *tihāī* and gives to it a new progression – and for the fact that it includes a chain of three *tihāīs* that in ex. 8.9 are enclosed by angle, square and round brackets.

The Kudau Singh school (*gharānā*) is believed to hold the widest repertoire of *stuti parans*. Indeed, Ram Kishore Das and Ramashish Pathak used to, and

Ramakant Pathak still does, recite many of them in their solo performances and even during a conversation – treating them just like quotations or sayings. Ramakant Pathak, for instance, during a conversation on the relationship of the *pakhāvaj* with Indra, clouds and rain, all of a sudden and spontaneously started reciting a *paran* connected to Indra to make clearer to me what he was saying. Ramashish Pathak had a huge repertoire of *stuti parans* and *chandas* (poetry) describing gods and goddesses and he could recite long chains of such compositions because, as he told me,[13] his guru and maternal grandfather Vishnudev Pathak, founder of his *paramparā*, was a brilliant musician with a deep interest in literature; he composed numerous pieces of poetry (*chandas*) inspired by nature or to describe gods, and played them on the *pakhāvaj*.

Ravishankar Upadhyay established the same link between *stuti parans* and *chandas* but stressed that *stuti parans* come from ancient devotional poetry (*chandas*), quoting as an example of this relationship the first line of the Śrī Rāma *stuti*[14] of Tulsīdās (16th century) (ex. 8.10) and then reciting the *chanda* (metre) through *pakhāvaj bols.*

Example 8.10 The first line of the Śrī Rāma *stuti* of Tulsīdās

	3			4				3			4			
Śrī	Rā	a	ma	Cha	n	dra	kṛi	pa	ā	lu	bha	ju	ma	ṇa
	3			4				3			4			
	ha	ra	n	bha	av	bha	y	Dhā	-	run	ṇa	ṁ	-	-

He specified that it had been composed in *jhūlnā chanda*, having a division of three plus four, and added that even though they come from gods' prayers *chandas* have become a means of composing.

It was with such a function that Dalchand Sharma mentioned *chandas* to me, because in Nathdwara style they are conceived as rhythmic patterns called *chandātmā*, inspired by poetry and based on specific figures such as five, seven and nine. They are used to elaborate the thematic material during improvisations. To provide an example he quoted the beginning of the *Rudrāṣṭakam*[15] of Tulsīdās (ex. 8.11 a) and rendered the *chanda* through *pakhāvaj* words as it was (ex.8.11 b), and in a slightly varied way in double speed (*dugunī laya*).

Example 8.11 a The first line of the *Rudrāṣṭakam*; b its rendition through *pakhāvaj bols*

		2		3			2		3			2		3			2		3		
a.	Na	ma	-	mi	-	śā	mi	-	śān	-	nir	vā	-	nā	-	ru	pa	-	ma	-	-
		2		3			2		3			2		3			2		3		
b.	tā	tā	ka	tā	ki	ṭe	tā	ka	tā	ki	ṭe	tā	ka	tā	ki	ṭe	tā	ka	tā	ki	ṭe

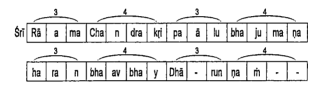

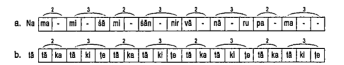

The Avadhi branch of the Kudau Singh *gharānā* considers the *stuti parans* and *pakhāvaj* playing in general as strongly connected with spiritual practices and yogic powers. Ram Kishore Das played many such *parans* and often underlined this relationship. Pagal Das, maybe the most famous representative of this school, was said to be able to cure a stammerer by putting on his lips the wheat (*āṭa*) which he had used on his *pakhāvaj* and which he had infused with the power of specific *parans* (Kippen 2000: 121). According to a widespread story, Kudau Singh tamed a mad elephant by playing a *gaj* (elephant) *paran.*[16]

A particular group of this kind of *parans* is that including the word '*jay*', victory – *jay śabda ki paran* (Ranade 2006: 160) – which often uses only lexical words. One such *paran*, *Rāma Sītā Hanumān paran* (ex. 8.12), was taught to me by Ram Kishore Das as a composition by Bhagwan Das. It is a hymn of victory (*jay*) to Sītā (Sīa), Rāma (Rām) and Hanumān, referred to with his alternative name of Bajrangī Bālī.

Example 8.12 *Rāma Sītā Hanumān paran*, *Cautāla* 12 beats

$_{x}$Jay-Sia-	Rām-Jay-	$_{o}$Sia-Rām-	Sia-Rām-	$_{2}$Jay-Sia-	Rām-Jay-
$_{o}$Sia-Rām-	Sia-Rām-	$_{3}$Jay-Sia-	Rām-Baj	$_{4}$rangīBā	lī-ki-
$_{x}$Jay	Jay-Jay-	$_{o}$Jay-Sia-	Rām-Baj	$_{2}$rangīBā	lī-ki-
$_{o}$Jay	Jay-Jay-	$_{3}$Jay-Sia-	Rām-Baj	$_{4}$rangīBā	lī-ki-

It has a very simple structure. The first part is composed of a phrase repeated twice and the *tihāī* is a simple variation of it including the name of Hanumān. Compositions (*prabandha*) similar to this one, called *Jayavardhana*, victory increasing, and 'consisting of a garland of victory words such as "*vijaya*" and "*jaya*" sung with victory as its purpose', are listed in the early medieval treatise *Bṛhaddeśī* (Rowell 1987: 166).

Parans, images and poetry

Parans telling a story or describing different kinds of situations by using exclusively the *bols* of the *pakhāvaj* are quite numerous. Instances of this group are the *gaj* (elephant) *parans*, simulating the movements and pace of an elephant, the various compositions devoted to the rain and describing or reproducing the sound of the thundering clouds, such as, for instance, the *bijulī* (lightening) *paran*, or the *bijulī kadak paran* (thunder-clack) (Mistry 1999: 76), and those telling an episode of the life of Kṛṣṇa and his dances with Rādhā and the *gopīs*, or describing episodes of the *Mahābhārata* where the protagonists are the Pandava brothers, such as, for instance, the *Arjun Bhīm yuddh paran*[17] (ex. 8.13).

Example 8.13 *Arjun Bhīm yuddh paran*, *Cautāla* 12 beats division of seven (*miśra jāti gati*)

dhāgenadhāgetiṭe X	tāgenatāgetiṭe	kredhet-din-din- O	nagenanagetiṭe
katiṭekatākatā 2	dhā—tā-	dhā-kredhān-dhān- O	dhā-kretān-tān-
dhā-kredhān-dhān- 3	dhā-kredhān-dhān-	dhā-kretān-tān- 4	dhā-kredhān-dhān-

When Ram Kishore Das taught me this *paran*, he explained that it depicts the moment in which Bhīma kills Kichaka, the army commander of the King Virata – in whose court the two brothers were disguised as a cook and music teacher – while Arjuna plays the *mṛdaṅga* to mask the sounds of the fight. He showed me, by miming it, that the *bols* ***dhā-kre dhandhan*** indicated Bhīma beating Kichaka with his club (*Mahābhārata* 4, 22).

The presence of a similar meaning in the *bols* was also highlighted by Dalchand Sharma while speaking about a *gaj paran* in which Pagal Das played the stroke ***dhet*** in such a way that it could be understood that he was thinking of it as a weapon, more precisely as an *aṅkuśa*, the puncher used by the elephant driver in order to control the animal. To explain clearly what he meant, Dalchand Sharma recited the first part of that *paran* simulating, in correspondence with the *bol* ***dhet***, the action of pushing the *aṅkuśa* with increasing energy at first twice and then three times (ex. 8.14) (Video 2, min. 30:34–31:29).

Example 8.14 The beginning of a *gaj paran* played by Pagal Das

< *f* < *f*

aga-ra dhet-dhet- tā--na tā-dhā- keredhet- dhet-dhet- tāranna getedhā-

Dalchand Sharma added that it was a rare *paran* and that, observing the way it had been composed and the increasing presence of the *bol* ***dhet***, it could be evinced that Pagal Das's interpretation was right; that *paran*, like many others, had to be conceived as a multilayered composition, having a pure musical level and a visual level suggesting specific images or acts, such as the pushing of the *aṅkuśa* on the shoulder of an elephant.

The typology of *parans* which I have included in the second or descriptive category represents a clear connection of the contemporary schools with the ancient tradition of the *mṛdaṅga*, both for the themes and the symbols that they mostly propose and for the fact that they are not intended as purely musical compositions but as images, sonic iconographies and theatrical representations. On the one hand, these *parans* are clear instances of the deep link between drum strokes and words emphasized by musical treatises and explain the importance attributed to the *mṛdaṅga* by the *Nāṭyaśāstra* and dramatic literature. On the other hand, the significant use they make of symbols and metaphors such as the elephant, clouds, rain and water in general highlights the auspicious role attributed to the drum and its relation with kingship and sovereignty. The enduring presence of ancient symbols in Indian culture may be understood in the light of the fact that they were strongly connected with royalty and that the figure of the king was crucial in Indian society until the 19th century. Furthermore, they are associated with the rainy season which is a crucial season in Indian life (see Chapter 5, pp. 86–87).

Although I was already aware of the many levels of interconnection between Indian arts, religion and philosophy, I understood that they were also significant aspects of the *pakhāvaj* heritage by observing Ram Kishore Das – later I had a similar experience with Dalchand Sharma – reciting particular *parans* while showing their meaning with the movements of his hands. It was revealing to see him transforming the *bols* of a *paran* into an image or an action, and explaining how many of these compositions are conceived to create pictures or tell short stories. His unveiling of the images hidden within the *parans* made me recognize the links of this music with poetry and induced me to realize their visual and poetical content. Through seeing these compositions not only as musical material but as images or poetry, I realized that they were depicting or narrating, in their own language, the main symbols and metaphors which were at the core of the ancient tradition of the *mṛdaṅga* and Sanskrit literature and were represented in temples and miniatures as well.

Example 8.15 *Bādal bijulī paran, Cautāla* 12 beats

p X dhā-tira	kiṭataka	O tā-tira	kiṭataka	2 tā-tira	kiṭataka
O tā-tira	kiṭataka	*ff* 3 talak--	*f* tā-la-	4 tā-la-	dhet- tā-
X kiṭataka	takadhuma	O kiṭataka	dhī-lang	2 dhī-ge-	tā-ge-
O ṭaketedhe	-tedhā-	3 takiṭedhe	kiṭataka	4 ṭakadhuma	kiṭetaka
X dhadigana	dhā--dhe	O kiṭe dhā-	dhā-dhā-	2 tā-la-	tā-la-
O dhet-tā-	kiṭataka	3 ṭakadhuma	kiṭetaka	4 dhadigana	dhā-dhā-
X dhā	dhā-dhā-	O dhā	dhā-dhā-	2 dhā	kiṭataka
O ṭakadhuma	kiṭetaka	3 dhadigana	dhā-dhā-	4 dhā	dhā-dhā-
X dhā	dhā-dhā-	O dhā	kiṭataka	2 takadhuma	kiṭetaka
O dhadigana	dhā-dhā-	3 dhā	dhā-dhā-	4 dhā	dhā-dhā-

Two main interconnected themes of *parans* show very clearly that the contemporary *pakhāvaj* incorporates ideas of the ancient tradition which are strongly associated with kingship, the theme of rain, expressed through the thunderclouds and lightning, and the theme of the elephant (*gaja*). Rain and its rhythmic movement are the subject of numerous compositions such as the *bādal bijulī paran* (ex. 8.15) – the *paran* of the cloud and the thunderbolt – one of the various rain *parans*.

The composition, developed over five *tāla* cycles, is descriptive. Indeed, when Ram Kishore Das taught it to me, he explained that the *bols* of the first eight beats (*mātrās*), which could be considered as a short *relā* (see p. 146) and should be played very softly, imitate the sound of light rain having a steady flux. By contrast, the *bols* ***tālak***, which should be played forcefully, represent the sudden sound of a bolt of lightning opening the way to a flock of rumbling clouds represented by the middle section of the *paran*. The closing *tihāī*, which is evocative of a dance, brings the thundering to an end and leads to a coming back of steady rain – the initial *relā* – or to a complete change of scene presented by a new *paran*.

The atmosphere and the context described by the *bādal bijulī paran* might be compared to a *rāgamāla* painting of *rāga* Megh, the *rāga* of the 'cloud' (Figure 8.3).[18]

Figure 8.3 *Megha Mallar Rāga*, folio from a *Rāgamāla* (*Garland of Melodies*), India, Rajasthan, Bikaner, 1605–1606. Opaque watercolour and gold on paper. Los Angeles County Museum of Art, gift of Paul F. Walter (M.86.345.1). Photo © Museum Associates/LACMA.

Clouds and rain *parans* are also clearly linked to the many descriptions of the rainy season, an important subject within ancient Indian literature, such as the following by the 11th-century poet Vidyākara:

> A cloth of darkness inlaid with fireflies;
> Flashes of lightning;
> The mighty cloud mass guessed at from the roll of thunder;
> A trumpeting of elephants;
> An east wind scented by opening buds of *ketakī*,
> And falling rain:
> I know not how a man can bear the night that hold all these
> when separated from his love.
> (*Subhāṣitaratnakoṣa*, Vidyākara)

Dalchand Sharma provided me with a very similar description by playing the *megh paran* composed by Purushottam Das (Video 1, min. 41:38–42:30). According to him, the composition describes the arrival of clouds, announced by thunder, and the fall of heavy rain bringing new water to the rivers. The *paran* includes two parts, the first one depicting the thundering clouds, based on *vīra rasa*, and the second one based on *śṛngāra-rasa*, describing the refreshing effect of the rain and the curvilinear flow of the rivers evoking the gait of women.[19]

The presence of iconic signs in the repertoire of the contemporary *pakhāvaj* has also been highlighted by Martinez (2001: 120) in his study on the semiotics of Hindustani music. Interestingly, he mentions *megh parans* and *stuti parans* as instances of compositions including such signs, or rhythmic diagrams, which he identifies as semiotic resources employed in the music of the 1st and early 2nd millennium and described in the *Nāṭyaśāstra* and the *Saṅgītaratnākara* (Martinez 2001: 119).

The deep metaphorical link of the *mṛdaṅga* or *muraja* with rain clouds is expressed through various images in the *Meghadūta* by Kālidāsa. The main character of the literary composition is *megha*, the rain cloud, and its deep rumbling is associated with the sound of the *muraja* played in temples for Śiva, or in the palaces of the nobles. In one instance the poet, speaking directly to the cloud, says that by 'playing the honourable role of drum at the evening offering to Śiva' it will receive the full reward for its deep thunder (*Meghadūta* I, 37), while in another instance says that 'drums whose sound resembles your deep thunder are beaten softly' (*Meghadūta* II, 5) on the terrace of a palace where deities of vegetation and fertility (*yakṣas*) are enjoying wine produced by a wish-fulfilling tree.

The name of the instrument and the mention of its sound activate different layers of associations and metaphors, which are musical as well as visual and performative. Furthermore, it has to be highlighted that they are all influenced, in other words, as in poetry the word *muraja* activates a cluster of visual and sonic similes, in visual arts the carvings or the paintings of a *mṛdaṅga* include sonic and poetical allusions.

The *paran*, as a category of self-sufficient composition, is reminiscent of the one stanza poem in Prākrit or Sanskrit *muktaka*, which generally paints miniature pictures and scenes or carefully builds up a description of a single theme (Lienhard 1984: 71). The *muktaka* constitutes the main unit of Indian poetry, it permits enjoyment of aesthetic experience (*rasa*), and like the *paran* has a second level of interpretation (*dhvani*) which may be perceived and understood only by connoisseurs (Lienhard 1984: 68–69). It is interesting to note that in the Mughal era, when the *pakhāvaj* emerged as the main drum, writers preferred free-standing verses (*muktaka*) over longer narratives (*prabandha*) since such kinds of composition were units of entertainment that could be presented in performance venues on different occasions (Bush 2015: 267). Similar practical reasons might have led musicians to compose in the form of *muktakas*.

The strong association between drums and poetry is again clearly shown by the process of composition. As already seen, the linking of material, from short phrases to extended pieces, is the principal method of construction in *pakhāvaj* drumming. Short phrases are composed by connecting patterns to patterns, compositions are created linking phrases and 'discourses', or long structures, are created by linking compositions and giving them, in this process, new meanings and beauty. The methods adopted by poets (*kavis*) to compose their works were in many ways very similar to the one adopted by *pakhāvajīs*. As explained by Lienhard, classical poets built their works on original concepts but had to follow conventions which prescribed in detail how the various pre-established themes were to be dealt with; their methods were based on the reconstruction and reorganization of existing material into new combinations (Lienhard 1984: 22).

The drummer, like a poet, on the basis of pre-established symbols and themes connected to kingship – such as clouds, lightning, elephants, monsoon, dancing peacocks – with his words (*bols*) creates stories, images and states of mind (*rasas*) with which he/she has to capture the audience. The *Nartananirṇaya* (16th century) by Puṇḍarīka Viṭṭhala, in line with a similar quotation of the *Saṅgītaratnākara*, states that the musician composing for drums should follow the same rules as the poet and adds that 'people speak of such an instrumental performer as a *kavitvakāra* (poetry-maker)' (*Nartananirṇaya* I, 44).

However, although the sound of drums was strongly associated with the king even at a general level, since it was meant to convey his power through its voice, the entire poetical world of the *mṛdaṅga* was based on themes, symbols and associations which might be understood and appreciated only by a limited group of refined courtly elite who knew its rules. Outside of that context the relationship of the *mṛdaṅga* with poetry was virtually non-existent as it is in most cases in contemporary India.

A knowledgeable king of the 20th century and his *parans*

While we have evidence of ancient themes inspiring current compositions, although contemporary *pakhāvaj* players claim that some compositions of their repertoire are centuries old, there is no evidence of actual ancient compositions being handed down through the centuries. Rāja Chakradhar Singh (1905–1947), ruler of Raigarh, constitutes a specific example of a 20th-century actor who attempted to establish a historical connection. His personality, representing the knowledgeable Indian king, and his approach to the performing arts deserve a particular mention. He was an expert musician deeply interested in dance and painting, studied Sanskrit, was well acquainted with the *śāstras*, was keen to observe the contemporary scene of performing arts, and was ever-eager to invite to his court the best musicians and dancers of his time (Ashirwadam 1990; Kothari 1989; Walker 2004).

Rāja Chakradhar Singh wrote various books and composed treatises such as the *Nartan Sarvasvam*, on dance, *Tāl Toe Nidhi*, a gigantic work on *tālas* from 1 *mātrā* to 360 *mātrās*, *Tāl Bal Puṡpakār*, on the art of playing *tablā*, and the *Muraj Paran Puṡpakār*, a collection of 430 *parans* for *pakhāvaj* and *tablā* (Ashirwadam 1990; Kothari 1989). He collected the many original and traditional compositions included in the *Muraj Paran Puṡpakār* from the doyens who played at Raigarh with the help of Bushan Mahārāja, a great scholar and his friend, who was able to notate the *parans* as quickly as they were uttered by musicians. According to Ashirwadam, author of an interesting and detailed monograph on the Raigarh court, as Bhatkhande and Paluskar started the mission of collecting and notating the valuable *rāgas* and *rāginis* in order to save parts of a repertoire which could otherwise have died due to the degeneration of the musicians and the *gharānā* system, Rāja Chakradhar Singh 'might have felt the dire necessity of doing something similar to the art of dance, which was neglected by scholars as well as society, thinking it to be immoral and degenerate' (Ashirwadam 1990: 130).

The *Muraj Paran Puṡpakār* includes *parans* of Baba Thakur Das, Ustad Khader Baksh, Munir Khan, Nathu Khan and several interesting compositions by both Bhushan Mahārāja and Rāja Chakradhar himself (Ashirwadam 1990; Kothari 1989). Other interesting features of the treatise are the watercolour paintings of some *parans* depicting their meaning and feelings (*rasas*) and the specimens of compositions written in the shape of elephants, starting from the tip of the trunk, spreading all over their body and going back to the *sam* at the end of the trunk. Every aspect of the *parans* was considered in detail, even their names which were compiled by the king and Bhushan Mahārāja with the help of Sanskrit scholars, after a careful analysis of their meaning and moods (Ashirwadam 1990; Kothari 1989).

Some of the *parans* composed by Chakradhar Singh were *joṛās* of pieces he had collected. Ashirwadam highlights the narrative and visual quality of some of these compositions and explains how Rāja Chakradhar Singh composed *joṛās* of such pieces filling them with a new symbolic meaning and images (Ashirwadam 1990: 158).

Equating *parans* with poetical compositions and drawing allusions between musical patterns and situations and images are practices that clearly stem from ancient Indian theories and methods, and Rāja Chakradhar evidently managed to handle such a close linking of the performing and visual arts with great ability and awareness, both theoretically and practically. Indeed, the presence of *parans* composed by the king himself such as the *Dalbādal* (bunch of clouds) *paran* or the *Gajavilāsa*, depicting the main features of the elephant (*gaja*) and his/her relationship with women, provide clear evidence of his knowledge of ancient poetry and its connections with the *pakhāvaj*.

What I consider particularly interesting about Rāja Chakradhar Singh is that he links the *pakhāvaj* to the *mṛdaṅga* and the ancient Indian world and symbols and does not make any specific reference to the ideas which had been attached to the drum during its Sanskritization in Mughal time. His work may clearly be considered as an instance of reconstruction or re-elaboration of the ancient tradition, since it happened in a period in which Hindu nationalists were recreating the history of India by looking back at its golden era before the Muslim invasions. However, while Paluskar and Bhatkhande reinterpreted the Indian musical tradition from a Brahmanical perspective with the aim of attributing to it a pure devotional function and solid theoretical basis – which they did not ascribe to courtesans and Muslim musicians who were the main keepers of the tradition – Chakradhar Singh approached the issue from the perspective of drums and dance, which he respected and appreciated like the ideal ancient king described in Sanskrit literature. Furthermore, he did it in a period in which the appreciation of dance was at its lowest ebb of fortune due to its association with courtesans and *devadāsīs* considered as prostitutes. While several publications celebrate him as one of the last important patrons of performing arts of the 20th century, none of them clearly states whether or not he was a member of nationalist groups.

The torrent and the rain

The other two types of compositions – both based on compositional procedures similar to those applied to the *parans* – are the *relā* and the *jhālā*. The *relā*, a term meaning 'a torrent or rushing stream',[20] is played at a fast speed and for this reason has been associated with the term 'rail' and the fast movement of trains. It is generally a short piece lasting one cycle (*āvarta*), performed in numerous variations and in sequence with similar patterns. Long *relās* are often called *paṛāl*.

The following two examples, taught to me by Ram Kishore Das, are based on the *bols* ***tirakiṭa*** and ***dhumakite***, which are the most suitable for this kind of composition, which should be played at high speed (ex. 8.16).

Example 8.16 *Relās, Cautāla* 12 beats

a.

x dhā-tira	kiṭataka	o tā-tira	kiṭataka	2 dhā-tira	kiṭataka
o tā-tira	kiṭataka	3 tirakiṭa	takatā-	4 kiṭetaka	dhadigana

b.

x dhumakiṭe	takadhuma	o kiṭetaka	dhumakiṭe	2 takataka	dhumakiṭe
o takataka	dhumakiṭe	3 dhumakiṭe	takadhuma	4 kiṭetaka	dhadigana

Part (a) in ex. 8.16, excluding the cadential formula ***kiṭetaka dhadigana***, is based on two almost identical patterns ***dhā-tira kiṭataka*** and ***tā-tira kiṭataka*** differing only in the presence of the bass open sound (*ge*) in the *bol* ***dhā***. Hence, it has a quite regular flow (see also ex. 8.15). By contrast, part (b) in ex. 8.16 displays a more complex interlacing of patterns and an interesting and irregular pace since it includes three patterns of different value: ***dhumakiṭe***, ***dhumakiṭetaka*** and ***dhumakiṭe takataka***.

Interestingly, the last repetition of the pattern ***dhumakiṭetaka*** fuses with the cadential pattern ***kiṭetaka dhadigana*** (ex. 8.16b).

While the *relā* is a kind of composition which is included even in the repertoire of *tablā*, the *jhālā*, a word which means 'rain',[21] is a typical composition exclusive to the *pakhāvaj*. The main feature of this composition, having a regular flow, is the prominent use of the *bols* ***tā*** and ***ghe*** (ex. 8.17).

Example 8.17 *Jhālā, Cautāla* 12 beats

x dhāge	gege	o tāge	gege	2 dhīge	gege
o nāge	gege	3 tāge	getā	4 getā	gege

The *jhālā* is thought to have derived from imitation of the *jhālā*, the fast section of instrumental composition played on string instruments such as the *vīnā* and the *rabāb* (Dick 1984d: 699), or from the last portion of the *ālāp* of *dhrupad* singing in which are sung phrases such as *rinanana rananana* (Baldeep Singh).[22] According to Dalchand Sharma, the *jhālā* is based on the proper balance (*samvād*) between the sounds produced by the right and the left hand, and has to convey the idea of rain falling at a constant rhythm or the steady flow of a river.[23]

Notes

1 It is the first *tāla* listed in the *Mṛdaṅg Vādan* of Purushottam Das.
2 Informal conversation held on 4 March 2012.
3 Ram Kishore Das taught me numerous pieces attributing them, whenever he knew the author, to one or another member of his school or others, and even Pagal Das and B. Das mention some of them in their book (1977).

4 Informal conversation held on 4 March 2012.
5 This important aspect was explained to me only by Dalchand Sharma.
6 Pagal Das (Das and Das 1977) mentions these names as related to *yati* and *parans* in his *Mṛdaṅg Tablā Prabhākar* and provides examples of a few of them.
7 Not all the schools of *pakhāvaj* use the same *bols* or write them in the same way, in particular the cadential formula ***kiṭetaka dhadigana***. As has been seen, each school conceives and writes these *bols* from its own specific aesthetical point of view. I have chosen to notate all the compositions according to the Nathdwara method to make the reading easier and more coherent.
8 *Ulṭā* (part. of *ulaṭnā*, q.v.), adj. (f.-*ī*, obl. *e*), reversed, turned back; inverted, head-downwards, upside-down, topsy-turvy; reverse, perverse; contrary, opposite (Platts 1884: 75).
9 According to Ramakant Pathak, Ram Kishore Das and Bhai Baldeep Singh.
10 This composition was provided to me by Dalchand Sharma.
11 This process is quite different from the theme and variations adopted in *tablā* and based on methods such as the permutation, substitution and repetition of the original elements (Gottlieb 1977; Kippen 2005).
12 The translation was provided to me by Prashant Maharana exponent of *dhrupad* and *odissi pakhāvaj* and student of Ram Kishore Das.
13 Interview conducted on 17 January 2012.
14 'O my mind! Sing praises of the merciful Śrī Rām, who takes away the dread of Samsara.'
15 'O lord, O Ishana! I prostrate before you who are the embodiment of Nirvana bliss.'
16 See Chapter 4, p. 70 on the meaning of the taming of an elephant in Buddhism. Ranade mentions two *parans* meant to influence the behavior of an elephant, the *hathiko roknā paran*, the *paran* which is expected to stop an elephant in its tracks, and the *hathiko nachnā paran*, which is expected to make an elephant dance (Ranade 2006: 159).
17 The *paran* of the fight of Bhīma and Arjuna was taught to me by Ram Kishore Das in 2002.
18 The *Saṅgīta Darpaṇa* (17th century C.E.) described this *rāga* as 'With a complexion like the blue lotus and a face like the moon, he is dressed in yellow and sought by thirsty cuckoos. With bewitching smile, he sits on the throne of the clouds. He is one amongst heroes, the youthful melody of the clouds'. (Dehejia 2009: 195).
19 Conversation held on 8 January 2012.
20 Platts (1884: 612). Dalchand Sharma explained to me the meaning of both *relā* and the *jhālā*.
21 *Jhālā* (cf. *jhārā*), s.m. Local rain, rain which falls on one spot (Platts 1884: 400).
22 Informal conversation held in March 2012.
23 Dalchand Sharma conversation of 13 March 2013.

9 The solo *pakhāvaj* recital

In Chapter 8 I analysed the different varieties of compositions included in the contemporary repertoire of the *pakhāvaj* and suggested how they incorporate and project ideas and symbols associated on the one hand with the ancient *mṛdaṅga* and courtly culture, and on the other hand with temple rituals. In this chapter I will study the way these compositions are usually put together in a solo *pakhāvaj* recital, as well as the symbolical association of the garland of flowers with the solo recital. Then, I will analyse the structure adopted by Dalchand Sharma and the features of his own approach arguing that it provides a sonic representation of the many facets and phases of evolution of the *mṛdaṅga-pakhāvaj*.

The structure of the solo recital

The solo recital constitutes an important part of the repertoire of the *pakhāvajīs* and, although it may vary according to the different schools and the musicians' personal choices, some compositions are very similar and the general structure is almost the same. This structure is not fixed in its details but functions as a frame to organize and develop the improvisation which follows a process similar to the one outlined for the building of a composition but at a different level. Indeed, the solo recital is developed by linking compositions of various kinds. Solos on the *dhrupad pakhāvaj* are usually based on the six main *tālas*, namely, *cautāla*, *dhamār*, *jhaptāla*, *sūltāla*, *tivra tāla*, *tīn tāla*, and sometimes *matta tāla*; the most frequently played are *cautāla* and *dhamār*. Although each *tāla* has its own features, the structure of the solo does not change.

The first element of a *tāla* to be presented in a solo rendition is the *ṭhekā*. It may be preceded by a short improvisation lasting a few *āvartas* or by a composition of the same length with a clear introductory character which Ramakant Pathak, Ramashish Pathak and Ravishankar Upadhyay called *uṭhān*, a term literally meaning 'act of appearing', 'rising'. Once the *ṭhekā* has been presented, the introduction is completed. In the following section, called *ṭhekā prastār* – the spreading of the *ṭhekā* – the *ṭhekā* is elaborated through a series of precomposed or improvised variations based on its main *bols*, usually played at twice the pace (*dugunī laya*) of the set beat cycle. While this is the most frequently used method to start a solo performance, a few musicians begin with the *ṭhekā layakārī* and then play the variations. In the *layakārī*, the *ṭhekā* is at first played at a very slow speed (*vilambit laya*) and then at progressively increasing *layas* such as *dugun*, *tigun*, *caugun*, *chegun*, *āṭhgun* and finally brought back to *vilambit laya* through a *tihāī*. A further alternative start may be an auspicious *stuti paran*, usually a *Gaṇeśa paran*, preceded by a short introduction and followed by the variations of the *ṭhekā*.

Once the variations of the *ṭhekā* have been satisfactorily completed the musician proceeds to a new section of the solo.

This is the central part of the performance and it is devoted to *parans* in their many typologies, often alternating the vocal recitation with the instrumental rendition. In this part the soloist may choose among many varieties of *parans* and elaborate and link them to others in numerous ways, although *layakārī* applied to part of a *paran* or to the entire composition is the most frequent choice. When the *layakārī* is applied to the entire *paran* it is played in *vilambit laya* and then at increased speeds exactly as has been explained for the *ṭhekā*. This procedure is quite interesting since compositions are played at twice the pace (*dugunī laya*) of the set beat cycle, which is at slow tempo (*vilambit laya*) and then at increasing speeds, while usually musicians play fast compositions from the beginning of the solo. The various *parans* may either be linked by various presentations of the *ṭhekā* or played in succession. Particularly complex *parans* may be highlighted by being preceded by the *ṭhekā* and first recited and then played.

While the section devoted to the *parans* generally includes compositions played in both *vilambit* and *drut laya*, the last section including *jhālās* and *relās* focuses on *drut laya* until the climax. Contrasting with *parans*, which often include different internal rhythmic divisions, *jhālās* and *relās* are quite regular compositions mostly based on an internal equal division and whose main feature is to create a continuous flow of strokes and sounds which may be easily played at high speeds. Due to these features they offer musicians the opportunity to introduce improvised sections based on divisions of the beat (*gati*) into three, five and seven, or *tiśra*, *khanda* and *miśra jāti gati*.

The overall structure of the solo recital moves from *vilambit* to *drut lay*. However, these are just the main and most common steps of a contemporary solo *pakhāvaj* recital which may include other elements. Ramashish Pathak, for instance, told me that in his tradition the *ṭhekā ke prastār* is usually followed by a section of improvisation (*upaj*) played and recited (*paṛhant*), and it will be seen that even the Nathdwara *ghārāna* lists a specific composition, called *dhenanaka bāj*, at the same point of the sequence, and another one, called *lay tāl torneka kata*, before the *jhālā*.

It is apparent that the place and the occasion of the performance may influence the organization and the development of the material. The solo recitals performed at the Benares Dhrupad Mela, for instance, although maintaining the outlined structure, do not flow like the recorded ones since musicians often interrupt the performance to introduce and explain the compositions they are going to perform, providing information about them and the peculiarities of their *gharānās*. Furthermore, since in that venue the religious aspects of *dhrupad* are particularly emphasized and fostered, some solos, in line with that vision, may include a long succession of *stuti parans*. This is the case, for instance, in the performance of Chatrapati Singh in the 1980s,[1] or the more recent concert of Rajkushi Ram in 2014.[2]

Lotuses, garlands of flowers and the solo *pakhāvaj*

It has been argued that the repertoire of the *pakhāvaj* is associated with literature and visual arts, and also that some compositional forms are based on geometrical images. One of the most recurrent of these images is that of the circle, which is a dominant form in Indian thought (Vatsyayan 1983). During our conversations, Dalchand Sharma emphasized that everything in Indian music and culture is circular like the sun, curvilinear and never straight, and to underline his point added that the weapon of Viṣṇu is the *cakra*, that the concept of the zero was a creation of the Indian mind, and that even worship procedures in some religious systems are based on the circle, being organized on the sequence of eight prayers every day. Indeed, the idea of circle in India includes the idea of cycle, and for this reason it is strongly associated with the concept of *tāla* which, conceived as a cycle (Chaudary 1997; Rowell 1998), is often represented as a circle including a flower having as many petals as the number of the beats (*mātrās*) and syllables composing the *ṭhekā* of a chosen *tāla*. Both the *Mṛdaṅg Sāgar* (Das 1911) and the *Mṛdaṅg Vādan* (Das 1982), the two books on the Nātdhwara school of *pakhāvaj*, present the *tālas* by means of such associations, and *tālas* represented as circles (*cakras*) appear also in the *Tāl toe nidhi* by Ashirwadam (1990). Another interesting representation may be found at the Minakshi Amman Temple (17th century) at Madurai, where not a single *tāla* but the 35 basic *tālas* are carved into the petals of a lotus flower (Gopal 2004: 73). According to Dalchand Sharma, the three concentric circles included in the *cakra tālas* of Nathdwara are connected to the ancient concept of *mārga*, a term indicating the density of events in the time span represented by the circles (Rowell 1998: 206). Ashirwadam describes the *cakras* in the *Tāl toe nidhi* by Chakradhar Singh in a similar way, explaining that all the *cakras* in the book follow the same pattern: in the inner ring are notated the *bols* of the *ṭhekā*, while in the middle and external rings are notated the *bols* of two *parans* in *dugun* and *caugun* respectively (Ashirwadam 1990: 136).

The visualization of *tālas* as lotuses agrees with the Indian symbolism which associates time and the manifestation of the cycles of life to the lotus flower, and leads us to imagine the various compositions as flowers and visualize their sequence in a solo recital as a garland of flowers. In fact, even the association of sequences of compositions to garlands (*mālā*) and garlands of flowers is recurrent, since, for instance, Ram Kishore Das used to compare the playing of the *pakhāvaj* to a *mālā*, a rosary, and an intricate and long composition of the Nathdwara school is called *puṣpamālā* (garland of flowers). According to Manorama Sharma, the accompaniment provided by *pakhāvajīs* to *rabab* players by playing *bols* 'like the garland of flowers being stringed together one after the other' (Sharma 1999: 476) was called *lada-guthāv*. Kippen writes that some *pakhāvaj* players refer to sequences of *bols* having a regular unbroken rhythm like a *laṛī*, a string, especially with something threaded on it, like pearls or flowers (2006: 169).

The association of the solo recital with a garland of flowers has to be understood as metaphorical and not as perfect correspondence. Indeed, the strongest and most interesting aspect of similitude between the garland of flowers and the solo is that they are both made up of a series of independent and self-sufficient elements linked to each other, by a real thread in one case and by the musician's creativity in the other. The way the two elements are metaphorically associated is paralleled by the comparison between the gradual development of the notes of the *rāga* in *dhrupad ālāp* and the decoration of the icon of a deity established by members of the Dagar family, as reported by Sanyal and Widdess (2004). They write that they

> compare the performance of *ālāp* with decorating the image of a deity in a Hindu temple. The process, called *śṛṅgāra* ('love'), comprises the gradual adding of garments, ornaments and garlands, until the whole image is concealed from view apart from the face.
>
> (Sanyal and Widdess 2004: 171)

Like the previous one, this metaphor is not based on a perfect correspondence either, since the notes of the *ālāp* are imagined as various kinds of ornaments.

However, to properly understand the image of the *cakra tāla* and the concept of the garland it is necessary to consider why the lotus has been assumed as a representation of time and cosmic life in ancient India and then relate this view to the idea of cyclic time conceived as a circle.

As already mentioned in Chapter 4, the lotus was primarily thought of as a symbol of waters and their creative and fertilizing power producing life, and secondarily as a symbol of the earth resting on the back of the cosmic waters. The meandering lotus creeper, which has no branching stems and the stalk of each flower and leaf rises directly from the rhizome, was chosen as an auspicious symbol of the never-ending flux of life generation in the universe (Coomaraswamy 2001; Mukerjee 1959: 120). Just like a lotus has its life cycle, universes are born, grow and decay; universes sprout and decay as flowers of the same plant. An interesting aspect of the *tāla cakras* that contrasts with the ancient view is that, while it conveyed the idea of life energy as an organic flux of existences and cycles of lives and universes represented as the meanders of the lotus creeper, the cycles of musical time are conceived as circular. Since, as argued and demonstrated by Clayton, the circularity of time in music does not result from perception but rests on ideologies (Clayton 2000: 18–23), it is necessary to reflect on the ideas shaping this concept in Indian music.

Issues such as the conception of musical time as cyclic and circular and the emergence of this idea in Indian music have been extensively treated by Rowell (1998), who argues that the concepts of temporal organization in the music of early India reflect the influence of prevailing cultural ideology and that among the most powerful pressures on the Indian arts have been cultural preferences for the circular disposition of space and the cyclical disposition of time. According to him, although the Vedas intended cosmic time as evolving in cycles, ancient Indian *mārga* music did not include the concept of cycle and was structured on a set of formal modular rhythmic patterns based on specific *tālas*. It was highly formalized ritual music, 'a ceremonial, symbolic representation of cosmic process – a sacrificial offering and an oblation' (Rowell 1998: 185). Rowell argues that the concept of musical time as circular appears – replacing the ancient *tāla* system of ritual (*mārga*) music – only during the medieval period in the repeated rhythmic cycles of the *deśī* music designed to facilitate improvisation (Rowell 1998: 180). On the basis of these arguments he supposes that 'the historical development of Indian music flowed from *mārga* to *deśī*, from theatrico-religious towards entertainment, from strict to relatively free, from Sanskrit to vernacular, from central to regional, from composed to improvised, and from modular to cyclical rhythm' (Rowell 1998: 223).

Rowell's hypothesis, however, is marked by an evolutionistic approach deriving from the fact that his analysis of the *mārga tālas* and the *tāla* system relies mostly on the 31st chapter of the *Nāṭyaśāstra* which did not cover the whole gamut of theatrical music nor, moreover, music in ancient Indian society in general. The *mārga tālas* provided the structure of the *gītakas*, a group of seven songs performed during the preliminaries of the drama (*pūrvaraṅga*); the *pūrvaraṅga* was devoted to the worship of the deity of the stage and preceded the enactment of the drama (Chaudary 1997: 157). Indeed, Bharata explained that the songs to be employed within the drama itself were the *dhruvās*, and clearly distinguished them from the ritual *gītakas* (Chaudary 1997; Ramanathan 2008: 4; Singh 2006).[3] *Gītakas* and *dhruvās*, alternatively called *gāndharva* and *gāna* and later *mārga* and *deśī*, were two divergent classes of songs which not only were played during different phases of the theatrical performance, but aimed at different results and had different structures. The aim of the *gāndharva* music was the imperceptible reward (*adṛṣṭa phala*) resulting from eulogizing the gods (Chaudary 1997: 157; Ramanathan 2008: 5; Tarlekar 1991–1992: 697). The purpose of *tāla* was to provide fixed measurement to the notes and to establish *sāmya*, or equipoise (Singh 2006). It was based on actions of the hands which had to be correctly rendered and like the rule-bound recitation of the Vedas it was not allowed to deviate from the set patterns (Chaudary 1997:159; Singh 2006; Tarlekar 1991–1992: 698). The meaning of the Sanskrit text was not important and the words were split to be in conformity with the *tāla* pattern in the songs (Tarlekar 1991–1992: 695); the melody took second place (Singh 2006; Tarlekar 1991–1992: 696).

Such an elaborate scheme was not found in *gāna* music where the purpose of *tāla* was to harmonize with the movement of the feet or the minds of these characters. *Dhruvā* songs were employed in the entry and exit of characters, to indicate a change in *rasa*, to communicate the mood of the character who had entered on stage and to show the gait of characters (Chaudary 1997: 452; Tarlekar 1991–1992: 695). The meaning of the text, uttered in Prakrit and other regional languages, had to be clear (Chaudary 1997: 450; Tarlekar 1991–1992: 697).

On the basis of such strong differences, clarified and discussed at length by Abhinavagupta in his commentary on the *Nāṭyaśāstra*, Singh emphasizes that *gāndharva* and *gāna*, or *mārga* and *deśī*, music, flourished side by side (Singh 2006), and Chaudary (1997), agreeing with him, writes that

> it would be contrary to both the popular and the textual traditions and norms to assert that in the age of Bharata, no melodies other than the *jātis*, no compositions other than the *gītakas* and no *tālas* other than the five *mārga tālas* had evolved or were in use.
>
> (Chaudary 1997: 69)

In the same line, Ramanathan adds further information writing that while in *gītakas* the *tāla* pattern was not repeated as a cycle, in *dhruvā* songs 'we find for the first time the *tāla* framework of a melodic line being formed by the repetition of a basic *tāla* structure a number of times. This cyclic notion of *tāla* continues till the present time' (Ramanathan 1987: 13).

Conjectural arguments in favour of the cyclicity of even *mārga* music are provided by Mohkamsing and Kintaert. According to Mohkamsing, evidence of the presence of the concept of cycle in *mārga* music is proved by the function of the *sannipāta* beat in the *āsārita* songs of the *gītakas* (Mohkamsing 2004), while Kintaert, arguing the polyrhythmic structure of the *mārga tālas* on the basis of the different *mātras* beaten by the right and left hands in the execution of the *tāla*, affirms that the idea of cyclic rhythm was not completely absent in the *gītakas* (Kintaert 1997).

In Chapter 5 I have argued that the period from the 2nd B.C.E. to the 6th century was an age of great changes which saw the birth of new political and religious ideas emerging from the lower strata of society. The *Nāṭyaśāstra* evolved in that period, intending to bring the different vernacular stage traditions into a unified and refined synthesis (Raghavan 1967). I have also argued that the concepts of *mārga* and *deśī* music have been changing over the centuries and that the two spheres of art and folk-music have always interacted like two communicating vessels and interconnected like the two pans of a scale. If the *gāndharva* and the *gāna* traditions flourished side by side, and even *gāndharvas* included at least some aspects relating to cyclicity, there are no arguments to affirm that ancient Indian music was exclusively based upon fixed rhythmic and modular patterns and that cyclical rhythm was developed at a later stage. Furthermore, although the idea of cyclic time is very ancient and 'accepted by the Indian culture as a whole' (Balslev 1984: 46), it was not the only one. Indeed, the philosophical speculation about time was developed by the six Brahmanical schools[4] and by Buddhist, Jaina and Tantra thinkers, disclosing a wide spectrum of often contrasting views (Balslev 1984: 40).

Time was conceived as linear or cyclical according to the perspective from which it was observed. In the context of such a variety of theories, the idea of the wheel has to be understood as a symbolic image of time from a soteriological point of view. In other words, it is meant to provide a visual representation of the unending process of transformation and transmigration involving everything in the universe. It does not look at time in its ontological reality but from the perspective of human life. From this point of view it represents the beginningless cycle of existence, the *saṃsāra*, in which the individual soul is entrapped in cycles of births, deaths and rebirths, and explains the process towards liberation from it (Balslev 1984; Eliade 1997). A very clear representation of time as a wheel with six spokes, corresponding to the worlds and the stages of transmigration of the individual soul, is the Buddhist *Bhāvacakra* or 'wheel of becoming'. The wheel is held by the jaws, hands and feet of Yama, the god of death, while the Buddha, standing on a cloud positioned outside of the wheel shows the way out of it by indicating with his forefinger the moon symbolizing enlightenment or liberation (*mukti*).[5]

Concerning this interpretation of cyclical time, it is worth noting that the idea of musical rhythm as circular appears during the 1st centuries of the 2nd millennium in the context of Sanskrit treatises on music and that the same texts interpret music as a path (*mārga*) to liberation. *Gāndharva* music produced unseen merit (*adṛṣṭa phala*) or appeasement of gods; it was music played to give pleasure to the gods (*Nāṭyaśāstra* 28, 9), whereas in treatises such as the *Saṅgītaratnākara* and later *Saṅgīta Dāmodara*, *mārga* music, which by then had absorbed numerous aspects of the so called *deśī* music, was explicitly defined as *vimuktida*, or as leading to liberation, a way to escape from the *saṃsāra* (*Saṅgītaratnākara* 2,162–168). It is noteworthy that the new interpretation of the function of music coincides with the spread and fortune of the *bhakta* cults, which considered music and particularly the singing of the praises of God as a means to fulfil union with the divine (Thielemann 2002), and with certain forms of Sufism that were and still are popular in India and which attributed a similar importance to music and conceived musical time as circular (Clayton 2000: 17–18).

It is not possible to gain a full understanding of any aspect of musical practice and thought without considering it in its socio-historical frame and as resulting from several processes, since 'music, like ideology, is constantly being re-created and redefined' (Clayton 2000: 23) and the two processes are constantly interacting. The patterns of transformation are several: the meeting of different cultures creates new ideas, ancient ideas are reinterpreted or recreated from new historical perspectives, new ideas merge with ancient ones and so on. As I have argued in Chapter 5 and Chapter 6, the development of the *pakhāvaj* itself is a very interesting example of this process of continuous elaboration of ideas and symbols. All the symbols and metaphors related to the lotus that may be found in the context of the *pakhāvaj* are derived from the ancient *mṛdaṅga.* The relation of the *mṛdaṅga* with the lotus was established by Svāti's myth of creation and by the fact that the first name of the drum was *puṣkara,* lotus. The plant was closely related to the goddess Lakṣmī and also to the elephant, who was the main animal associated symbolically to the drum[6] in various ways.

A similar process of stratification and re-elaboration may be recognized in the representation of the *pakhāvaj cakra tālas.* Indeed, I suggest that the concept of time intended as continuous unceasing flux and represented by the lotus creeper and the vision of time as a circle of transmigration merge in the *cakra tālas* during the second half of the 2nd millennium under the influence of *bhakta* cults. In other words, the medieval representation of time as a circle assimilated the lotus, ancient symbol of life and its flux, in a single image just as the *pakhāvaj* had incorporated the heritage of the *mṛdaṅga,* or the *bhakta* sects had assimilated the theatrical tradition of the *Nāṭyaśāstra,* reshaping its aim and making of the performing arts a pure means for salvation. Confirming this interpretation, a similar fusion or synthesis may be seen even in the construction and development of the solo *pakhāvaj* recital, which follows the ancient model of the garland, a substitute for the lotus creeper, and is regulated by the *āvarta,* circle.

The solo recital of the nathdwara *gharānā*

The solo recital of the Nathdwara *gharānā* follows the structure outlined above but a few particular aspects contribute significantly to create a very distinctive approach. The main aspect is that although its repertoire of *parans, relās* and *jhālās* is quite wide, the largest part of the solo recital pivots around simple and short compositions which are used as thematic material to be developed through elaboration (*prastār*) and improvisation (*upaj*) based on rhythmic figures (*chandātmā*). These compositions, which are based on different *bols,* highlight various aspects of the rich expressivity of the *pakhāvaj.* By contrast, precomposed pieces feature complex structures and complicated mathematical calculations based on simple *bols* and an extensive use of the stroke ***dhā.***

Dalchand Sharma emphasizes in his own way specific aspects of his tradition such as a careful and refined use of the many *rasas* expressed by each *tāla* and each composition, clarity of sound, extremely careful attention to the tuning of the drum, rich expressivity based on delicate and elegant dynamics, excellent control of *laya* and very clear and evocative vocal recitation (*paṛhant*) of the compositions.

The following sequence delineates the typical steps in the structure of Dalchand Sharma's recital, as he himself explained during our conversations – although the position of some elements in the sequence may change according to his and the audience's mood.

Stuti paran

Dalchand Sharma starts his solo concerts with a *stuti paran* or *vandanā.* Since it is an auspicious composition, an invocation to a chosen deity is played in order to get his/her protection and keep away any possible obstacle to a good performance, most of the contemporary solo *dhrupad pakhāvaj* recitals start with it. *Gaṇeśa*, being a god who removes obstacles, is the most often invoked. Indeed there are several varieties of *Gaṇeśa paran*, old or recent, all having the same basic features. Dalchand Sharma plays the Nathdwara *Gaṇeśa paran* or *Gaṇeśa vandanā* (ex. 9.1/Audio 9.1).

Example 9.1 *Gaṇeśa paran, Cautāla* 12 beats

x dhā	dhā	o din	tā	2 kite	dhā
o Ganapati	suramuni	3 vande	buddhivi	4 nā-yaka	gajamukha
x chaturbhujā	vighna-ha	o raneśobha	karaṇasa	2 hā-yaka	digataka
o tugataka	digada-digadiga	3 theīathe	īathei	4 atheīa	theī-diga
x takatuga	takadigada-	o digadigatheī	atheīa	2 theīathe	īatheī
o digataka	tugataka	3 digada-digadiga	theīathe	4 īatheī	atheīa

'Ganapati, the great sages hail you as the Lord of wisdom. Elephant faced, four-armed, remover of obstacles, you are the one who ensures auspiciousness'.[7]

The *paran* starts on the seventh beat of the *ṭhekā.* The first part is composed only of lexical words which describe and invoke *Gaṇeśa* with his alternative name of Gaṇapati; the second one – the *tihāī* – includes only *bols* and has a joyous mood and dance feeling expressed by the 12-times recurring *bol theī.* As emphasized by Dalchand Sharma, the *bol theī* is not originally part of the *dhrupad pakhāvaj* vocabulary but comes from *kathak* dance compositions, and its presence may be explained by the fact that the

Aṣṭachāp, the eight main saints of the Puṣṭimārg, inserted *pakhāvaj*'s *bols* into their poetry.[8] According to Dalchand Sharma, the *bol* ***theī*** in this *Gaṇeśa vandanā* has to be understood as an expedient used by the author to indicate a sentiment of joyfulness through the act of dancing, and more precisely the act of dancing out a blissful emotional state generated by love for the deity. Indeed, he added that the composition should convey the image of the devotee invoking the elephant god while dancing in a state of ecstatic love for him.

Like any other *paran*, even *stuti parans* are quite flexible: they can either be modified in order to fit other *tālas* or arranged in more complex structures.

A few *stuti parans* of the Nathdwara school such as *Pañcadeva stuti*, which Purushottam (1982) Das notated along with a few others in his *Mṛdaṅg Vādan*, are quite famous for their beauty. The *Mṛdaṅg Sāgar* reports that Rupram knew how to play compositions defined as the *parans* of the gods (Gaston 1997: 245) which were probably similar to the *stuti parans*.

Madhya lay ka prastār

After having paid homage to Gaṇeśa, Śiva or other deities, asking for protection and blessings, the musician turns towards himself/herself and his/her music. According to Dalchand Sharma, the *madhya lay ka prastār* or *ṭhekā ke prastār*, the development of the thematic material of the *ṭhekā* at medium speed, is the section in which the performer introduces himself/herself to the audience. Indeed, as he himself underlined, its old name was *peśkār*, a word which means to present, to introduce (Saxena 2006: 46).[9] The musician states that drumming is his/her specialty and shows his/her confidence by playing in a different *laya* and showing ease and command over a purposely unstable rhythm swinging on different speeds often increasing and decreasing, and taking various forms. In other words, in this section the *laya* does not proceed steadily but goes through different speeds accelerating (*dugunī laya* or *deṛhī laya*), decelerating (*barābar laya*) and often going off beat.

The *madhya lay ka prastār* is based on the *bols* of the *ṭhekā*; in the case of the *cautāla*, it focuses mostly on ***dhā***, ***dintā***, ***dhadigana***, and on a specific composition such as the following one[10] (ex. 9.2/Audio 9.2), featuring the *bols* ***dhā***, ***din*** and ***dhadi*** offbeat.

Example 9.2 *Madhya lay ka prastār, Cautāla* 12 beats

x dhā-din-	tā-dhādi	o ganadhā-	din-tā-	2 keredhā-	din-tā-
o kiṭetaka	dhādigana	3 dhā-din-	tā-kata	4 kat-dhāki	tedhā-ne
x dhā	dhādigana	o dhā-din-	tā-kata	2 kat-dhāki	tedhā-ne
o dhā	dhādigana	3 dhā-din-	tā-kata	4 kat-dhāki	tedhā-ne

Dhenanaka bāj

The solo recital continues with improvisation on a special composition of the Nathdwara school based on the *bols* ***dhe na na ka*** and hence called *dhenanaka bāj* (ex. 9.3/Audio 9.3):

Example 9.3 *Dhenanaka bāj, Cautāla* 12 beats

x *mf mp* tā-dhena	*mf* nakadhet-	o dhenanaka	dhet-dhet-	2 dhenanaka	*mf f* dhet-dhet-
o dhenanaka	*mf* dhet-dhena	3 nakadhet- *mf*	*mp* dhenanaka	4 dhenanadhi	nanataka

As carefully highlighted by Dalchand Sharma, a very important feature of these *bols* is that they express different feelings (*rasas*); while the strokes ***dhenanaka*** are soft and have to convey *śṛngāra-rasa*, the stroke ***dhet*** is powerful and has to project the energetic *vīra rasa*, and these two *rasas* have to be properly presented and emphasized during the execution. The composition is played at its regular speed and then elaborated through improvisation (*upaj*) based on rhythmic figures called *chandkari*, at first in *tigunī laya* (Audio 9.4) and then in *caugunī laya* (Audio 9.5).

Ram Kishore Das did not teach me any composition including these *bols*, and while they are described as among the most characteristic features of the Nathdwara school, according to Baldeep Singh of the Punjab school the repertoire of his tradition includes an extensive list of pieces based on the *bols* ***dhe na na ka***.

Paran

After the ***dhenanaka*** section Dalchand Sharma plays some traditional *parans*. This is also the moment when he exhibits another important quality of a good *pakhāvaj* player: the ability to propose a fine vocal rendition (*paṛhant*) of the compositions. The musician has to show the dynamics and the feelings implicit in them by reciting their words (*bols*). As Dalchand Sharma argues, this aspect, called *udgatan pattu*, was emphasized in treatises such as the *Saṅgītaratnākara* (Audio 9.6). In this section of his solo Dalchand Sharma plays various kinds of *parans*. He usually starts from compositions which create geometric figures, such as *ārohī avārohī parans*, *gopucchā parans* and *cakradār parans* similar to those I have explained in Chapter 8 (ex. 8.2, 8.3, 8.4 and 8.5), and then moves to *parans* with visual and literary content, such as the *megh paran* by Purushottam Das (see Chapter 8, p. 43), the *gaj paran* (see Chapter 8, ex. 8.14) and other *parans* which he selects for their literary content. However, while other sections of the solo are based on improvisation and follow a precise structure, this is mostly a sequence of compositions and the improvisation may consist of creating on the spot a string of precomposed *parans*.

Lay tāl torneka kata

Lay tāl torneka kata which, as Dalchand Sharma explained to me, means cracking the rhythm in a balanced way – from *torneka*, cracking, and *kata*, the pole of the scales – is the name of another special piece from the Nathdwara school. It comes from *havelī saṅgīt*, in particular from the section called *chalti* where the density of the rhythm increases temporarily. Purushottam Das took a pattern from there and made of it a composition which he played in his solo recitals. It is a very short composition which includes only a few *bols*: ***katetetā -dhetetā***. It is an interesting piece since, contrasting with the general practice, the closed *bol* of the left hand ***ka*** is on-beat while the resonant *bol* of the right hand ***tā*** is offbeat, and this feature provides great scope for improvisation (*upaj*).

Dalchand Sharma assimilated the idea of this piece to the two main phases of the carving of an image, the first one, in which the block of stone is broken in order to take out rough shapes, thus producing disorder, and the second one, in which the sculptor refines the carving, eventually taking out of the stone the form that he had in his mind. In order to explain the feeling that it should project, he associated it to the pain felt by a man walking barefoot and suddenly stepping on some stones but soon having relief from it. Thus, the concept of this piece is to create tension, or rhythmic instability, and then relax, resulting in a new rhythmic balance.

Example 9.4 *Lay tāl torneka kata, Cautāla* 12 beats

x katiṭetā	-dheṭetā	o katiṭetā	-dheṭetā	2 katiṭetā	-dheṭetā
o katiṭetā	-dheṭetā	3 katiṭetā	-dheṭetā	4 katiṭetā	-dheṭetā

The composition (ex. 9.4/Audio 9.7, min. 00:06–00:42) is first presented in the set base speed (*ekguni laya*) and then elaborated through improvisation in *tiśra* (Audio 9.7, min. 00:42–01:50), *miśra* (Audio 9.8, min. 00:04–00:25) and *catuśra jāti gati* (Audio 9.9, min. 00:06–00:49).

Chandkari

The term *chandkari* means rhythmic patterns but refers also to a specific kind of *paran* which Dalchand Sharma called *pūjā parans*, since they evoke the ritual offering of flowers through a creative use of the *bol* ***dhā***. The school of Nathdwara has a huge repertoire of such compositions; some of them, having four or six ***dhās***, have been selected by Dalchand Sharma for his recitals and renamed as *puṣpabṛṣṭi*, or rain of flowers, as he himself told me. During his recitals he explains this piece and then recites it, showing by the movement of the arms and hands the act of throwing flowers over the icon of a deity (Video 2, min. 27.45–29.39).

The composition/improvisation is built on the *bols* of the *samā paran* (ex 8.1), which are slightly varied in each repetition, but the most important part of the piece are the *tihāīs* and the following *cakradār* showing an increasing presence of ***dhās***. Indeed, the first *tihāī* includes only one ***dhā*** (ex. 9.5a), the second two ***dhās*** (ex. 9.5b), and the third three ***dhās*** (ex. 9.5c); they lead to a six *vibhāgs* phrase introducing a *cakradār*, based on the same *bols* of the *tihāīs*, in which the number of ***dhās*** increases gradually from one to four (ex. 9.5d) and whose triple repetition produces the effect of a grand finale and the accomplishment of the offering.

Example 9.5 The *tihāīs* and the *cakradār* in *Puṣpabṛṣṭi*, *Cautāla* 12 beats

a.	[kiṭetakadhādigana	**dhā-------**	--------] x 3
b.	[kiṭetakadhādigana	**dhā-------**	**dhā---**] x 3
c.	[kiṭetakadhādigana	**dhā---dhā---**	**dhā---**] x 3
d.	[tā-kiṭetakadhādigana	**dhā---**	
	tā-kiṭetakadhādigana	**dhā-dhā---**	
	tā-kiṭetakadhādigana	**dhā-dhā-dhā---**	
	tā-kiṭetakadhādigana	**dhā-dhā-dhā-dhā---**	
	tā-kiṭetakadhādigana	**dhā-dhā-dhā-dhā---**	
	tā-kiṭetakadhādigana	**dhā-dhā-dhā-dhā-------**	-digana] x 3

Thapiyā ka bāj

Thapiyā ka bāj, or playing of the *thāp*, the alternative name for the *bol* ***tā***, is the traditional name attributed by the Nātdhwara school to the section generally called *jhālā*. According to Dalchand Sharma the term *jhālā*, or *jhārā*, means rain, and its main idea is to evoke the steady and balanced rhythm of rain.

The specific feature of this section of the solo is the continuous flow of sound based on the bass sound of the left-hand resounding *bol* ***ge*** played in strings such as ***tāgegege***, including more than one repetition of it, and other bols such as ***di*** and ***na*** (Audio 9.10, min 00:03–01:04). The improvisation is developed through rhythmic patterns of various length whose sequence produces a continuous shift of the strong accents produced by the *bol* ***tā***, over a steady flow of bass sounds (***ge***). *Layakārī* provides another means of improvisation (Audio 9.10, min 01:05–02:03). *Bols* such as ***dhumakiṭe*** or ***dheredhere*** matching with the character of this piece are those including the bass sound ***ge***, and may be played to create variations.

Relā

The *relā* occupies the last section of the solo. As already said (in Chapter 8) the term means torrent, and this is the fastest part of the recital. The compositions are usually based on *bols* allowing fast fingering. Dalchand Sharma often plays simple *relās* which he develops by creating numerous sound variations produced by striking various areas of the skin in different ways, and through a sensitive use of dynamics (Audio 9.11). In his concerts he often associates the *relā* to rain and 'shows' the heavy or light rain by a careful use of fingering and dynamics.

While other schools such as the Kudau Singh *gharānā* define the *paṛāl* as a long *relā*, in the Nathdwara tradition the *paṛāl* is a special kind of composition based on the *bols* ***tā di tun na*** and the *gopucchā* (cow-tail) *yati* (ex. 8.2/ Audio 8.1). According to Dalchand Sharma, compositions belonging to this group may be played at the end of the solo recital together with the *relā*.

The analysis of the contemporary repertoire of the *pakhāvaj* from a multidimensional perspective confirms the data provided by historical, religious and iconographical research. The study of the visual and literary content of the compositions discloses the deep links of the *pakhāvaj* with courts and kings, besides its important and presently most highlighted role in temple worship. Indeed, while prayers such as the *stuti parans* and compositions based on the prosody of religious texts show the impact of temple traditions on the repertoire of the *pakhāvaj*, *parans* including images and metaphors associated with kingship and sovereignty demonstrate its relationship with royal courts. Furthermore, these images and metaphors strongly linked with Sanskrit literature suggest that the function and the qualities attributed to the *mṛdaṅga* in early medieval courts had been transferred to the *pakhāvaj* in the Mughal period, when it was identified with the *mṛdaṅga*. It is also extremely interesting that not only were its symbolical aspects absorbed during the process of incorporation of the heritage of the *mṛdaṅga*, but so were the visual and narrative functions attributed to its language. They have survived the religious zeal of the nationalist movements of the 19th century and still tell stories connected with kings and sovereignty. In fact, they are a unique feature of the *pakhāvaj* and as such help to understand its history.

Seen from a multidimensional perspective, the sequence of the solo recital of Dalchand Sharma speaks of kings, gods, of the King-God Nāthjī and the Nathdwara tradition, of musicianship and of the musician's relationship with his audience; combining compositions connected with the temple and the court with new pieces and a new approach introduced to meet the needs and tastes of the audiences of republican and globalized India, it provides a sonic representation of the many facets of the *mṛdaṅga-pakhāvaj* and the various phases of its evolution.

Notes

1 The recording of the solo recital of Rāja Chatrapati Singh was given to me by Prabhu Datt, nephew of Amarnath Mishra and member of the staff organizing the Benares Dhrupad Mela.

2 Video available at: www.youtube.com/watch?v=3GLVLBkEDM (Accessed 28 November 2016).
3 The distinction was further clarified and discussed at length by Abhinavagupta in his commentary on the *Nāṭyaśāstra*.
4 *Nyāya, Vaiśeṣika, Sāṃkya, Yoga, Mīṃānsā* and *Vedānta*.
5 The six-spoked wheel also appears in the commentary of the *Yoga Sūtra* by Vyāsa (Balslev1984: 47). The same concept is expressed in the Upaniṣads (*Bṛhadāranyaka Upaniṣad* 6, 2, 16-*Chāndogya Upaniṣad* 5, 10, 3–7) and the *Bhagvad Gītā* (VIII, 23–26).
6 Interestingly, the elephant–lotus association is employed in *cakra* diagrams of the human body in relation to two particular *cakras*: *mūlādhāra cakra* and *viśuddha cakra*.
7 The translation is mine.
8 See also Sharma, Yadav and Sharma 1997: 168; Thielemann 1999: 345.
9 Ram Kishore Das had a different opinion. Indeed, he told me that the *peśkār* had been introduced into the *pakhāvaj* repertoire by Pagal Das.
10 Ram Kishore Das taught me this composition naming it *ṭhekā ke bāṇṭ*, a definition which means division and seems to imply an elaboration similar to the *bol bāṇṭ* of vocal *dhrupad*.

10 Conclusion

I was introduced into the world of the *pakhāvaj* by Svāmī Ram Kishore Das. Since our first meeting in his house, he insisted on the strong relationship of the *pakhāvaj* – conceived as a high-status drum – with worship, kingship, literature, arts and yoga, supporting his affirmation with myths and quotations from the epics. Furthermore, he maintained that his school included mostly ascetics, who played the *pakhāvaj* for worship or as meditative practice (Chapter 1).

In order to answer the many questions arising from his extremely interesting and fascinating representation of the *pakhāvaj*, combining the ancient past with present time, I have conducted fieldwork research on contemporary *pakhāvaj* playing and interviewed several representatives of almost all of the main schools (Chapter 3). All the musicians showed familiarity with the mythology linked to the *mṛdaṅga* and the episodes of the epics in which it is mentioned, and quoted verses in Sanskrit or vernacular languages related to the drum or to explain the relationship of some compositions with prosody. They considered their drum to be a divine instrument and, in fact, often kept it among the deities in the temple-room of their houses. The picture which emerges of these musicians is quite different from that of other performers of Indian classical music belonging to the category of accompanists, and results from the specific qualities of the drum they play. The high rank and religious aura of the *pakhāvaj* – which are generally recognized by performing artists – derive primarily from its being the drum played by major gods such as Gaṇeśa, Śiva and Viṣṇu, and in the *sancta sanctorum* of Vaiṣṇava temples. However, as the *pakhāvajīs* themselves pointed out, it is also due to its ancient association with kings, sovereignty and auspiciousness.

Thus, the themes that came up were consistent with the world of the *pakhāvaj* depicted by Ram Kishore Das, but did not provide any rational explanation for its auspiciousness, its association with kings and gods or the fact that its repertoire includes compositions which are in various ways linked to royal courts and temples.

I realized I had to deepen my research on the history of the *pakhāvaj*, its myths and symbolism. Since the literature on the history of the *pakhāvaj* and the ancient *mṛdaṅga* was scanty, I turned my attention to studies related to the cultural and religious context of ancient and premodern Indian society. A critical assessment and analysis of these studies (Chapter 2), which I have integrated with research on visual sources, have helped me to identify the concept of the King-God as the main key to answer my research questions and explain the symbolic world proposed by the contemporary *pakhāvaj* players.

I studied the main ideas linked to the *mṛdaṅga* and their evolution in changing social and religious contexts. First (Chapter 4) I focused on the concept of auspiciousness, the cults of fertility and the main symbols and metaphors associated with it. I described the ancient *mṛdaṅga* set, analysed the myth of the origin of drums narrated in the *Nāṭyaśāstra* and, with the help of iconographic and literary sources, provided a new interpretation according to which the *mṛdaṅga* symbolically corresponds to Gaja-Lakṣmī, goddess of fertility, auspiciousness and sovereignty. I argued that the sound of the *mṛdaṅga* was not conceived as purely aesthetic, that its value was not exclusively based on the beauty of its sound, but that it also had to produce auspiciousness and represent kingship. I suggested that the idea of the music which developed in the royal courts of ancient India was at the same time aesthetic and ritual; in other words, that the concept of aesthetics included the evocation of fertility and auspiciousness as empowering forces. I also argued that the qualities and powers of the sound of the *mṛdaṅga* relied not only on their purely sonic/acoustical properties but also on the symbolical associations attached to the instrument. The *mṛdaṅga* was linked to Gaja-Lakṣmī, a goddess representing auspiciousness and sovereignty, and to clouds and elephants, which were important symbols of kingship, and the rain which fertilizes the earth. Thus, it was a living emblem of kingship and the repository of royal power and authority, and to play it meant to activate the auspicious powers and forces connected to sovereignty. I also proposed an alternative interpretation arguing that auspiciousness, clouds and rain have been linked not only to fertility but also to enlightenment, with the sound of the *mṛdaṅga* being a symbol of spiritual fulfillment.

Then I explained the relationship of Śiva and Viṣṇu with kingship and the royal drum (Chapter 5). At the core of this argument are the concept of the King-God and the associated secular–sacred dichotomy; on the basis of myths, literary and visual sources, I suggested a new narrative on the evolution of the *mṛdaṅga* and its relationship with kingship and godship.

I reported on the evolution of the organology of the *mṛdaṅga*, examined the reasons why it was associated with the two main representatives of power in Indian life, and provided an interpretation of the cluster of symbols and metaphors which constitute its most essential aspects. I suggested that the concepts of the sacred and the secular, as they were conceived in the world of kings of ancient and medieval India of the 1st millennium, changed significantly during the 2nd millennium C.E. and, accordingly, the relationship between kings and gods changed. During the 1st millennium

C.E. kings were divinized figures, and gods such as Śiva and Viṣṇu were conceived as kings; the sacred and the secular almost coincided, and music, dance and eroticism, intended as auspicious and fertilizing, played an important role in their lives and rituals. The identification of secular and sacred, and kings and gods, entailed the adoption of the royal ceremonial, hence, music and dance in their erotic and auspicious aspects, and the *mṛdaṅga* as symbol of kingship in the temple's ritual worship.

During the 2nd millennium, the spread of Islam and new devotional cults throughout the subcontinent contributed to the establishment of a new balance between the sacred and the secular; in the new scenario gods predominated and kings became representatives of deities on the earth, needing divine legitimation. However, the identification of Śiva and Viṣṇu as kings remained and with it the worship procedures based on royal ceremonial. Most of the numerous devotional cults – Śaiva, Vaiṣṇava, Sikh, Sufi – which spread during that period did not reject music and eroticism but included them in their rituals; they were reinterpreted in a spiritualized form, and adopted into a ritual worship which was conceived as a devotional act, a service to God, and no longer as an empowering auspicious ritual. During this process, the *mṛdaṅga*, in its many new regional varieties, was transformed from an emblem of kingship into a symbol of God. Indeed, the emergence of vernacular (*deśī*) traditions and their legitimation as courtly or sacred (*mārga*) through a process of Sanskritization was an important phenomenon happening in that period, and I argued that the *pakhāvaj* was a regional drum, appreciated by Mughal nobles for its masculine and powerful sound, which was identified with the ancient *mṛdaṅga* so as to legitimate it as a royal drum (Chapter 6). In fact, this process happened under the Emperor Akbar and in the context of Mughal discovery of the splendours of the ancient Indian kingdoms, and their tradition and Sanskrit texts. I further highlighted the Mughals' contribution to the evolution of the *pakhāvaj* suggesting that it completed its organological development during their empire, becoming a drum very similar to the contemporary instrument during their empirical reign, and that some of the most important ideas and aspects which are still strongly associated with the *pakhāvaj*, such as its vigorous and heroic character, had been attributed by them.

The devotional aspect of music emphasized by the *bhakta* cults of the second half of the 2nd millennium C.E. was assumed as the essence of Indian music by the nationalist movements of the second half of the 19th century. Temple music was elected as the exclusive representative of the sacred – intended as religious and devotional – and was contrasted with the entertaining music of the debauched royal courts; devotional music was assumed as a symbol of Hindu culture with the result that music is still today a synonym of devotional religion. While the new vision of music entailed significant changes in the life of musicians and the status of musical instruments, the *mṛdaṅga*, due to its secular association with temple music, remained almost unaffected, and for this reason it is still considered a high-status drum.

The many aspects of my research have converged at Nathdwara, a contemporary temple town ruled by the King-God Nāthjī in which one of the major schools of *pakhāvaj* evolved (Chapter 7). Numerous important aspects of the heritage of this school are rooted in the temple tradition of Nathdwara, in which music is a crucial element of ritual worship. The study of the history and the aesthetic approach of this *gharānā*, which evolved in connection with ritual worship, have given me the opportunity to observe and analyse musical ideas and creative processes connected to the cult of a King-God from the point of view of a contemporary temple/palace. The chance to discuss with Dalchand Sharma the aesthetics of the *pakhāvaj* playing in the temple of Nathdwara has allowed me to comprehend the ritual function of music according to the Vallabha sect, as well as the main features of the specific style and repertoire developed there, with the aim of pleasing the King-God Nāthjī.

On the basis of all this information I analysed (Chapter 8) the various classes of composition included in the contemporary repertoire of the *pakhāvaj*. I approached them not as purely musical compositions but as multilayered pieces including visual and literary content. I suggested that the main compositional forms have strong relationships with different types of images, with poetry and prayers, and that the voice of the *pakhāvaj* had been structured in a language capable of suggesting movements, such as the gait of elephants and women, images, such as the peacocks dancing at the sound of the thundering monsoon clouds, and telling stories from the epics. I argued that these aspects of the *pakhāvaj* are rooted in early medieval courtly culture in which its ancestor *mṛdaṅga* was considered as the sonic representation of kingship, and that some of the most important symbols of sovereignty are strongly associated with it and incorporated in its compositions. These unique facets of the *pakhāvaj* and its language have never been pointed out before, and this is the first study of its repertoire from multiple perspectives, including visual and narrative aspects.

Having studied such musical forms I analysed the structure of solo recital and its symbolical association with the garland of flowers. Then, I focused the analysis on the solo recital in the Nathdwara *gharānā* and according to Dalchand Sharma (Chapter 9), highlighting a few unique compositions of this tradition and the strong impact of the aesthetic approach of the temple music of the Vallabha sect in the repertoire. Furthermore, considering the visual and narrative aspects included in the *pakhāvaj*'s compositions, I suggested that the sequence of the solo recital of Dalchand Sharma, including pieces connected with the many contexts in which the *mṛdaṅga-pakhāvaj* has been played over time, provides a sonic representation of its many facets and phases of evolution.

Thus, I studied the contemporary repertoire of the *pakhāvaj* and its relationships with ancient courtly culture and temple music. Indeed, the fact that for centuries it has been emblematic of kings and gods, and hence an important presence in both courts and temples, has left clear traces in various facets of its heritage, from the myths of origin associated with it, to its auspiciousness and repertoire.

Most of the aspects which I have analysed in this study have been changing over time: the body of the drum, its repertoire, the function of music, the concepts of the sacred and the secular and their relationship. Accordingly, I have studied the *mṛdaṅg-pakhāvaj* as a process, in other words, as a living aspect of a culture in a continuous process of change. However, notwithstanding the evolution of the ideas associated with the drum, since kingship was the main political and administrative power in India until the last century, and gods have been and still are conceived as kings, the association of the *mṛdaṅga* with kings and gods has remained unchanged until today. The element which more than any other confirms this association is the name *mṛdaṅga*; indeed, the analysis of the changes in the body of the drum, in spite of the persistence of its name and the fact that it has always been the most important drum, has allowed me to argue that the name *mṛdaṅga* represented sovereignty, divine status and auspiciousness, and that different vernacular drums, over time, had been consecrated as the most important court or temple drums by being attributed with the name *mṛdaṅga*. The evolution of the *mṛdaṅga* shows that while its body changed significantly according to historical periods and geographical areas, and the cluster of ideas and symbols associated with it slightly changed too, the name *mṛdaṅga* remained unchanged over time to guarantee authenticity and authority to the instruments to which it was attributed.

One perspective of research which it has not been possible to include in this study, due to the lack of notated examples in textual sources, is the evolution of *mṛdaṅga* compositions over the centuries. Such information would have been useful to the understanding of the development of compositional forms during the Middle Ages and to the study of the relationship of drumming and images, which has emerged from this research and has never before been studied. Indeed, the main subject of Indological and ethnomusicological analysis in the context of the relationship of music and images has been the *rāgamālās*, in which such relationship is based on paintings and *rāgas*, in other words on paintings giving visual forms to melodic types.

In this study, I have suggested that the deep relationship of drumming with images – intended as painted and verbal as well as enacted representations – had tribal or folk roots; it was structured and codified in the context of theatre, and established by the *Nāṭyaśāstra* and Sanskrit literature in a period between the last centuries of the 1st millennium B.C.E. and the first centuries of the 2nd millennium C.E.. The ancient drama tradition was then incorporated and reinterpreted during the 2nd millennium by the emerging Vaiṣṇava cults, who adopted it as a means of propagating their creed, and their theatrical forms are still enacted. The strict association of drumming with images is still clearly visible, for instance, in the many festivals of Orissa in which gods and goddesses are represented by masked performers whose movements are guided and sonically expressed through specific *bols* of the drum; it was explained to me by an Odissi *pakhāvaj* player member of a hereditary family of musicians of the temple of Puri, who first showed me the way that the drum is played in the temple, and then played a few of the different rhythmic figures which provide sonic form to the various deities parading in the streets of the town during festivals, and guide their gait. My ongoing research in Kerala on Kūḍiyāṭṭaṃ, Teyyāṭṭaṃ and *kaḷams*, drawings made with coloured powders on the floor, confirm the strict association of drumming with images, and suggest further research on drumming, images and dance in other theatrical forms such as, for instance, the Ankhiya Bhaona of Assam. This would provide important information on the evolution of this relationship and the different ways it has been approached in various regions of South Asia and contribute to the development of a wider picture.

Other useful research in this direction should be focused on tribal and folk cults, still practised in various areas of the subcontinent, in which ritual drumming empowers sacred paintings such as, for instance, the wall paintings of the Rathvas of Gujarat, the Warli of Rajasthan and the Saora of Orissa. It would provide extremely interesting information and would help to distinguish the different layers of development of this relationship, and the mutual influences of Hindu and Muslim approaches to drumming at the levels of ritual music and classical music. Another important aspect of the relationship of music and images is the practice of playing music for an icon. Indeed, it is part of my ongoing research on ritual music in Kerala temples, the preliminary results of which have been providing fascinating and extremely interesting information. Music has been adopted as a ritual element by almost all Indic religious traditions from at least the 1st millennium C.E. onward; the comprehension of the meaning and the aim of the playing of music for the image or icon, as well as its meaning in the overall ritual procedure, would be useful to an understanding of its religious value and the meaning of music-making in India.

Bibliography

Ahmad, N. (Trans.) (1956). *Kitab-i-Nauras: By Ibrahim Adil Shah II*, New Delhi: Bharatiya Kala Kendra.

Ahuja, N.P. (2001). 'Changing Gods, Enduring Rituals: Observations on Early Indian Religion as Seen through Terracotta Imagery', *South Asian Archaeology*, Vol. II. Historical Archaeology and Art History. Paris, pp. 345–354.

Aiyar, K.N. (1914). *Thirty Minor Upanishads*, Madras: Theosophical Society.

Ali, D. (2006). *Courtly Culture and Political Life in Early Medieval India*, New Delhi: Cambridge University Press-Foundation Book Ptv.

Ambalal, A. (1987). *Krishna as Shrinathji: Rajasthani Paintings from Nathdwara*, Ahmedabad: Mapin.

Ambedkar, B.R. (1947). *India in Kalidasa*, Allahabad: Kitabistan.

Asher, C.B. and Talbot, C. (2006). *India before Europe*, Cambridge: Cambridge University Press.

Ashirwadam, P.D. (1990). *Raigarh Darbar*, New Delhi: Agam Kala Prakasham.

Auboyer, J. (1965). *Daily Life in Ancient India*, London: Phoenix Press.

Babiracki, C.M. (1991). 'Tribal Music in the Study of Great and Little Traditions of Indian Music', In Nettl, B. and Bohlman, P. (Eds.), *Comparative Musicology and Anthropology of Music* (pp. 69–90). Chicago: University of Chicago Press.

Bahattacharya, D. (1999). *Musical Instruments of Tribal India*, New Delhi: Manas Publications.

Bake, A. (1987). 'La musica dell'India', In Wellesz, E. (Ed.), *Musica antica e orientale* (Vol. I, pp. 217–250). Milano: Feltrinelli.

Bakhle, J. (2005). *Two Men and Music*, New York: Oxford University Press.

Balslev, N.A. (1984). 'Time in Indian Philosophy', *Proceedings of the Scandinavian Conference Seminar of Indological Studies*, Stockholm 1982.

Bandopadhay, S. (2010). *Manipuri Dance: An Assessment on History and Presentation*, Gurgaon: Shubhi Publication.

Banerjea, J.N. (1956). *The Development of Hindu Iconography*, Calcutta: Calcutta University Press.

Bansat-Boudon, L. (1992a). *Poètique du Thèâtre Indienne: Lectures du Nāṭyaśāstra*, Paris: Publications de l'École Française d'Extrème Orient.

Bansat-Boudon, L. (1992b). 'Le cœur-miroir: Remarques sur la théorie indienne de l'expérience esthétique et ses rapports avec le théâtre', In *Les cahiers de philosophie 14: L'Orient de la pensée. Philosophies en Inde* (pp. 133–154).

Barthakur, D.R. (2003). *The Music and Musical Instruments of North Eastern India*, New Delhi: Mittal Publication.

Beach, M.C. (2002). *Mughal and Rajput Painting*, Cambridge: New Cambridge History of India.

Beck, G.L. (2011). *Sonic Liturgy: Ritual and Music in Hindu Tradition*, Columbia: University of South Carolina Press.

Bhatnagar, V. (2003). *Shringar: The Ras Raj. Indian Classical View*, New Delhi: Abhinav Publication.

Blochmann, H.A. and Jarrett, H.S.C. (Trans.) (1894). *The Ain I Akbari by Abdul Fazl 'Allami*, Calcutta: Asiatic Society of Bengal.

Booth, G.D. (2008). 'Space, Sound, Auspiciousness, and Performance in North Indian Wedding Processions', In Jacobsen, K.A. (Ed.), *South Asian Religion on Display* (pp. 63–76). London: Routledge.

Bor, J. (1986/87). 'The Voice of Sarangi: An Illustrated History of Bowing in India', *Journal of the National Centre for the Performing Arts*, Vol. XV–XVI. Bombay.

Brancaccio, P. (2011). *The Buddhist Caves at Aurangabad: Transformations in Art and Religion*, Leiden/Boston: Brill.

Brown, K. (2000). 'Reading Indian Music: The Interpretation of Seventeenth-century European Travel-Writing in the (Re)construction of Indian Music History', *British Journal of Ethnomusicology*, Vol. 9, No. 2, pp. 1–34.

———. (2003). *Hindustani Music in the Time of Aurangzeb*, (Phd), London: School of Oriental and African Studies, University of London.

Brown, R.E. (1965). *The Mridanga: A Study of Drumming in South India*, (PhD), Los Angeles: University of California.

Buhnemann, G. (1988). *Pūjā: A Study in Smarta Ritual*, Vienna: De Nobili Research Library.

Bush, A. (2004). *The Courtly Vernacular: The Transformation of Brajbasha Literary Culture (1590–1690)*, (PhD), Chicago: University of Chicago.

———. (2010). 'Hidden in Plain View: Brajabhasa Poets at the Mughal Court', *Modern Asian Studies*, Vol. 44, No. 2, pp. 267–309.

———. (2015). 'Listening for the Context: Tuning in to the Reception of Riti Poetry', In Orsini, F. and Butler Schofield, K. (Eds.), *Tellings and Texts: Music, Literature and Performance in North India* (pp. 249–282). Cambridge: Open Book Publishers.

Butler Schofield, K. (2010). 'Reviving the Golden Age Again: "Classicization", "Hindustani Music" and the Mughals', *Ethnomusicology*, Vol. 54, No. 3, pp. 484–517.

Caitanya, K. (1976). *A History of Indian Painting: The Mural Tradition*, New Delhi: Abhinav Publications.

———. (1979). *A History of Indian Painting: Manuscript, Mughal and Deccani Traditions*, New Delhi: Abhinav Publications.

———. (1982). *A History of Indian Painting: Rajasthani Traditions*, New Delhi: Abhinav Publications.

Carman, J.B. and Marglin, F.A. (1985). *Purity and Auspiciousness in Indian Society*, Leiden: Brill.

Caudhury, V.R. (2000). *The Dictionary of Hindustani Classical Music*, Delhi: Motilal Banarsidass.

Chaubey, S. (1958). *Musicians I Have Met*, Lukhnow: Prakashan Shanka.

Chaudary, S. (1997). *Time Measures and Compositional Types in Indian Music*, New Delhi: Aditya Prakashan.

Clayton, M. (2000). *Time in Indian Music: Rhythm, Metre, and Form in North Indian Rag Performance*, Oxford: Oxford University Press.

Clothey, F.W. (2006). *Religion in India: A Historical Introduction*, New York/ Oxon: Routledge.

Collins, C.D. (1982). 'Elephanta and the Ritual of the Lakulīśa-Pāśupatas', *Journal of the American Oriental Society*, Vol. 102, No. 4, (Oct.–Dec.), pp. 605–617.

Coomaraswamy, A.K. (1929). 'Early Indian Iconography', *Eastern Art*, Vol. 1, No. 3, pp. 175–189.

———. (1942). *Spiritual Authority and Temporal Power*, New Haven: American Oriental Society.

———. (1991). *The Dance of Shiva*, New Delhi: Munishram Manoharlal.

———. (2001). *Yakshas*, New Delhi: Motilal Banarsidass.

———. (2004). 'The Nature of Folklore and Popular Art', In Coomaraswamy, A.K. (Ed.), *The Essential* (pp. 213-224). by Coomaraswamy R.P. Bloomington: World Wisdom.

Dallapiccola, A. L. and Isacco, E. (1977). *Ragamala*, Paris: Exhibition catalogue, Galerie Marco Polo.

Danielou, A. (1943). *Introduction to the Study of Musical Scales*, Benares: The India Society.

———. (1949). *Northern Indian Music*, Vol.1, London: Christopher Johnson.

———. (1954). *Northern Indian Music*, Vol.2, London: Halcyon Press.

———. (1970). 'Rhythm and Tempo in the Puranas', in *Aspects of Indian music*, New Delhi: Publication Division, Ministry of Information and Broadcasting, Government of India, Patiala House. All India Radio Symposium.

———. (1987). *While the Gods Play*, Rochester: Inner Traditions International.

Danielou, A. and Bhatt, N.R. (1959). *Le Gītālaṃkāra*, Pondichery: Institute Francoise d'Indologie.

Das, B. and Das, S.R. (Pagal Das) (1977). *Mṛdaṅg Tablā Prabhākar*, Hatras: Sangeet Karyalaya.
Das, G. (1911). *Mṛdaṅg Sāgar*, Bombay: Subhodini Press, Bhagvallal Tribhuvan.
Das, P. (1982). *Mṛdaṅg Vādan*, New Delhi: Sangeet Natak Akademi.
Davidson, R.M. (2002). *Esoteric Buddhism: A Social History of the Tantric Movement*, New York: Columbia University Press.
Davies, R. (1989). 'Enlivening Images: The Śaiva Rite of Invocation', In Dallapiccola, A.L. (Ed.), *Shastric Traditions in Indian Arts* (pp. 351–359). Stuttgart: Steiner Verlag Weisbaden.
Day, C.R. (1891). *The Music and Musical Instruments of South India and the Deccan*, Londo: Novello, Ewer & Co.
De Bruijn, T. and Bush, A. (2014). *Culture and Circulation: Literature in Motion in Early-Modern India*, Leiden: Brill.
Dehejia, V. (2009). *Adorning the Body: Dissolving Boundaries between Sacred and Profane in Inda's Art*, New York: Columbia University Press.
Delahoutre, M. (1994). *Lo spirito dell'arte Indiana*, Milano: Jaca Book.
Delvoye, N. (1990). 'The Verbal Content of Dhrupad Songs from the Earliest Collections: The Hazar Dhrupad or Sahas-Ras, a Collection of 1004 Dhrupads Attributed to Nayak Bakhsu', *Dhrupad Annual*, Vol. 5, pp. 93–108.
———. (1992). 'The Verbal Content of Dhrupad Songs from the Earliest Collections: Kitab-i-nauras (Part 1)', *Dhrupad Annual*, Vol. 6, pp. 93–108.
———. (1993). 'The Verbal Content of Dhrupad Songs from the Earliest Collections: Kitab-i-nauras (Part 2)', *Dhrupad Annual*, Vol. 8, pp. 1–23.
Deshpande, M.M. (1997). 'Who Inspired Pāṇini? Reconstructing the Hindu and Buddhist Counter-Claims', *Journal of the American Oriental Society*, Vol. 117, No. 3, pp. 444–465.
Deva, C.D. (1989). *Musical Instruments in Sculpture in Karnataka*, New Delhi: Motilal Banarsidass.
Deva, C.D. (2000). *Musical Instruments of India: Their History and Development*, New Delhi: Munishram Manoharlal.
Dick, A. (1984a). 'Hudukka', In Sadie, S. (Ed.), *The New Grove Dictionary of Musical Instruments* (pp. 257–258). London: Macmillan.
———. (1984b). 'Dholak', In Sadie, S. (Ed.), *The New Grove Dictionary of Musical Instruments* (p. 562). London: Macmillan.
———. (1984c). 'Dundubhi', In Sadie, S. (Ed.), *The New Grove Dictionary of Musical Instruments* (pp. 634–635). London: Macmillan.
———. (1984d). 'Mṛdaṅga', In Sadie, S. (Ed.), *The New Grove Dictionary of Musical Instruments* (pp. 694–695 and 696–699). London: Macmillan.
———. (1984e). 'Pataḥa', In Sadie, S. (Ed.), *The New Grove Dictionary of Musical Instruments* (pp. 21–22). London: Macmillan.
Donaldson, T. (1975). 'Propitious-Apotropaic Eroticism in the Art of Orissa', *Artibus Asiae*, Vol. 37, No. 1/2, pp. 75–100.

Eck, D. (2007). *Darshan: Seeing the Divine Image in India*, Delhi: Motilal Banarsidass.

Eliade, M. (1997). *Immagini e simboli*, Milano: Tea.

Ellingson, T. (1979) *The Mandala of Sound:Concepts and Sound Structures in Tibetan Ritual Music*, PhD Thesis, University of Wisconsin-Madison.

Ellingson, T. (1990). 'Nasad:dya: Newar God of Music', In De Vale, S.C. (Ed.), *Selected Reports in Ethnomusicology: Issues in Organology, Vol. VIII* (p. 221–272). Los Angeles: University of California.

Erdman, J.L. (1985). *Patrons and Performers in Rajasthan*, Delhi: Chanakya Publications.

Farrell, G. (1999). *Indian Music and the West*, Oxford: Oxford University Press.

Francom, T. (2012). *A Sociomusicological Analysis of the Paran*, (M Thesis), University of Toronto.

Gangoly, O.C. (1935). *Ragas & Raginis. A Pictorial & Iconographic Study of Indian Musical Modes Based on Original Sources*, New Delhi: Munshiram Manoharlal.

Gangouly, K.M. (Trans.) (1883–1896). *The Mahabharata of Krishna-Dwaipayana Vyasa*, www.sacred-texts.com/hin/maha/index.htm.

Garzilli, E. (2003). 'The Flowers of the Ṛgveda Hymns: Lotus in V.78.7, X.184.2, X.107.10, VI.16.13, and VII.33.11, VI.61.2, VIII.1.33, X.142.8', *Indo-Iranian Journal*, Vol. 46, No. 4, pp. 293–314.

Gaston, A.M. (1981). *Shiva in Dance, Myth and Iconography*, New Delhi: Oxford University Press.

———. (1989). 'The Hereditary Drummers of the Śrī Nāthjī Temple: The Family History of Pakhāvajī Guru Purushottam Das', *Dhrupal Annual*, Vol. IV, pp. 15–35. Varanasi: All India Kashi Raj Trust.

———. (1997). *Krishna's Musicians: Musicians and Music Making in the Temples of Nathdwara Rajasthan*, New Delhi: Manohar.

Ghosh, M. (Trans.) (1950). *The Nāṭyaśāstra: A Treatise on Hindu Dramaturgy and Histrionics, Vol. 1*, Calcutta: Royal Asiatic Society.

Ghosh, M. (Trans.) (1961). *The Nāṭyaśāstra: A Treatise on Hindu Dramaturgy and Histrionics, Vol. 2*, Calcutta: Royal Asiatic Society.

Gnoli, R. (1968). *The Aesthetic Experience according to Abhinavagupta*, Varanasi: Chowkhamba Sanskrit Studies.

Gonda, J. (1956a). 'Ancient Indian Kingship from the Religious Point of View', *Numen*, Vol. 3, No. 1, pp. 36–71.

———. (1956b). 'Ancient Indian Kingship from the Religious Point of View', *Numen*, Vol. 3, No. 2, pp. 122–155.

———. (1957a). 'Ancient Indian Kingship from the Religious Point of View', *Numen*, Vol. 4, No. 1, pp. 24–58.

———. (1957b). 'Ancient Indian Kingship from the Religious Point of View', *Numen*, Vol. 4, No. 2, pp. 122–164.

———. (1963). *The Indian Mantra, Oriens, Vol.13*, Leiden: Brill.

———. (1969). *Aspects of Early Vishnuism*, Delhi: Motilal Banarsidass.

———. (1981). *Veda E Antico Induismo*, Milano: Jaca Book.

Gopal, S. (2004). *Mridangam:. An Indian Classical Percussion Drum*, Delhi: B.R. Rhythms.

Gottlieb, R.S. (1977). *The Major Traditions of North Indian Tabla Drumming, Vol. 2*, Munchen-Salzburg: Musicverlag E. Katzblichler.

Graves, E. (2009). *Rhythmic Theology: Khol Drumming in Caitanya Vaisnava Kirtan*, (PhD), Medford, Massachusetts: TUFTS University.

Greig, J.A. (1987). *Tarikh-i Sangita: The Foundations of North Indian Music in the Sixteenth Century*, (PhD), Los Angeles: University of California.

Gupt, B. (1986). 'Valmiki's Rāmāyaṇa and the Nāṭyaśāstra', *Sangeet Natak Journal*, Vol. 81–82, July–Dec, pp. 63–76.

———. (2006). *Dramatic Concepts, Greek and India: A Study of Poetics & Nāṭyaśāstra*, New Delhi: D.K.Printworld.

Gupta, S.K. (1983). *Elephant in Indian Art and Mythology*, New Delhi: Abhinav Publications.

Haas, G. (Trans.) (1912). *The Daśarūpaka: A Treatise on Hindu Dramaturgy*, Columbia: Columbia University Press.

Haberman, D.L. (2001). *Acting as A Way of Salvation: A Study of Raganuga Bhakti Sadhana*, New Delhi: Motilal Banarsidass.

Hart, G.L. (1975). *The Poems of Ancient Tamil*, London: University of California Press.

———. (1999). *The Four Hundreds Songs of War and Wisdom*, New York, Chichester: Columbia University Press.

Hawley, J.S. (2009). *The Memory of Love: Surdas Sings Krishna*, New York: Oxford University Press.

Heesterman, J.C. (1985). *The Inner Conflict of Tradition: Essays in Indian Ritual, Kingship, and Society*, Chicago: University of Chicago Press.

Ho, M. (2006). *The Liturgical Music of the Pusti Marg of India: An Embryonic Form of the Classical Tradition*, (PhD), Los Angeles: University of California.

———. (2009). 'A True Self Revealed: Song and Play in Pushtimarg Liturgical Service', *The World of Music*, Vol. 51, No. 2, pp. 23–43.

Hopkins Washburn, E. (1916). 'Indra as God of Fertility', *Journal of the American Oriental Society*, Vol. 36, pp. 242–268.

Huntington, S. (1994). 'Kings as Gods, Gods as Kings: Temporality and Eternity in the Art of India', *Ars Orientalis*, Vol. 24, pp. 30–38.

———. (2001). *The Art of Ancient India*, Boston/London: Weather Hill.

Inden, R. (1985). 'Kings and Omens', In Carman, J.B. and Marglin, F.A. (Eds.), *Purity and Auspiciousness in Indian Society* (pp. 30–40). Leiden: Brill.

Ingalls, D.H.H. (1965). *An Anthology of Court Sanskrit Poetry* (p. 130). Cambridge: Harward University Press.

Iravati. (2003). *Performing Artists in Ancient India*, New Delhi: D.K. Printworld.

Jain, S. (1997). 'On the Indian Ritual of Abhisheka and Mahamastakabhisheka', *Annals of the Bhandarkar Oriental Research Institute*, Vol. 78, No. 1/4, pp. 61–86.

Jhaveri, D. and Devi, K. (1989). *Maṇipurī Tāla Prakāś*, Varanasi/New Delhi: Chaukhambha Orientalia.

Jindel, R. (1976). *Culture of a Sacred Town: A Sociological Study of Nathdwara*, Bombay: Popular Prakshan Private Limited.

Jones, J. (2009). *Performing the Sacred: Song, Genre, and Aesthetics in Bhakti*, (PhD), Chicago: University of Chicago.

———. (2014). 'Music, History and the Sacred in South Asia', In Bohlman, P. (Ed.), *The Cambridge History of World Music* (pp. 202–222). Cambridge: University of Cambridge.

Kaimal, P. (1999). 'Śiva Naṭarāja: Shifting Meanings of an Icon', *The Art Bulletin*, Vol. 81, No. 3 (Sept.), pp. 390–419.

Kalidos, R. (1999). 'Dance of Viṣṇu: The Spectacle of Tamil Āḻvārs', *Journal of the Royal Asiatic Society*, Third Series, Vol. 9, No. 2, pp. 223–250.

Katz, J.B. (1987). *The Musicological Portions of the Saṅgītanārāyaṇa: A Critical Edition and Commentary*, (PhD), Oxford: Wolfson College.

Kersenboom, S. (1987). *Nytiasumangali*, New Delhi: Motilal Banarsidass.

Kintaert, T. (1997). 'Ancient Indian Polyrhythms', *Sangeet Natak Journal*, No. 124, pp. 15–29.

———. (2010). 'On the Cultural Significance of the Leaf of the Indian Lotus: Introduction and Uses', In Franco, E. and Zin, M. (Eds.), *From Turfan to Ajanta: Festschrift for Dieter Schlingloff on the Occasion of His Eightieth Birthday* (pp. 481–512). Lumbini: Lumbini International Research Institute.

———. (2012). 'On the Role of Lotus Leaf in South Asian Cosmography', *Vienna Journal of South Asian Studies*, Vol. 54, pp. 85–120.

Kippen, J. (2000). 'Hindustani Tāla', In Arnold, A. (Ed.), *The Garland Encyclopedia of World Music* (pp. 110–137). New York: Routledge.

———. (2005). *The Tablā of Lukhnow*, New Delhi: Manohar Publishers.

———. (2006). *Gurudev's Drumming Legacy: Music, Theory and Nationalism in the Mṛdaṅg aur Tablā Vādanpaddhati of Gurudev Patwardhan*, Burlington: Ashgate.

———. (2007). 'Tāl Paddhati of 1888: An Early Source for Tabla', *Journal of the Indian Musicological Society*, Vol. 38, pp. 146–234.

Klostermaier, K. (1986). 'Dharmamegha Samādhi: Comments on Yogasūtra IV, 29', *Philosophy East and West*, Vol. 36, No. 3, pp. 253–262.

Kothari, S. (1989). *Kathak: Indian Classical Dance Art*, New Delhi: Abhinav Abhinav Publications.

Kramrish, S. (Trans.) (1928). *The Vishnudharmottara (Part III): A Treatise on Indian Painting and Image-Making*, Calcutta: Calcutta University Press.

———. (1976). *The Hindu Temple*, New Delhi: Motilal Banarsidass.

Krishnaakinkari (2012). *Sri Pushtimargiya Asthayam Seva Kirtan Pranalika*, Nathdwara: Vrajakishori Publications.

Krisnha Murthy, K. (1985). *Archaeology of Indian Musical Instruments*, New Delhi: Sundeep Prakashan.
Kubo, T. and Yuyama, A. (Trans.) (2009). *The Lotus Sutra*, Berkley: Numata Center for Buddhist Translation and Research.
Kulshreshtha, S.R. (1989–1990). 'Music and Dance in Buddhist Literature', In *Proceedings of the Seventh World Sanskrit Conference* (pp. 215–223). Torino: A.I.T.
Lama, D. (2001). *Stages of Meditation*, London: Ryder, Random House.
Lath, M. (1988). 'Folk and Classical Music: A Dichotomy that Does Not Quite Work in India', *Sangeet Natak Journal*, Vol. 88, pp. 44–46.
Lidova, N. (1996). *Drama and Ritual of Early Hinduism*, New Delhi: Motilal Banarsidass.
Lienhard, S. (1984). *A History of Classical Poetry: Sanskrit-Pali-Prakrit*, Wiesbaden: Otto Harrassowitz.
Lybarger, L.H. (2003). *The Tabla Solo Repertoire of Pakistani Panjab: An Ethnomusicological Perspective*, (Phd), Toronto: University of Toronto.
Madan, T.N. (1985). 'Concerning the Categories Subha and Suddha in Hindu Culture. An Explanatory Essay', In Carman, J.B. and Marglin, F.A. (Eds.), *Purity and Auspiciousness in Indian Society* (pp. 11–29). Leiden: Brill.
Malamoud, C. (2005). *La danze delle pietre. Studi sulla scena sacrificale nell'India antica*, Milano: Adelphi.
Malkeyeva, A. (1997). 'Musical Instruments in the Text and Miniatures of the Bāburnāma', *RIdIM/RCMI Newsletter*, Vol. 22, No. 1 (Spring), pp. 12–22.
Marcel-Dubois, C. (1941). *Les instruments de la musique de l'Inde ancienne*, Paris: Presses Universitaires de France.
Marglin, F.A. (1985a). *Wives of the King-God*, New Delhi: Oxford University Press.
———. (1985b). 'Types of Oppositions in Hindu Culture', In Carman, J.B. and Marglin, F.A. (Eds.), *Purity and Auspiciousness in Indian Society* (pp. 65–83). Leiden: Brill.
Martinez, J.S. (2001). *Semiosis in Hindustani Music*, Delhi: Motilal Banarsidass.
Miner, A. (1994). *The Saṅgītopanisatsāroddhāra: A Fourteenth Century Treatise on Music from Western India*, (PhD), Philadelphia: University of Pennsylvania.
Misra, S. (1981). *Great Masters of Hisndustani Music*, New Delhi: Hem Publishers.
———. (1990). *Some Immortals of Hisndustani Music*, New Delhi: Harman.
Mistry, A.E. (1999). *Pakhawaj and Tabla: History, Schools and Traditions*, Mumbay: New Rajkamal Printing Press.
Mohkamsing, N. (2004). 'Beating Time. Concepts of Rhythm in the Nāṭyaśāstra', *IIAS Newsletter*, Vol. 33, pp. 22.
Mukerjee, R. (1959). *The Culture and Art of India*, London: George Allen & Unwin Ltd.

Naimpalli, S. (2005). *Theory and Practice of Tabla,* Mumbai: Popular Prakashan.

Narayanan, V. (1985). 'Srivaisnava Ritual and Literature', In Carman, J.B. and Marglin, F.A. (Eds.), *Purity and Auspiciousness in Indian Society* (pp. 55–64). Leiden: Brill.

Neog, M. and Changkakati, K. (2008). *Rhythm in the Vaisnava Music of Assam,* Guwahati: Publication Board Assam.

Neuman, D.M. (1977). 'The Social Organization of a Music Tradition: Hereditary Specialists in North India', *Ethnomusicology,* Vol. 21, No. 2, May, pp. 233–245.

———. (1985). 'Indian Music as a Cultural Model', *Asian Music,* Vol. 17, No. 1 Autumn–Winter, pp. 98–113.

———. (1980). *The Life of Music in North India,* New Delhi: Manohar.

Nijenhuis, E. (1974). *Indian Music: History and Structure,* Leiden/Koln: Brill.

———. (1977). *Musicological Literature,* Wiesbaden: Otto Harrassovitz.

Nijenhuis, E. and Delvoye, F. (2010). 'Sanskrit and Indo-Persian Literature on Indian Music', In Delvoye, F., Harwey, J. and Nijenhuis, E. (Eds.), *Hindustani Music: Thirteenth to Twentieth Centuries* (pp. 35–64). New Delhi: Manohar Publishers.

Olivelle, P. (1998). *The Early Upaniṣad,* Oxford/New York: Oxford University Press.

Orsini, F. (2014). '"Krishna is the Truth of Man": Mir 'Abdul Bilgrami's haqq'iq-i-Hindi (Indian Truths) and the Circulation of Dhrupad and Bishnupad', In De Bruijn, T. and Bush, A. (Eds.), *Culture and Circulation: Literature in Motion in Early-Modern India* (pp. 222–246). Leiden: Brill.

Orsini, F. and Butler Schofield, K. (Eds.) (2015). *Tellings and Texts: Music, Literature and Performance in North India,* Cambridge: Open Book Publishers.

Pacciolla, P. and Spagna, A.L. (2008). *La gioia e il potere: Musica e danza in India,* Nardò: Besa.

Pal, P. (1983). 'The Divine Image and Poetic Imagery in Gupta India', *Art Institute of Chicago Museum Studies,* The Art Institute of Chicago Centennial lectures, Vol. 10, pp. 209–296.

Pande, A. (1993). *The Natyashastra Tradition and Ancient Indian Society,* Jaipur: Kusumanjali Book World.

———. (1996). *A Historical and Cultural Study of the Natyashastra of Bharata,* Jaipur: Kusumanjali Book World.

Paulose, K.G. (2014). *Theatre Classical and Popular,* http://kgpaulose.info/index.php/from-the-press/12-articles/41-theatre-classical-and-popular.

Peerera, E.S. (1994). *The Origin and Development of Dhrupad and Its Bearing on Instrumental Music,* Calcutta: K.P. Bagchi.

Pieruccini, C. (2002). 'Occhi Di Loto', In Botto, O., Boccali, G. and Rossi, P.M. (Ed.), *Atti del Seminario 'La Natura ne Pensiero e nella Letteratura e nelle Arti dell'India.* Torino: Associazione Italiana Studi Sanscriti, pp. 35–50.

Platts, J. (1884). *A Dictionary of Urdu, Classical Hindi and English*, London: Library Association Publishing.

Pollock, S. (1984). 'The Divine King in the Indian Epics', *Journal of the American Oriental Society*, Vol. 104, No. 3, (Jul–Sept), pp. 505–528.

———. (1985). 'The Theory of Practice and the Practice of Theory in Indian Intellectual History', *Journal of the American Oriental Society*, Vol. 105, No. 3, Indological Studies, pp. 499–519.

———. (1996). 'The Sanskrit Cosmopolis, 300–1300 C.E. Transculturation, Vernacularization, and the Question of Ideology', In Houben, J.E.M. (Ed.), *Ideology and Status of Sanskrit: Contributions to the History of the Sanskrit Language* (pp. 197–248). Leiden: Brill.

———. (1998). 'The Cosmopolitan Vernacular', *The Journal of Asian Studies*, Vol. 57, No. 1, pp. 6–37.

———. (2006). *The Language of the Gods in the World of Men: Sanskrit, Culture and Power in Premodern India*, Berkley: University of California Press.

Powers, H.S. (1984). 'Mṛdaṅga', In Sadie, S. (Ed.), *The New Grove Dictionary of Musical Instruments* (pp. 695–696). London: Macmillan.

Prajnanananda, S. (1963). *A History of Indian Music*, Calcutta: Ramakrishna Vedanta Math.

———. (1973). *Historical Development of Indian Music*, Calcutta: K.L. Mukhopadhyay.

Prasad, R. (Trans.) (1998). *Patanjali's Yoga Sutras: With the Commentary of Vyasa and the Gloss of Vachaspati Mishra*, New Delhi: Munshiram Manoharlal.

Premlata, V. (1985). *Music through the Ages*, New Delhi: Sandeep Prakashan.

Printchman, T. (2003). 'The Month of Kartik and Women's Ritual Devotion to Krishna in Benares', In Flood, G. (Ed.), *The Blackwell Companion to Hinduism* (pp. 327–342). Oxford: Blackwell.

Qureshi, R.B. (1986). *Sufi Music of India and Pakistan: Sound, Context and Meaning in Qawwali*, Cambridge: Cambridge University Press.

———. (1997). 'The Indian Sarangi: Sound of Affect', *Yearbook for Traditional Music*, Vol. 29, pp. 1–38.

———. (2002). 'Mode of Production and Musical Production: Is Hindustani Music Feudal?', In Qureshi, R.B. (Ed.), *Music and Marx* (pp. 81–105). New York: Routledge.

Radicchi, A. (1967). *La musica di Mālavikāgnimitra II, 4*, Firenze: Holski.

Raghavan, V. (1955). 'Why the Mridanga Is so Called?', *Journal of the Music Academy of Madras*, Vol. I-IV, pp. 135–136.

———. (1956). 'Variety and Integration in the Pattern of Indian Culture', *The Far East Quarterly*, Vol. 15, No. 4 (Aug.1956), pp. 497–505.

———. (1967). 'Sanskrit Drama: Theory and Performance', *Comparative Drama*, Vol. 1, No. 1 (Spring), pp. 36–48.

Raja, D. (2005). *Archival Music and the Gharanas*, New Delhi: Sangeet Natak Akademi, XXXIX, n.4, pp. 3–18.

———. (2012). *The Pakhawaj: Bramha's Handiwork*, http://swaratala.blogspot.in/2012/03/pakhawaj-bramhas-handiwork.html.

Rajagopalan, L.S. (2010). *Temple Musical Instruments of Kerala*, New Delhi: Sangeet Natak Akademi/Prontworld Ltd.

Rajan, C. (1997). *The Complete Works of Kalidasa*, New Delhi: Sahitya Academy.

Rajan, A. 2009, 03 september. 'Song of the oarsman', *The Hindu*. Chennai.

Rama Murthy, D.R. and Rao, D.V. (2004). *The Theory and Practice of Mridanga*. Hyderabad: Sangeet Natak Akademi.

Ramanathan, N. (1987). *Tala: A Conceptual and Structural Analysis*, Bombay: Sanmukha.

———. (1999). *Musical Forms in Saṅgītaratnākara*, Chennai: Sampradaya.

———. (2003). 'Textual Studies and Musical Forms', *Papers of the Seminar Music Research: A Focus on Musical Forms*, Mumbai.

———. (2008). *Form in Music*, www.musicreasearch.in.

Ranade, A. (1997). *Hindustani Music*, New Delhi: National Book Trust India.

———. (1998). *Essays in Indian Ethnomusicology*, New Delhi: Munshiram Manoharlal.

———. (2006). *Music Contexts: A Concise Dictionary of Hindustani Music*, New Delhi: Promiolla & Co Publishers in association with Bibliophile South Asia.

Ratanjankar. (2007). 'Traditional Methods of Musical Training and Modern Music Classes', *Sangeet Natak Journal*, Vol, XLI, No. 4, pp. 3–12.

Redington, J.D. (1990). *Vallabhācarya on the Love Games of Kṛṣṇa*, New Delhi: Motilal Banarsidas.

Rhys Davids, T.W. (Trans.) (1890). *The Questions of King Milinda, Volume XXXV of 'The Sacred Books of the East'*, Oxford: Claredon.

Richardson, D.A. (1979). *Mughal and Rajput Patronage of the Bhakti Sect of the Maharajas, the Vallabha Sampradaya, 1640–1760 A.D.*, (PhD), Tucson: University of Arizona.

Rodhes Bailly, C. (2000). 'Śrī-lakṣmī. Majesty of the Hindu King', In Bernard, E. and Moon, B. (Eds.), *Goddesses Who Rule* (pp. 133–146). Oxford: Oxford University Press.

Rowell, L. (1987). 'The Song of Medieval India: The *Prabandhas* as Described in Mataṅga's *Bṛhaddeśī*', *Music Theory Spectrum*, Vol. 9, No. 1, pp. 136–172..

———. (1998). *Music and Musical Thought in Early India*, New Delhi: Munshiram Manoharlal.

Rukmani, T.S. (2007). 'Dharmamegha-Samadhi in the Yoga Sutras of Patanjali: A Critique', *Philosophy East and West*, Vol. 57, No. 2 April, pp. 131–139.

Saha, S. (2006). 'A Community of Grace: The Social and Theological World of the Puṣṭi Mārga Vārtā', *Bulletin of the School of Oriental and African Studies, University of London*, Vol. 69, No. 2, pp. 225–249.

———. (2007). 'The Movement of Bhakti along a North-West Axis: Tracing the History of the Puṣṭimārg between the Sixteenth and Nineteenth Centuries', *International Journal of Hindu Studies,* Vol. 11, No. 3, (Dec.), pp. 299–318.

Samuel, G. (2008). *The Origins of Yoga and Tantra: Indic Religions to the Thirteenth Century,* Delhi: Cambridge University Press.

Sanderson, A. (2009), 'The Śaiva Age. The Rise and Dominance of Śaivism during the Early Medieval Period', In Shingo, E. (Ed.), *Genesis and Development of Tantrism* (pp. 41–350). Tokyo: Institute of Oriental Culture.

Sankaram, T.S.(1994). *The Rhythmic principles & Practice of South Indian Drumming,* Toronto: Lalit Publishers.

Sankrityayan, A. (2004). 'Dhrupad of the Dagar Tradition and Nada Yoga', In *CD Dhrupad-Ragas: Bhupali,Shankara of Dagar Brothers of Udaipur.* The Royal Collection of Mewar, Maharana Kumbha Sangeet Kala Trust.

———. *The Fundamental Concepts of Dhrupad,* http://klangzeitort.de/uploads/documentation2/Ashish%20Sankrityayan.pdf.

Sanyal, R. (1986). 'The Banaras Dhrupad Mela-s', *Dhrupad Annual,* Vol. 1, pp. 116–120.

Sanyal, R. and Widdess, R. (2004). *Dhrupad: Tradition and Performance in Indian Music,* Burlington: Ashgate.

Sarmadee, S. (1984/1985). 'Mankutuhal and Rag Darpan: Reflections of a Great Seventeenth Century Musician', *Istar Newsletter,* Vol. 3–4, pp. 18–26.

———. (Trans.) (2002). *Tarjuma-i-manakutuhala and Risala-i-Ragadarpana: Of Faqirullah,* New Delhi: Indira Gandhi National Centre for the Arts.

———. (Trans.) (2003). *Ghunyatu'l Munya: The Earliest Persian Work on Indian Classical Music,* New Delhi: Northern Book Centre.

Sathyanarayana, R. (Ed.) (1960). *Abhinavabharatisārasaṅgrah of Mummadi Cikkabhūpāla,* Mysore: Sri Varalakshmi Academies.

———. (1987). 'Indian Music. Myth and Legend', *Journal of Indian Musicological Society,* Vol. 18, No. 1 June 1987, pp. 1–67.

———. (1988). *Music of Madhva Monks of Karnataka,* Chennai: Gnana Jyoti Kala Mandir.

———. (Trans.) (1994). *Nartananirṇaya, Vol. 1,* New Delhi: Indira Gandhi National Centre for the Arts.

Saxena, S.K. (2006). *The Art of Tabla Rhythm,* New Delhi: Sangeet Natak Akademi.

Sen, A.K. (1994). *Indian Concept of Rhythm,* New Delhi: Kanishka Publishers.

Sharma, K.C., Yadav, K.C. and Sharma, P. (1997). *Surdasa: A Critical Study,* New Delhi: Eastern Book Linkers.

Sharma, M. (1999). *Music India,* New Delhi: A.P.H. Publishing Corporation.

Sharma, P.L. (1989). 'Myths in Sangitashastra', In Metha, R.C. (Ed.), *Music and Mythology: A Collection of Essays,* Books 1–2 (pp. 5–13, Book 2). Baroda: Indian Musicological Society.

———. (Ed.) (1992). *Bṛhaddeśī of Śrī Mataṅga Muni*, New Delhi: Motilal Banarsidass.
———. (2007). 'Is Music and Dance an Integral Part of Natya?' In Srinivasan, A. (Ed.), *Approaches to Bharata's Natyashastra* (pp. 107–124). New Delhi: Sangeet Natak Akademi.
Shepherd, F.A. (1976). *Tabla and the Benares Gharana*, (Phd), Middletown: Wesleyan University.
Shringy, R.K. (Trans.) (1978). *Saṅgītaratnākara of Śārṅagadeva Vol. 1*, Delhi: Munshiram Manoharlal.
Shulman, D. (2005). 'Axial Grammar', In Arnason, J.P., Eisenstadt, S.N. and Wittrock, B. (Eds.), *Axial Civilization and World History* (pp. 367–397). Leiden: Brill.
Singh, B. (2012). 'What is Kīrtan?', *Sikh Formations*, Vol. 7, No. 3, pp. 245–295.
———. (2006). 'Abhinavagupta's Contribution to the Solution of Some Problems in Indian Musicology', In Paranjape, M. and Visuvalingam, S. (Eds.), *Abhinavagupta: Reconsiderations* (pp. 333–342). New Delhi: Samvad India Foundation.
Singh, O.P. (1983). *Iconography of Gaja-Lakshmi*, Varanasi: Bharati Prakashan.
Sinh, P. (Trans.) (1914). *The Hata Yoga Pradipika*, Allahbad: Panini Office.
Sitanarasimhan. (2004). 'Nataraja in Tamil Tradition', *East and West*, Vol. 54, No. 1–4 (Dec.), pp. 303–312.
Sivaramamurti, C. (1974). *Nataraja in Art, Thought and Literature*, New Delhi: National Museum.
———. (1982). *Śrī Lakshmi in Indian Art and Thought*, New Delhi: Kanak Publications.
Sivaraman, U.K. (2008) 'Mridanga Cintamani', Swathi Sanskriti Series. Set of 7 DVDs.
Smith, W. (1999). 'Images of Divine Kings from the Mukteśvara Temple, Bhubaneswar', *Artibus Asiae*, Vol. 51, No. 1/2, pp. 90–106.
Srinivas, M.N. (1956). 'A Note on Sankritization and Westernization', *The Far Eastern Quarterly*, Vol. 15, No. 4, pp. 481–496.
Srinivasan, D.M. (2005). 'The Mauryan Gaṇikā from Dīdārgañj (Pāṭaliputra)', *East and West*, Vol. 55, No. 1/4 (Dec.), pp. 345–362.
Srivastava, I. (1980). *Dhrupada: A Study of Its Origin, Historical Development, Structure and Present State*, New Delhi: Motilal Banarsidass.
Staal, F. (1963). 'Sanskrit and Sanskritization', *The Journal of Asian Studies*, Vol. 22, No. 3, pp. 261–275.
Stewart, R. (1974). *The Tabla in Perspective*, (PhD), Los Angeles: University of California.
Subramaniam, L. (2006a). 'Court to Academy: Karnatic Music', *Economical and Political Weekly*, Vol. 33, No. 2, pp. 125–138.
———. (2006b). 'Faith and the Musician "Ustads" in Modern India', *Economical and Political Weekly*, Vol. 41, No. 45, (Nov. 11/17), pp. 4648–4650.

Subramaniam, V. (1980). *The Sacred and the Secular in India's Performing Arts: Ananda Coomaraswamy Centenary Essays,* New Delhi: APH Publishing.

———. (1998). 'Religion and the Performing Arts: A Critique of Ananda K. Coomaraswamy', *Sangeet Natak Journal,* Vol. 129–130, pp. 16–26.

Tanaka, T. (2008). 'The Samāj-Gāyan Tradition: Transmitting a Musico-Religious System in North India', In Senri Ethnological Studies Yoshitaka, T. (Ed.), *Music and Society in South Asia: Perspectives from Japan,* Osaka: National Museum of Ethnology, pp. 87–101.

Tapasyananda, S. (2004). *Śrī Vallabhācarya: His Life, Religion and Philosophy,* Madras: Sri Ramakrishna Math.

Tarlekar, G.H. (1987). 'Some Puranic Legends Relating to Music', *Journal of the Indian Musicological Society,* Vol. 18, No. 2 December Indian Musicological Society, pp. 47–51.

———. (1991–1992). 'The Distinction between Gandharva and Gana', *Annals of the Bhandarkar Oriental Research Institute,* Vol. 72/73, No. 1/4, Amrtamahotsava (1917–1992) Volume (1991–1992), pp. 689–699.

Terada, Y. (2005). 'Performing Auspiciousness: Periya Melam Music in South Indian Marriage Ceremony', *Wacana Seni Journal of Arts Discourse,* Vol. 4, pp. 103–138.

———. (2008). 'Temple Music Traditions in Hindu South India: "Periya Mēḷam" and Its Performance Practice', *Asian Music,* Vol. 39, No. 2, (Summer/Fall), pp. 108–151.

Thapar, R. (1978). 'Interpretation of Ancient Indian History', In *Ancient Indian Social History* (pp. 1–22). New Delhi: Orient Longman Limited.

———. (2002). *The Penguin History of Early India: From the Origins to AD 1300,* London: Penguin Books.

———. (2010). *India's Past and Present: How History Informs Contemporary Narrative,* Canada: International Development Research Centre. Available at: www.youtube.com/watch?v=J8HhLJzpx3Y (Accessed on 22 July 2016).

Thielemann, S. (1997). *The Darbhanga Tradition: Dhrupad in the School of Pandit Vidur Mallik,* New Delhi: Indica Books.

———. (1999). *The Music of South Asia,* New Delhi: A.P.H. Publishing Corporation.

———. (2001). *Musical Traditions of Vaiṣṇava Temples in Vraja: A Comparative Study of Samāja and Dhrupada Tradition of North Indian Classical Music,* New Delhi: Sagar Printers and Publishers.

———. (2002). *Divine Service and the Performing Arts in India,* New Delhi: A.P.H. Publishing Corporation.

Thite, G.U. (1997). *Music in the Vedas: Its Magico Religious Significance,* New Delhi: Sharada Publishing House.

Tingey, C. (1994). *Auspicious Music in a Changing Society: The Damāi Musicians of Nepal,* London: School of Oriental and African Studies.

Todd, J. (1920). *Annals of Antiquities of Rajasthan,* London: Oxford University Press.

Trivedi, M. (2010). 'Music Patronage in the Indo-Persian Context: A Historical Overview', In Bor, J., Delvoye, N., Harvey, J. and Nijenhuis, T. (Eds.), *Hindustani Music: Thirteenth to Twentieth Centuries* (pp. 65–93). New Delhi: Manohar Publishers.

Truschke, A. (2012). *Cosmopolitan Encounters: Sanskrit and Persian at the Mughal Court*, (PhD), New York: Columbia University.

Vajracharya, G.V. (2003). *Watson Collection of Indian Miniaturse at the Elvehjem Museum of Art*, Madison: University of Wisconsin Press.

———. (2013). *Frog Hymns and Rain Babies: Monsoon Culture and the Art of Ancient South Asia*, Mumbai: The Marg Foundation.

Valmiki. *Ramayana*, www.valmikiramayan.net/.

Van Der Meer, W. (1980). *Hindustani Music in the 20th Century*, The Hague/Boston/London: Martinus Nijhoff Publishers.

Varadapande. (1978). *Traditions of Indian Theatre*, New Delhi: Abhinav Publications.

———. (1982). *Krishna Theatre*, New Delhi: Abhinav Publications.

———. (1983). *Religion and Theatre*, New Delhi: Abhinav Publications.

Vatsyayan, K. (1968). *Indian Classical Dance in Literature and the Arts*, New Delhi: Sangeet Natak Akademi.

———. (1982). *Dance in Indian Painting*, New Delhi: Abhinav Publications.

———. (1983). *The Square and the Circle of the Indian Arts*, New Delhi: Roli Books International.

———. (1996). *Bharata: The Natyashastra*, New Delhi: Sahitya Academy.

Verdia, H.S. (1982). *Religion and Social Structure in a Sacred Town: Nathdwara*, Delhi: Research Publications.

Vijay Lakshmi, M. (1996). *A Critical Study of Saṅgīta Makaranda of Nārada*, New Delhi: Gyan Publishing House.

———. (2004). *Aumpatam: A Work on Music*, New Delhi: Poonam Goel Raj Publication.

———. (2011). *An Analytical Study of Saṅgītasamayasara of Sri Pārśvadeva*, Poonam Goel Raj Publication, New Delhi: Raj Publications.

Vir, R.A. (1977). *Learn to Play on Tabla 1–2*, Delhi: Pankaj Books.

———. (1983). *Musical Instruments of India. History and Development*, Delhi: Pankaj Books.

Virupaksha, S. (Trans.) (1995). *Sāṃkhya Kārikā of Iśvara Kṛṣṇa with the Tattva Kaumudī of Śri Vācaspati Miśra*, Milapore/Madras: Ramakrishna Math.

Wade, B. (1998). *Imaging Sound: An Ethnomusicological Study of Music, Art, and Culture of Mughal India*, Chicago/London: University of Chicago Press.

Walker, M.E. (2004). *Kathak Dance: A Critical History*, (PhD), Toronto: University of Toronto.

Warder, A.K. (1988). *Indian Kāvya Literature*, Delhi: Motilal Banarsidass.

Wegner, M.G. (1992). 'Invocations of Nāsadyaḥ', In Kölver, B. (Ed.), *Aspects of Nepalese Traditions* (pp. 125–134). Stuttgart: Franz Steiner.

White, D.G. (1996). *The Alchemical Body*, Chicago: University of Chicago Press.

———. (2003). *Kiss of the Yogini*, Chicago: University of Chicago Press.

Whitney Sanford, A. (2008). *Singing Krishna: Sound Becomes Sight in Paramanand's Poetry*, New York: State University of New York Press.

Widdess, R. (1994a). 'Festivals of Dhrupad in Northern India: New Contexts for an Ancient Art', *British Journal of Ethnomusicology*, Vol. 3, pp. 89–109.

———. (1994b). 'Involving the Performer in Transcriptions and Analysis: A Dialectic Approach to Dhrupad', *Ethnomusicology*, Vol. 38, No. 1, pp. 59–79.

———. (1995). *The Ragas of Early Indian Music: Modes, Melodies and Musical Notation from the Gupta Period to c.1250*. Oxford: Clareidon Press (OUP).

———. (2006). 'Performance and Meaning: The Case of a Stick-Dance from Nepal', *Ethnomusicology Forum*, Vol. 15, No. 2, pp. 179–213.

———. (2013). *Dapha. Music, Performance and Meaning in Bhaktapur, Nepal*, Burlington: Ashgate.

Willard, N.A. (1834). *A Treatise on the Music of Hindostan*. Calcutta: Printed at the baptist Mission Press.

Wilkins, W.J. (1913), *Hindu Mythology. Epic and Puranic*, Calcutta and Simla: Thacker, Spink & Co.

Woodroffe, J. (1994). *The Garland of Letters*, Madras: Ganesh & Co.

Zimmer, H. (1947). *Myths and Symbols of Indian Art and Civilization*, New York: Pantheon Books.

Zimmermann, F. (1987). 'Monsoon in Traditional Culture', In Fein Jay, S. and Stephens, P.L. (Eds.), *Monsoon* (pp. 51–76). Chichester: Wiley-Blackwell.

Index

Note: Locators in *italics* refer to figures. Locators followed by an 'n' and a number refer to a footnote, e.g. 108n11 refers to footnote 11 on page 108.